Rescuing Slaves of the Watchtower

How to lead Jehovah's Witness prisoners into the light of Christ

Joe B. Hewitt

Copyright Joe B. Hewitt 2011
All Rights Reserved
Printed in the United States of America
by Lightning Source, Inc., LaVergne, TN
Cover design by Dennis Davidson
Unless otherwise indicated all Scripture taken
from the King James Version of the Holy Bible. Used by permission.

ISBN 978-1-61315-006-1
Library of Congress Control Number: 2011928344

Hannibal Books
P.O. Box 461592
Garland, TX 75046-1592
www.hannibalbooks.com
1-800-747-0738

Table of Contents

Introduction: Chipping Away at the Stones and Mortar..........5
Chapter 1: Rescue Is Possible..................................9
Chapter 2: How Not to Witness to the JW's.....................27
Chapter 3: Touch the Mortar Joint.............................33
Chapter 4: Of What Is the Society Afraid?.....................47
Chapter 5: Watchtower Hierarchy...............................51
Chapter 6: Jehovah's Witnesses' Mind Games....................63
Chapter 7: Callous Cruelty....................................71
Chapter 8: Still Anti-Education...............................75
Chapter 9: Confront the Real Truth............................79
Chapter 10: Replacing Error with Truth........................99
Chapter 11: Corrections......................................107
Chapter 12: The Truth about Blood............................123
Chapter 13: The Soul, the Spirit, and the Afterlife..........133
Chapter 14: God's Chosen People..............................151
Chapter 15: Repair the Reflexes..............................163
Chapter 16: Enjoy Christian Freedom..........................179
Appendix A: Evangelism Approaches............................189
Appendix B: Understanding the Trinity........................205
Appendix C: An Objective Look at Cults.......................235
Appendix D: The Word...239
Additional Resources...243
Glossary of Terms..245
References...249
Index..255

What Others Are Saying about This Book

This book is an excellent resource for those who would reach out to people caught up in the Jehovah's Witness organization. Joe Hewitt speaks from a deep reservoir of personal knowledge and passion to get the liberating gospel of Christ past the seemingly impenetrable wall that the Watchtower often projects. I commend *How to Rescue Prisoners of the Watchtower* for the tragic human victimology it exposes, the insight it provides, and the numerous creative presentations of the gospel it offers.

Rudy Gonzalez, Ph.D.
Dean, Southwestern Baptist Theological Seminary
Fort Worth, TX

Joe Hewitt writes from the unique position of having lived out in his own experience the conditions about which he writes. The message is clear and compelling. This book will be an immeasurable blessing to those who are dealing with and witnessing to those who are trapped in the Jehovah's Witness culture.

Jimmy Draper, president emeritus
LifeWay Christian Resources

Introduction

Chipping Away at the Stones and Mortar

"You lie and you teach your people to lie." I laid that charge against the most religious of religious organizations.

My mother—as had her father—believed the Watchtower Society spoke for God. The Society taught her to lie and deceive; she taught me to do the same. Jehovah's Witnesses believe they serve Jehovah by using almost any means necessary. She feared the condemnation of the Society and believed its leaders had the authority to consign her to eternal destruction.

I had been a disciplined Jehovah's Witness, but I also had been a boy with trouble on my mind. "I'm afraid I won't see life because of my kids," my mother had said, as she used the Watchtower terminology for eternal life on earth. Because of our misbehavior the elders might disfellowship her; this would eliminate any chance of her *seeing life.*

The total control the Watchtower Society had on my mother continued the rest of her life. I was rescued from being a slave of the Watchtower, but its teachings still permeated my brain. That resulted in years of grief for me and caused my mother to consider me as one dead. On orders of the JW leaders she was forced to shun me.

In meetings across the United States and Mexico as I have worked to alert people about the dangers of the Watchtower, I have asked, "How many of you have had Jehovah's Witnesses visit your home?" Usually almost every hand goes up. Most families in North America have a relative, friend, or neighbor under the Watchtower's control. These relatives, friends, or neighbors are slaves in need of rescue. In this book my purpose is to help you rescue these loved ones from mental and emotional bondage and to equip and guard your children against being lured into the cult.

Besides backing up all the above charges this book will demonstrate that The Watchtower Society is a thief, as it steals intellectual property by plagiarizing modern translations of the Bible. The Society rephrased some, substituted synonyms, and termed *the best translation ever* its own New World Translation of the Holy Scriptures.

Jehovah's Witnesses believe the Watchtower Society is God's organization and speaks for Him. Therefore, the JW approves of anything the Society says or does. The JW may deny he believes that the end justifies the means. You can deceive or outright lie to any worldly person. After all, such persons do not deserve to know the truth (*Aid to Bible Understanding*, Watchtower Bible and Tract Society of New York 1971, page 1060 under description of *Lie*.)

They can't be prosecuted for it, but leaders of the Jehovah's Witnesses have stolen words such as *truth, gospel,* and *god* and changed their meanings. In some places they interprct the Bible the exact opposite of what it means. They pick and choose certain Old Testament laws to obey and ignore the rest.

Jehovah's Witnesses claim to have peace in their hearts, but their lives are filled with anxiety. They have no confidence or assurance of having forgiveness and the eternal blessing of God. Rather they frequently are warned that failure to measure up as a JW will cause them to be destroyed in the Battle of Armageddon, which they warn will occur at any moment.

The Jehovah's Witness sees lying, doctrinal contradictions, hypocrisy in the leadership, double standards between the hierarchy and membership, sexual abuse of children ignored or covered up, and the hundreds of millions of dollars of income from efforts of volunteer workers going who-knows-where. He sees innocent children left to die rather than receive a blood transfusion. But the JW does not allow these thoughts into her conscious perception. She would feel guilty and believe her thoughts to be sinful thoughts. She also realizes that she is a small entity compared to the gigantic Watchtower Society fervently believed in by almost seven-million people around the world. She is powerless to resist or work for change. She learns to adapt by treating her conscience the same way the Society treats her: shush it up; get your mind on something else; stay busy studying Watchtower literature and doing kingdom work; dare not question the authority of God's earthly organization.

Belief in the divine authority of the Watchtower Society is the stone and mortar that holds the Watchtower together.

Can we rescue Jehovah's Witnesses from intellectual and emotional bondage? Yes, we can. Can we break down the stone and mortar of the Watchtower and lead its prisoners into the light of Christ? Absolutely! This book tells you how.

Note: Rather than use the word *he* as the generic third person pronoun or the sometimes cumbersome *he/she*, I have alternated using *he* and *she*.

Chapter 1

Rescue Is Possible

As one trained from childhood by the Jehovah's Witnesses, I can show you how people fall under the complete control of the Watchtower and also how they can be rescued from the hold the Watchtower has on them.

As one of the early disciples of Charles Taze Russell, founder of the Watchtower Bible and Tract Society before the turn of the 20th century, my maternal grandfather trained my mother in Watchtower doctrines. In turn my mother trained me.

In countries in which Jehovah's Witnesses are active, almost every family suffers because one or more members are under control of the Watchtower Society. These individuals seem almost to be locked up in a prison—not a prison of stone but one of mind control even more oppressive than that of a dungeon.

According to Watchtower statistics almost seven million Jehovah's Witnesses exist worldwide; each year the organization adds a quarter-of-a-million or more new members. Yet the net growth is nowhere near that much. So what happens to hundreds of thousands of active Jehovah's Witnesses who each year slip through the statistical cracks?

People escape from the Watchtower by the thousands. During one decade alone—1975-1985—nearly one million JW's dropped out or were tossed out.[1]

JW's Drop Out Because of Physical and Mental Exhaustion

Becoming a Jehovah's Witness takes about six months of study. The newly baptized JW eagerly attends five meetings a week and spends at least 10 hours a month knocking on doors and *witnessing* to people. But that soon grows old; exhaustion replaces enthusiasm. Most of the JW's emotional and physical energy is devoted to the *theocratic ministry*. The person has little time or strength left for family or work. The individual just can't keep up the pace, so he or she drops out.

Like being out on parole the exhausted ones escape physically from the Watchtower, but emotionally they are the walking wounded. Part of their training sensitizes them to guilt. JW elders try to manipulate them back into the fold by pushing the guilt-buttons of the exhausted ones. The exhausted one feels as though she is an utter failure. She believes she has failed Jehovah God. Instead she has failed the Watchtower, *Jehovah's Earthly Organization.* The guilt is overwhelming.

Then to make matters worse, the exhausted person is bombarded with telephone calls from and visits by JW friends to get her to return. These drive her deeper and deeper into depression. Of any religious group Jehovah's Witnesses have the highest incidence of mental illness and suicide among their membership.

Out of service for the Watchtower, the exhausted one's mind still is captive; he or she still is convinced the Watchtower doctrines are true and that the Watchtower Society is Jehovah God's earthly authority. She feels she herself is the evil one—the failure. While an active JW she never measured up. She always failed, according to the impossible standards set by the Watchtower. So she damns herself an admitted, utter failure who is doomed to die in the *sudden destruction of Armageddon* which she believes will occur any day.

The exhausted one lives a miserable existence. She may try to get back into good standing at the Kingdom Hall, the meeting place of JW's. She can stand before the congregation and repent, confess her failures, and beg for reinstatement. She then may be put on probation and be allowed to sit on the back row. Nobody talks to her. After about a year she asks for reinstatement and goes before the board of elders. If she's accepted back, she usually finds that she is marked and treated with suspicion. She lives with guilt and futility. Or she learns to lie to herself and convinces herself she *really does* measure up and joins the ranks of the self-righteous.

However, once a person has dropped out, most fail a second time and then a third. Finally the person gives up and adopts the attitude: *If I'm doomed to die in Armageddon anyway, I might as well do as I please and leave God out of my life altogether.* Emotionally and spiritually he still is locked up in the stone-cold Watchtower.

If on the other hand the JW is male and has not dropped out, he has the opportunity to progress through the ranks of *publisher* (a baptized JW in good standing), a *servant,* (equivalent to deacon), and perhaps even *elder* (member of the congregation's governing board).

JW's Are Kicked Out

The Watchtower Society would have you believe that all those kicked out are *disfellowshiped* for immorality. Not so. Many have been kicked out for smoking.[2] Back when hippies distinguished themselves with wire-rimmed glasses and beards, JW's were disfellowshiped for wearing those glasses, which the Watchtower considered *worldly* attire. Charles Taze Russell, founder of the Watchtower, wore a long beard, but that apparently made no difference. JW's still have been disfellowshiped for wearing beards.

JW's also are kicked out for participating in independent Bible study, for questioning Watchtower dogma, for associating with a former JW whom they are supposed to shun, and for many other reasons ordinary people would find trivial or grossly unfair.

JW's Leave in Disgust over Immoral JW Leaders

Some Jehovah's Witnesses leave the organization when they see hypocrisy and double standards among members of the leadership. The most serious example is sexual molestation of children followed by organized cover-up. This blatant hypocrisy has pierced the hard shell of many JW's and has caused them to leave *the organization* in disgust.

As with other religious organizations, child molesters flock to the JW's, in which they can work themselves into positions of trust and have access to children. A familiar pattern has emerged. For years a priest sexually abuses children. Somebody blows the whistle; more victims present themselves. The offending priest finally goes to jail. If he doesn't go to jail, at least he is hauled off to a monastery in which he no longer has contact with children.

A pedophile becomes trained as a children's worker or youth director in a church. He sexually abuses children. A child tells on him. The parent reports to the police; the pedophile goes to jail. After he gets out of prison, he is labeled and tracked as a sexual predator.

The JW's, however, deal with sexual-abuse problems differently. They will disfellowship a person who disagrees with Watchtower dogma, who smokes, who wears skirts too short, or who engages in the catch-all transgression—*worldly activity*. But the Jehovah's Witnesses protect child molesters in a cocoon of impossible rules and in an attitude that often punishes the victim.

If a child reports to an elder that she has been sexually molested, the elder will confront the accused. If he denies it, the elder tells the family that two witnesses must exist; otherwise, nothing can be done. The family members then insist that something be done about the child molester. They are told to *wait on Jehovah*. If they refuse to keep the matter quiet, the elders accuse the family of causing dissension in the congregation. If the family members persist, they are kicked out of the congregation, branded as *troublemakers*, and shunned. The child molester continues his dirty deeds but is careful to do nothing in front of two witnesses.

Another typical scenario is one in which a person of influence in the congregation is guilty of sexually abusing a child. Typically the child's parents report the crime to the elders. The elders call the accused in to a *judicial* hearing. If no witnesses to the offense are produced, the elders refuse to believe such a charge against him and hush it up. Because of their power, influence, and role, the elders can do what they want. They may believe the influential offender is being persecuted; they may turn on the complaining parent. Usually the parents will continue to ask justice from the elders. As far as the elders are concerned, the case is closed, because no witnesses exist. If the parents persist, the elders have the authority to order the parents onto the carpet for a *judicial hearing* and accuse them of *causing dissension among the brethren*. This punishment of the victim often causes the parents to quietly leave the congregation. If they go and later unite with another congregation of JW's, their file containing a record of judicial hearings and accusations goes there also.

An Australian JW congregation disfellowshiped Jan Groenveld because she blew the whistle on pedophiles and wouldn't hush it up. She insisted that the elders do something about an abuser in the congregation. They refused. She went to the press. The JW elders declared her dead; she was shunned. The child abuser remained under the elders' protection.

Because of so many cases of sexual molestation of children, including those by Jehovah's Witnesses, Internet websites are devoted to telling the heartbreaking stories of victims and their families. Two of these websites are *www.silentlambs.org* and *www.lambsroar.org*.

The Love and Norris law firm of Fort Worth, TX, specializes in cases involving Jehovah's Witnesses and sexual molestation of children. The firm says, "If you are a victim of sexual abuse at the hands of a perpetrator in a Jehovah's Witnesses congregation, we may be able to help you. Consistently, the Watchtower Society and Jehovah's Witnesses congregations have responded to an abuse outcry with concern for the organization's loss of reputation or prestige, rather than concern for victimized children.

"Statistically, a known pedophile WILL abuse again. By failing to acknowledge the problem, investigate vigorously, and cooperate with criminal law enforcement authorities, the Watchtower Society has failed to protect its own children from sexual predators. By harboring pedophiles, the Society potentially becomes responsible for the damage suffered by abused children."[3] Google on the Internet lists 65,200 sources under "Sex Abuse by Jehovah's Witnesses".

A July 12, 2002, BBC report included a story about Bill Bowen, a JW elder in Kentucky for nearly 20 years. He said the Watchtower keeps a secret list of 23,720 sex offenders in the organization. The organization is well-aware of the problem but doesn't want the public to know about it, according to Bowen. The Society reasons that by covering it up, only one person is hurt; by letting out the information, the image of the entire organization is hurt. The JW's will take action against the sex offender only if two witnesses are produced or if the offender confesses. Even if a member of the congregation is convicted of child abuse, they keep it secret, Bowen told the BBC interviewer.

Bowen said when a sexual-abuse report is turned in, elders are instructed to call the Watchtower Society's *legal department.* He said on one occasion he phoned the legal desk and asked how he should deal with a suspected case of abuse in his congregation. The Society's representative told Bowen to ask the suspect again if the accusation was true. If the accused said, "No," then Bowen was to "walk away from it. Leave it for Jehovah. He'll bring it out."

The BBC report also contained the story of Alison Cousins, a young JW from Scotland. She reported to the elders that her father had sexually abused her. She later learned that he had abused her sister as well. The elders listened but did nothing. They sent her back home. For three years her father continued the abuse. Finally in desperation Alison went to the police. Her father was tried and convicted. The police had been the last to know about the abuse. It had been well-known in the Kingdom Hall but kept secret.

JW's Escape Only to Plunge into Spiritual Limbo

I was one of those who left the Jehovah's Witnesses and went into spiritual limbo. Starting at age 10 I began my long journey. I stood on street corners in Wichita, KS, with the canvas strap of a book bag over my shoulder. I held up a copy of *The Watchtower* magazine and called out to passersby, "*The Watchtower*, Announcing Jehovah's Kingdom."

Most people just ignored me. Others would look askance at the little kid and his canvas bag of magazines. A few were hateful and rude. "If you don't like this country, why don't you leave?"

Others pointed a finger and shouted, "Nazi" or "Jap". In my mind I would repeat what I had been taught. *They persecute us just like they persecuted Jesus. It shows that we are doing Jehovah's will,* I told myself over and over, but the unkind words still hurt.

I trained in the *Theocratic Ministry* in the Kingdom Hall on the second floor of an old Wichita downtown business building. At age 11 I made my first public talk to an audience of 200. I faithfully went from door to door and distributed the Watchtower Bible and Tract Society's magazines and books.

The Society helped enable kids like me to go door-to-door. Usually I went with an adult, but often, to get my 10 hours in, I would go alone. My equipment was a book bag with *Watchtower* and *Awake* magazines, a few booklets, and the newest hardbound book, a windup phonograph, and a yellow laminated *testimony card*. The testimony card introduced me as an ordained minister of the gospel and asked whether the person would listen to a three-minute phonograph message from Judge Joseph Rutherford.

Before I went out in the *field service,* I visited the *Territory Servant's* window at the Kingdom Hall and checked out a territory card. One side showed a map of the area, usually two or three square blocks; the other side had addresses and blanks on which to record attitudes of the residents. If one was interested enough to listen and perhaps to accept a piece of literature, that person received the highest rating—"Good Will". If a person reacted rudely or tried to rebut the Watchtower teachings, we were instructed to write "Goat". That person, we believed, would be separated on Judgment Day from the righteous "Sheep" and would be consigned to destruction.

Some doors slammed in my face. A few rude people shouted at me, "Get off my property."

Some cursed me. One man turned water sprinklers on me. But all that made me feel justified. I was persecuted as Jesus had been. To be kind many people accepted the literature. People typically said, "I'm a Catholic. I'm not interested." Or, "I'm a Baptist" or "Methodist" or "Presbyterian" or just plain "I'm not interested." I had been taught that all those church folks worshiped Satan because they didn't pray to Jehovah. If they prayed to "God", Jehovah would not accept their prayers, because Satan, too, was a god, so Jehovah would send their prayers to Satan.

I did what I was told. I did not realize I was on my way to a spiritual limbo.

Obvious Double Standard Encourages JW's to Defect

I went to the five meetings a week required of *publishers*. I prayed daily to Jehovah. I tried to think moral thoughts and to behave as expected. Of course I failed and felt continuous guilt. Yet I saw other JW kids my age who didn't measure up as well as I did who apparently weren't bothered by guilt. Some, especially children of the elders and other leaders in the congregation, were downright mean and could get away with anything. The double standard existed among the children, too.

My Uncle Al Gordon rose to be one of the most prominent leaders in the Kingdom Hall. He claimed membership in *The Elect*, the 144,000 who held exclusive tickets to heaven. Ordinary JW's looked up to him with awe. To me Uncle Al was as mean as a snake. He expressed kindness to my mother, his youngest sister, but I never saw him show kindness to anyone else. He was rude to his wife and daughter and heaped verbal abuse on his step-granddaughter. He kept the 16-year-old step-granddaughter so cowed, she moved in nervous jerks. She was afraid to speak or move.

I saw the double standard among influential JW's and in Uncle Al's hypocrisy. Those contradictions bothered me but not enough to make me doubt the Watchtower Society, *Jehovah's earthly organization.*

I have talked to many ex-JW's who told me the same story. They saw double standards and hypocrisy that started weakening the cold stone of the Watchtower. Without consciously realizing it, this realization enabled them to begin their escape. Some escape the Watchtower and go immediately into Christian liberty. Others, as I did, go out into spiritual nothingness.

After Reading the Bible in Context JW's Begin Their Escape

A violent beating led to my reading the Bible in context without Watchtower aids.

Kids in my school knew that I refused to salute the flag. When people asked why, I had a canned response. "We respect the flag and what it stands for, but the Bible tells us we should not bow down to any graven image." That meant the flag was an image; to salute it would be the same as to bow down to an idol and worship it, according to the Watchtower Society, our official interpreter of what things meant.

One sunny afternoon when I was 15, a group of six boys surrounded me in the gravel driveway of the neighborhood convenience store, at which we hung out and drank sodas. On a stick one boy held a dirty little U.S. flag. "You're going to salute this flag," he said as he held the flag in my face.

They all shouted at me, "Salute this flag." My little canned speech made no difference. They berated me and called me a traitor because Jehovah's Witnesses refused military service. I opened another can and said, "Jesus said, my kingdom is not of this world; if my kingdom were of this world then would my servants fight." They continued to shout and started shoving. I was surrounded by flailing fists and kicks. I would have let them kill me before I would salute the flag; for a while I thought they might. They beat me down to the ground. I'll never forget the taste of blood and gravel in my mouth as they kicked me. I never knew what caused them to quit kicking and leave. Too groggy to get up I lay there awhile. Beaten and bloody I slowly rose. I hurt all over.

As I limped the half-mile home, my heart hurt more than my beaten body did. Again I questioned God. I knew the boys had done wrong. No justification existed for their rage. But still I had a dilemma. I loved my country; I loved God. *Why couldn't I be loyal to both?* My faith needed to be strengthened.

At home I went to my Bible. At that time JW's used the King James translation. I looked up the Scripture I had quoted, *My kingdom is not of this world: if my kingdom were of this world, then would my servants fight* (John 18:36).

Then I read the whole verse in context. It didn't say at all what the Watchtower claimed. Jesus explained why His disciples didn't fight His arrest in the Garden of Gethsemane, . . . *if my kingdom were of this world, then would my servants fight, that I should not be delivered to the Jews* . . . .

Suddenly, the possibility that I had been lied to hit me with greater force than did the boys' kicks in the head.

The realization that the Society had lied to me began my escape from the Watchtower.

In an attempt to strengthen my faith as a Jehovah's Witness I had gone to the Bible. I didn't consult anyone. I did it on my own. If I had asked my mother or stepfather or one of the congregation leaders, they would have given me Watchtower literature and books and would have assured me that this literature contained answers to my dilemma.

Physically and emotionally I was hurting. For a change I didn't use the Watchtower sieve as a filter for what the Bible said. I just believed what the Bible plainly said.

For sure I had been lied to. The Watchtower had misquoted Jesus, taken His words out of context, and applied them to something entirely different. The Watchtower told its young men to refuse military service. If they already were in military service, the Society instructed them to refuse to salute officers and obey orders.

I looked in the Bible to see what Jesus said about soldiers. Jesus had contact with soldiers but never told them to desert. He never told them to refuse to salute their officers. Jesus never told anyone to refuse military service.[4]

I decided to see what some of the disciples said about military service. In the concordance in the back of the Bible I looked up John the Baptist.

John the Baptist likewise never encouraged soldiers to rebel against their superior officers, shed their uniforms, and refuse to serve. Rather John told the soldiers to be honest in the discharge of their duties and to be content with their wages.[5]

The apostle Paul likened Christians to soldiers. He spoke favorably of their dedication to duty. Paul never told Christians to refuse military service. He did not tell soldiers to quit obeying orders and to go to prison; rather Paul told Christians to obey civil authority.

If I had announced to the Witnesses my discovery and told them that I believed a Christian was permitted to serve in the Armed Forces, even if I accepted all the other Watchtower doctrines, I would have been disfellowshiped and consigned to death in Armageddon. On no point of doctrine can a Witness disagree with the Society.

I studied further the apostle Peter's attitude toward military service. He went to Caesarea to see Cornelius, a centurion and officer in charge of 100 men in the Roman Imperial Regiment. The Bible calls Cornelius *devout* and said he was a man who feared God, gave generously to those in need, and prayed. Peter preached to Cornelius, some of his soldiers, and his household. They became Christians and were baptized.[6]

If Peter had been a JW elder, he would have told them all to quit the army and go to prison or worse. Peter did no such thing. Rather, according to history, Christianity spread rapidly throughout the Roman Empire largely because so many soldiers believed in Christ and shared their faith as they were transferred to other posts.

Then I decided to examine the rule against saluting the flag. I looked more closely at Exodus 20:3-5, *Thou shalt have no other gods before me. Thou shalt not make unto thee any graven image, or any likeness of any thing that is in heaven above, or that is in the earth beneath, or that is in the water under the earth: Thou shalt not bow down thyself to them, nor serve them.*

I could not see how it could apply to the flag. If it applied to a flag, it also would apply to a photograph, a painting, or a map.

The Witnesses thought photographs, paintings, and maps were OK. But they taught that to salute the flag was to bow down to an image. I could love my mother without worshiping her. I could have a picture of my mother without worshiping it. I could love my country without worshiping it. I could salute the flag, which stood for America, without worshiping the flag.

But I didn't salute the flag. I kept these new convictions a secret. I still went to the Kingdom Hall. I gradually quit the *Witness Work*. That was obvious because my weekly reports turned in at the Kingdom Hall showed no time spent in field service.

I continued to read the Bible with an open mind. I read in the New Testament that people who heard the gospel and became converted were joyful. This wasn't the same picture I saw in the Witnesses. New Believers in the New Testament time seemed as though they were people who were released from bondage. New Jehovah's Witnesses seemed as though they were those who went into bondage.

After the Watchtower Society lied to me and other JW's, we repeated those lies.

Many different things cause JW's to begin to read the Bible in context. For me a beating spurred me on. For Helen Ortega suspicion and mistreatment by fellow JW's influenced her to start with Bible-reading.

I met Helen Ortega at one of the Ex-Jehovah's Witnesses for Jesus conventions in New Ringgold, PA. A lifelong Jehovah's Witness, Helen had a good reputation as an active publisher in the Kingdom Hall and was highly regarded as *theocratic* (an active, moral, and obedient JW). In private, however, Helen started something forbidden. She read the Bible on her own without the Watchtower's guidance. She became increasingly interested in what the Bible had to say. The idea of heaven fascinated her.

Even the Watchtower's Bible, the *New World Translation of the Holy Scriptures* (NWT), for the believer contains promises of eternal life in heaven. The JW guide, however, will explain that heaven is only for *The Elect*, the *Little Flock*, the 144,000. Still, Helen couldn't get heaven out of her mind. After months of private Bible study and prayer Helen found only one answer for her deep feeling about heaven. She must be one of The Elect.

At Passover time when Kingdom Halls around the world celebrate *The Lord's Evening Meal*, Helen attended but not as usual. At this most important meeting of the year JW's try to get all their members there; they even invite visitors—those they consider to be *people of good will* studying with JW's. As usual the elders passed the bread and wine. As usual no one partook. The bread and wine were only for The Elect. In the vast majority of Kingdom Halls none of The Elect show up. But that evening Helen took the bread and wine.

Gasps arose from the congregation. *What is Helen doing? If she is of The Elect, someone must have fallen.*

Afterward members and elders surrounded Helen and fired questions at her. She explained her convictions about heaven and that she now believed she would go there. After that event her lifelong friends began to regard her with suspicion. Some avoided her. The elders confronted her. They demanded to know: *Is she really of The Elect?* She explained how she had understood the Scriptures about heaven, which revealed to them that she had been reading the Bible on her own. They ordered her to quit reading the Bible on her own. Rather than obey them she read the Bible more and more. Eventually she decided the doctrine that only 144,000 could go to heaven was not scriptural. When she told the elders about her conclusion, they disfellowshiped her, branded her as an *apostate,* and shunned her. Even her family turned against her.

She continued to read the Bible. She realized that salvation is by grace alone; she trusted in Jesus Christ and claimed His promise of a home in heaven. After months of emotional conflict with her family members who remained loyal JW's, they eventually saw her Christian joy and sense of liberation from the Watchtower; they, too, trusted in Christ.

Helen Ortega was willing to accept, believe, and live by all the Watchtower dictates except one. The elders chose to reject her.

In 1983 Paul Blizard, a third-generation JW, phoned me from Brady, TX. He had read my book, *I Was Raised a Jehovah's Witness,* and recently left the Watchtower. Paul had become a Christian. He told me the heartbreaking story of his betrayal by the Witnesses.

At insistence of the elders, who believed Armageddon would arrive in 1975, Paul dropped out of high school to devote full time to the *witness work*. A bright young man, he rose quickly in the local congregation. Then he was promoted to the prestigious position of a *Bethelite*—honored to work without pay in the printing plant at Watchtower Headquarters in Brooklyn.

After several years in Bethel he left and married a JW and former missionary. Paul and Pat had two boys and longed for a girl. Finally in 1980 Pat gave birth to their daughter, Jenny. The baby had a blood disorder and became so anemic, doctors said she had to have a blood transfusion.

The Blizards refused to allow the transfusion. They sadly surrendered their beloved child to die. However, the medical team notified authorities, who took legal guardianship of Jenny. Because JW's, to prevent a blood transfusion, routinely took chil-

Rescue Is Possible

dren away from hospitals, a judge issued a restraining order that would not allow the Blizards to take the child away.

Paul and Pat secretly felt great relief that their baby would be saved. Their consciences were clear. They had done everything they could to obey the Watchtower dictates, but now the situation was out of their hands. JW elders didn't agree.

In the hospital the elders approached the Blizards and presented a plan to slip into the hospital and kidnap Jenny. Paul and Pat refused to disobey the court order; they knew to do so would doom their daughter to death. Paul explained that if he pulled the plugs on devices that kept his daughter alive and if he removed her from treatment, he might be charged with homicide. The elders told him he would have to take the chance. At any cost he had to prevent the child from taking blood.

Fed up with their callous disregard for his daughter's life, Paul ordered the elders to leave. As they left, one elder called back, "I hope she gets hepatitis from the blood."

Paul Blizard was willing to accept, believe, and live by all the Watchtower rules with only one exception—the prohibition of a blood transfusion. He objected to that only in special circumstances. Too bad. The elders still regarded him as an outcast.

Years earlier Paul and Pat had obtained a New American Standard Bible, which they studied in secret lest a JW report them to the elders. Paul knew well about the network of informers in the Kingdom Hall. He had been one himself; he thought part of his theocratic duty was to root out weak and straying members.

Paul's own father had turned him in. The elders convened a judicial hearing and found Paul guilty. With the threat of excommunication looming over his head Paul repented of his unauthorized Bible study and confessed.

The JW's make a big deal out of confessing and use it not only to purge an individual's conscience but also as a subtle weapon to implicate other people by mentioning their complicity in the repentant person's wrongdoing.

After Paul's trial and confession, he promised to obey all the Watchtower rules. The elders stripped him of all duties at the

Kingdom Hall. Now Paul had a record. His file, with all that damning information, would follow him to any Kingdom Hall wherever he went.

After the hospital showdown, Paul and Pat remembered their secret Bible studies and the humiliation that followed. They had disobeyed the Watchtower and were *personas non grata* anyway, so they went back to studying the forbidden Bible. Paul also remembered another forbidden book, *Thirty Years a Watchtower Slave* by William J. Schnell. Possession of that book or my book, *I Was Raised a Jehovah's Witness*, means immediate expulsion from Jehovah's Witnesses. Years earlier Paul secretly had read Schnell's book and discarded it as *apostate* propaganda. (Jehovah's Witnesses consider as an *apostate* any ex-JW who speaks against the Watchtower.) After the traumatic experience with Jenny and the elders in the hospital, Paul's mind searched back for pieces of the puzzle. He remembered what Schnell in his book had said. Paul, too, had been a Watchtower slave. The pieces fit. The truths he had read in the New American Standard Version (NASV) of the Bible returned to him. They fit as well.

In the Bible Paul and Pat learned that Jesus is The Truth and trusted in His grace. When the elders learned about Paul and Pat's decision to trust in Jesus Christ, they disfellowshiped them; Paul and Pat then were shunned by old friends and family. But they rejoiced in their newfound Christian liberty.

When I flew in for the first Ex-Jehovah's Witnesses for Jesus convention in New Ringgold, PA, Alex DeMayo of Runnemede, NJ, picked me up at the Philadelphia airport. On the ride we got acquainted and traded accounts of how we got out of the Watchtower.

For 18 years Alex was a faithful *Witness*. Several people reported to the elders that his daughter's skirts were too short. Elders forced him to stand "on the carpet" before them and be reprimanded. The humiliation hurt his pride, but he continued on as an obedient JW. Later, after he had forgotten that incident, for no particular reason he bought his wife a dozen roses. He just wanted to express his love for her. He didn't realize Mother's Day was just a few days away. Someone informed the elders that Alex celebrated Mother's Day. Elders summoned him to another judicial hearing. The elders accused him of *worldliness* because they said he had celebrated a pagan holiday. The callous cruelty of the elders made Alex, for the first time, realize that *just maybe* the Watchtower could be wrong in some instances. He began to think for himself and with an open mind began to read the Bible in context.

Now believing that the Watchtower possibly could be wrong, he accepted an invitation to attend a Christian church and hear Bill Cetnar speak on the errors of the Watchtower. Just to set foot in a church was a major move, because the Society taught that to do so would mean he immediately would be demon-possessed.

Bill Cetnar had been a high official in the Watchtower organization and had escaped. He knew the innerworkings of the Society and the duplicity, hypocrisy, and manipulation of volunteer labor that went on at Bethel (the Watchtower headquarters in Brooklyn). Bill Cetnar talked about Jesus, Who claimed to be *ego aime*—the I AM. That prompted Alex to delve more deeply into independent Bible study. Soon he escaped from the Watchtower's domination and accepted Jesus Christ as LORD and Savior.

"For 18 years I knocked on doors and witnessed to people. During that time I failed to bring one person into the Jehovah's Witnesses, no matter how hard I tried," Alex told the people gathered for the convention. In the two years since his conversion to real Christianity, he had helped several people, including his wife and daughter, trust Christ as Savior.

People do escape from the Watchtower. The way of escape is like a big funnel. The big end is a crisis of belief brought on by unjust actions or lies by the Watchtower or congregational leaders. These accumulate in the big end of the funnel and are concentrated toward the little end. There the Word of God corrects the theological errors and provides a way of escape.

Chapter 2

How Not to Witness to the JW's

Bible Ping-Pong Doesn't Work

If the above various situations funnel people toward the Word of God, why not just start out with Bible truth? Why be concerned with all those swirling around in the big bowl of the funnel? These would include:

- JW's that have dropped out because they can't keep up the pace
- Those who have been kicked out
- Those who left in disgust over immoral leaders, and
- Those who for other reasons think the Watchtower possibly could be wrong.

Usually we can't go directly to them with Bible truth, because they have been conditioned not to perceive what we say.

The narrow end of the funnel is the place to which they are headed, but we can't rush them. Their minds still are clouded with the conviction that the Watchtower is Jehovah's earthly organization. So we have to go back to the place in which they are and work our way into the narrow end—the Word of God.

People don't escape from the Watchtower because you defeat them at biblical ping-pong, in which you quote a verse, then the other person quotes a verse, back and forth. The JW is an expert at this. He practices at the Kingdom Hall. Again and again he has been drilled on each subject. His reflexes are sharp. He can quote two or three Scriptures while you look up one. True, the Scriptures he quotes often are taken out of context and misapplied; he depends on his speed to beat your accuracy. Remember, he believes the Scripture means *what the Watchtower says it means*. So don't play Bible ping-pong with a Jehovah's Witness. It's counterproductive. He doesn't listen to you anyway. While you talk, he's thinking of what he'll say next.

Furthermore, what you say doesn't make any difference. His mind is made up. To him, the Watchtower is God's earthly organization. He rejects anything you say that disagrees with the Watchtower. It's as if someone approached you, a loyal American, with a proposition to commit treason and betray your country. You wouldn't listen. Neither will the JW.

To the JW you are a messenger of Satan with a proposition to join his army in opposition to the True God.

His mind is set. He won't listen to anything you say. If he politely nods his head, just assume that what you say doesn't even go in one ear, let alone pass through a totally disengaged brain. If you try to tell the JW his beliefs are wrong, he thinks you are tempting him to turn against God, friends, and family. His heart fills with fear that he would be separated from all them and then be shunned by them. The JW takes those perceived threats seriously, no matter how logical your argument.

After I became a Christian, on those rare occasions when we were together, in the interest of family peace my stepfather and I avoided the subject of religion. If he brought up the subject and wanted to argue, I would engage him. On one of those occasions, I quoted John 3:16. As usual the discussion descended into an argument and culminated in him getting angry.

"John 3:16. John 3:16. You people always quote John 3:16," he said and then went on to say that I was young and didn't know what I was talking about.

Bible ping-pong didn't work with him. I'm sorry to say nothing else worked either. He died a devout Jehovah's Witness who still believed that God's truth arrived through an invisible Jesus at Watchtower headquarters in Brooklyn.

The rescue process must proceed in small steps. Take my case, for example: I saw a double standard among JW's. I saw hypocrisy. My heart had conflict. Things did not add up. Still I was a loyal Jehovah's Witness.

Finally, because of a preponderance of the evidence, I considered the remote possibility that the Watchtower could be wrong. Then after reading the Bible I clearly saw that I had been lied to. That's when the heavy stones of the Watchtower prison began to loosen and I started my escape.

I saw that the Watchtower's prohibition of military service didn't emerge in the wash. I saw that the prohibition from saluting the flag was baseless. To cherish a photo of a loved one was harmless but still much closer to idolatry than was saluting the flag.

When I urge avoiding Bible ping-pong, I don't mean to flee the battle. If a JW wants to challenge you, explain what you believe. Follow the apostle Paul's example. Paul was a great theologian, but when he shared his faith with someone, he didn't wax eloquent with high-sounding theological words. Rather, he told of his personal experience on the road to Damascus. You may not have seen a blinding light and fallen to the ground, but if you are a Christian, you have had an experience of conversion. Tell the JW your own, personal Christian testimony. She won't listen, but some of what you say will stick. Perhaps later someone else will share his or her testimony with her; it will produce a cumulative effect. I believe that if every Christian would share his or her testimony with every JW who knocks on the door, within 10 years the JW's' numbers would be cut in half.

Until the JW considers the fact that the Watchtower possibly could be wrong, asking questions is more effective than is quoting Scripture. For example one might ask a JW, "What is the Watchtower Society's policy on sex abusers of children in the Kingdom Hall?" or "Are Jehovah's Witness children not allowed to play sports?" Or "Can a person be disfellowshiped for playing chess?" Be prepared to be lied to. When you catch a JW in a lie, confront her with it. Ask, "How many lies does the Watchtower have to tell to become a liar?"

Being Rude Doesn't Help

When I knocked on a door for the Watchtower and someone treated me rudely, I felt vindicated—being persecuted the same as Jesus had been. Being rude to a JW proves to him that he is in Jehovah's will. Being rude to a JW is like work-hardening iron. The more the blacksmith pounds a piece of iron, the harder it gets. If it's too hard, he has to anneal it by getting it red hot and patiently letting it cool very gradually.

When you interact with a JW, whether the JW is a stranger or a family member, be patient and courteous. Imagine what your conversation, from the Jehovah's Witnesses' point of view, would sound like if played back.

You don't have to be wimpy to be courteous. For example: One of the JW's favorite tools is to *change the subject.* Talking Scripture early on is inadvisable. However, sometimes the JW insists on it. You may be talking about the Bible doctrine of only one God. The JW will agree. She can show you many Scriptures that back it up. You might ask, "Why does your NWT Bible say in John Chapter One that Jesus was 'a God?'" She will explain that only *in a sense* was Jesus a God, like Satan is the god of this world; many pagan gods exist. "So was Jesus a good God or a bad god?" you might ask. Or, "Jesus a God, plus Jehovah The God, equals how many Gods? More than one God for sure."

Suddenly the JW will announce that some people in the car are waiting on her and that she has to go, or she will change the subject entirely and ask, "What about hell? You don't believe in a literal, burning hell, do you?"

Then is the time to politely say, "Let's stay on the subject." Pointing out that the JW has dodged a question by attempting to change the subject is not unfair.

JW's practice *verbal gymnastics.* They drill and practice at the Kingdom Hall, so they're ready to take you on. You are responsible for keeping them from jumping out of bounds.

Treating the JW Like an Enemy Doesn't Help

Because a close loved one of yours has been brainwashed into the cult, you might justifiably feel anger toward the Watchtower and Jehovah's Witnesses. If you express your outrage to a JW, it will drive her to a deeper commitment to the Watchtower Society. Keep your anger to yourself and be as courteous as possible.

Remember, the JW is a victim. Use tact, love, and concern to help her become free of the Watchtower. You will see a changed person. I have seen changes as dramatic as those in the apostle Paul, who changed from a terrorist who persecuted Christians to a humble preacher and great hero of the faith.

Jesus said to Saul of Tarsus, *Saul, Saul, why persecutest thou me? it is hard for thee to kick against the pricks.*[7] Saul was an enemy of Christianity, yet Jesus loved him. Saul apparently had been exposed to the gospel by family members who were Christians, so his conscience was "pricking" him. The Lord alluded to the practice of a person driving an ox that pulled a cart. The driver would "prick" the ox with a sharp stick to make the animal pull or change directions. God had been "pricking" Paul to get him to go in the right direction. Like an obstinate ox, rather than turning Paul had "kicked against the pricks".

Treat the Jehovah's Witness with the same compassion as Jesus treated Saul; bear in mind that the JW is also "kicking against the pricks". If he sees lying and duplicity in the Watchtower and love and compassion in Christians, the pricks of conscience will become greater.

Chapter 3

Touch the Mortar Joint

When I realized the Watchtower had lied to me, I was like a poor, hurt prisoner in a stone prison. I timidly reached a finger to probe the mortar that held the stones together. To my surprise the old mortar crumbled. It was a scary experience. All my life I thought the stone walls of the Watchtower were impregnable. Now the mortar started to crumble. Maybe now I would be crushed if it fell down on me.

As I read the Bible alone with my mind finally open, the Watchtower crumbled and I escaped.

You can chip away the crumbling mortar of the Watchtower by showing Watchtower double standards and hypocrisy. You can say, "The Watchtower lies and teaches its followers to lie." The JW will deny it, but you can back up your charge. In his heart he knows the Watchtower lies, but he dares not let that thought surface in his mind. If you press on and show proof, those thoughts eventually will fight their way to the surface.

You can tell the JW about child sex abuse and cover up; you can back it up. You can tell some of the accounts written here of JW's who have been grossly mistreated. You can demonstrate how the Society treats people without compassion and encourages the elders to do so. You can tell the horrors of dying children whose parents refused them blood transfusions.

You can talk to the JW about the Watchtower's false prophecies about Armageddon. "Everyone makes mistakes," he will answer. However, according to the Bible, prophets of God don't. If one who claims to speak for the LORD, as the Watchtower does, makes wrong prophecy, it proves he is a false prophet. One strike and you're out.

In defense the JW might point out hypocrisy among professing Christians and try to indict the entire Christian community. The great difference is that the Watchtower Society itself promulgates the errors and lies. Things might be different if the Society were straight and true and only a few renegade Witnesses lied and acted like hypocrites. The Society itself is the chief liar. The Governing Body sanctioned lying.

Lying was invented by Satan. *When he (the devil) speaketh a lie, he speaketh of his own: for he is a liar, and the father of it.*[8] Institutionalized lying then must be the children of lies. Jesus was positive in condemning "all liars". He lumped them in with the cowardly, the unbelieving, the vile, the murderers, the sexually immoral, those who practice magic arts, and idolaters who will go into the lake of fire and experience the second death.[9]

Lying Is OK, the Watchtower Says

When I was 13, I wanted a job that required employees to be 16. I was big for my age and had a lot of work experience. I had washed dishes in a restaurant on the graveyard shift. I had delivered morning and evening newspapers. I had caddied at golf courses. In those jobs age made no difference. But this job required that I be 16, the interviewer told me.

"I'm 16," I lied.

"You'll need a birth certificate or some kind of proof," the interviewer said. I didn't know whether I had a birth certificate. If so, it wouldn't say I was 16, so I told her I didn't have one.

"Do you have an old family Bible? If you do, and your birth date is recorded in it, that will do fine."

I went home and told my mother what the interviewer had said. My mother and stepfather had many Bibles. She found one that hadn't been written in and recorded my birth, with a date that would make me a little over 16-years old. I took the Bible to the interviewer and got the job.

My mother was a moral woman, but her morals were based on the Watchtower Society. To her, telling a lie to a *worldly* organization wasn't really a lie. It was OK to tell untruths to *the world*. She never would have lied to a Jehovah's Witness. But she did not hesitate to lie to others and encouraged me to do the same if I had a good reason and no malice.

After the fall of communism in 1989 and the eastern bloc countries became more open, Jehovah's Witnesses became more active in those countries. Bulgaria considered the JW's a cult; this primarily occurred because of their refusal to take blood transfusions. To allow their injured children to die rather than permit blood transfusions was repugnant to the Bulgarians.

The Watchtower made application in Bulgaria for recognition as a legally registered religion. The Bulgarian government refused to recognize the Watchtower.

In 1998 the Watchtower reached an agreement with the Bulgarian government: If it would recognize the Jehovah's Witnesses as a religion, the Watchtower would not punish a JW for taking a blood transfusion in Bulgaria. The Watchtower was lying.

David Reed, ex-JW author, in his newsletter, *Comments from the Friends*, said, "However, the Watchtower made it plain to the news media that they will not change anything regarding members who receive blood transfusions. It is not acceptable and will be punished by disfellowshiping the offender."[10]

Watchtower Gives a License to Lie

The Watchtower's dictionary of terms, *Aid to Bible Understanding*, gives the organization's official description of a *lie*. "LIE. The opposite of truth. Lying generally involves saying something false to a person who is entitled to know the truth and doing so with the intent to deceive or to injure him or another person."[11]

When my mother forged a document that lied about my age, she lied to a *worldly* entity *not entitled to know the truth*; she didn't do it with intent to injure. This happened many years before the Watchtower terms were codified in *Aid to Bible Understanding.*

The Watchtower lies, encourages its people to lie, and calls it *theocratic strategy.* I experienced that strategy.

In a confrontation with three JW elders, I said, "No one has ever decided, just from reading the Bible alone, that only 144,000 people will go to heaven."

One of the elders spoke up. "I have."

"You have?" I asked.

"Yes. Just from reading the Bible alone."

"You read in Revelation how 144,000 Jews, all male, from 12 tribes of Israel received a special seal from God. You read that and came to the independent conclusion that only 144,000 people could go to heaven?"

"That's right," he answered.

"All those Jews were virgins," I said. "They were all without guile. But the Watchtower teaches that the 144,000 are both men and women—some married and some not. You got all that just from reading the Bible about the male virgin Jews with no one to help you understand it?"

"Well, one of the brothers did help me understand it," he conceded.

He didn't want to talk about that anymore, so I asked, "Who translated the Watchtower's Bible?"

The three elders quickly delivered the canned speech that explained that they wouldn't name the translators because they didn't want to give honor to men.

"I know who the translators were. Not one of them understood Hebrew or Greek. The most educated of the committee was Frederick Franz, who dropped out of the University of Cincinnati after two years," I said.

Touch the Mortar Joint

"They were eminent Greek and Hebrew scholars," the verbose elder gave the standard Watchtower reply.

"There was not a Greek or Hebrew scholar in the whole bunch," I said.

"I know Greek," he countered. "I'm a Greek scholar."

"How do you know Greek? Did you study Greek in school?"

"Yes."

"Where?"

"In Athens. I grew up in Athens. I graduated from high school in Athens. I spoke Greek," he said proudly.

"You understand modern Greek," I said. "Do you understand *koine* Greek?"

"What's that?" he asked.

"*Koine* Greek is the language of the New Testament. It was the common Greek spoken throughout the Roman Empire. You say you're a Greek scholar. You're not a Greek scholar. But I'll tell you what you really are. You are a liar."

The occasion for our conversation was a Jehovah's Witnesses Assembly at a Rockwall, TX, middle school. I had put gospel tracts on the windshields of the cars in the parking lot. The three elders had started taking them off. I confronted them and demanded that they leave the tracts alone.

"You guys demand your constitutional rights. You insist that you be able to put out your literature unhindered. Now practice what you preach and leave my literature alone."

"OK. OK," one elder said. "I'm sorry. We'll leave your stuff alone."

"I've got to leave for a few minutes. I want you to promise me you'll leave my tracts alone while I'm gone." (My church to which I had to go briefly was only five minutes away.)

"Oh, we won't bother your tracts," he said as he oozed sincerity.

I drove to the church as quickly as possible and returned to see all three elders grabbing tracts off windshields and stuffing them in their pockets.

To them I didn't deserve to know the truth, so they had a license to lie.

How Many Lies Qualifies You as a Liar?

The Watchtower has lied about its Bible. It says a group of eminent Greek and Hebrew scholars translated the NWT. Not one Greek or Hebrew scholar was among them. The chief of the translation committee was Frederick Franz, who admitted under oath in a court of law in Scotland in 1954 that he neither could translate nor read Hebrew. Franz had dropped out of the University of Cincinnati after two years and was the most educated member of the translation committee.

The Watchtower lied to the United States government when it issued forged vaccination certificates for its international missionaries. The Watchtower lied to the Bulgarian government when it said it would not punish a Bulgarian JW for taking a blood transfusion. The Watchtower lied to the Mexican government when it told young men of draft age to buy fake military training certificates so they wouldn't have to serve in the Mexican Armed Forces.

Jehovah's Witnesses tell lies. The Watchtower tells lies. Liars tell lies.

Dishonest Deception

One of the questions prospective JW's ask is, "If I become one of Jehovah's Witnesses, would I be expected to preach as they do?" The Watchtower's official answer would make a politician proud. "When one becomes filled with the knowledge of the promised earthly Paradise under Christ's Kingdom, one wants to share it with others. You will, too."

The lengthy answer includes ". . . Telling others about the Paradise earth and its blessings is to be done willingly, out of a heart filled with a desire to share the good news . . .."[12] The Watchtower's offer is one the new JW can't refuse. She can spend at least 10 hours a month preaching and distributing Watchtower literature willingly or be disfellowshiped and consigned to death at Armageddon.

A new JW is definitely expected to preach like the others and live up to eight times more *Thou Shalt Not*s than the Ten Commandments. The Watchtower's political answer is deception at best.

The Watchtower teaches Jehovah's Witnesses, when talking to prospects, to keep quiet about blood, not celebrating holidays, and forsaking family and friends. Controversial teachings occur later after the prospect is committed. It's akin to the "bait-and-switch" strategy in selling.

When I was a young man with a young family and still hadn't settled on a vocation, I took a job selling sewing machines in Fort Worth. The company at which I worked advertised a "Rebuilt Singer Sewing Machine" for $25. It was a great bargain. People answered the ad; the company sent salesmen to follow up. I was supposed to "sell" the rebuilt Singer, then pull out the new, modern machine and "switch" the sale to the more expensive model. I sold lots of sewing machines. But often the customer couldn't afford more than the $25 rebuilt Singer, so I sold it to them. The company lost money on each of those sales, so I was fired.

JW's practice "bait-and-switch." The prospect buys into sweet fellowship, true friends, and prospects of eternal life on Paradise earth, but it gets switched to a long list of "Don't you dare, or you'll die at Armageddon" and "You'd better remain faithful and obedient, or you're doomed."

JW's Have Their Share of Hypocrites

JW's would have you believe that theirs is a near-perfect society in which people love each other, don't cheat, and don't lie. We know they lie to *the world*, to people who *don't deserve to know the truth*. But do they cheat and lie to each other? Much to the embarrassment of other members, cheats and liars are in every religious group. Regardless of their claims to purity, JW's have the same kind of people. They talk one way and act another.

The year I turned 14, a JW farmer I will call Mr. Miller begged my mother to allow me to go to his Western Kansas wheat farm and work for him for the summer.

"I'll treat him like my own son," Mr. Miller said.

He said he would pay me for my work and would take good care of me. I wanted to go. A great adventure that I considered a prelude to manhood excited me. I hoped Mama would say *yes*.

The JW's, both in his local congregation and the Wichita, KS, congregation, highly regarded Mr. Miller. I lived with him for three months and from close up received a lesson on hypocrisy.

Mr. Miller's home was isolated out in the Western Kansas prairie far beyond electrical transmission lines. However, he had his own electrical generation system, a completely modern home, and well-lighted farmstead that included a private grain elevator. The house had four bedrooms—one for his invalid wife, one for Mr. Miller, one for the full-time cook who also took care of Mrs. Miller, and an extra bedroom that was not being used. Since he had assured my mother he would treat me as though I was his own son, I assumed the other bedroom would be mine. Wrong. Mine was a cot in the basement.

We routinely ate together—Mr. Miller, the cook, and me, so I often was in the kitchen. Even as an inexperienced kid I could perceive the more-than-friendly looks between Mr. Miller and the cook, a stout but shapely woman young enough to be his daughter. She hid her pretty face behind round eyeglasses. I also saw him go into her bedroom more times than he emerged.

Mr. Miller never beat me, but he threatened to do so when I wanted to go home early. He raised a big fist over my face and loomed over me. I was fed up with being treated like a slave but was intimidated and afraid to disobey him.

I drove his tractor and his truck and herded his cattle. One of my jobs was to stand on a 12-inch plank 40-feet up in his grain elevator and keep a grain chute from getting blocked. The grains of wheat on the plank were like ball bearings, so I was in constant fear of slipping and falling.

Every day for three months I worked with him. Mr. Miller never went to the Kingdom Hall and never went into the field service, yet to my knowledge he was not rebuked as I or any other ordinary JW would have been. He was a man of means and a man of influence—the kind that gets special consideration in many organizations, including the Watchtower.

When my three months were up, Mr. Miller sat me down and announced his accounting. He deducted room and board and paid me $30 for my summer's work. It was in the form of a check made out to my mother. Mr. Miller put me on a bus for Wichita; that was the last I saw of him.

Certainly Mr. Miller was not representative of JW's, but he demonstrated that they are not so loving and kind to each other as they claim. He had treated me, a fellow JW, with contempt. He lied to my mother. Just two rooms away from his invalid wife he flaunted immorality.

Like members of other organizations, if they have influence or money, some JW's get away with dishonesty and deception. Mr. Miller had both.

JW's Have Typical Marks of a Cult

One of the Jehovah's Witnesses' most conspicuous beliefs and one of the marks typical of a cult is that *only they have the truth*. The only way anyone has hope for salvation is by being part of their organization. However, when a prospective convert asks whether JW's believe they are the only ones who will be saved, the Watchtower's official answer is, "No."

The Watchtower Society says millions who have died will be resurrected and "have an opportunity for life. Many now living may yet take a stand for truth and righteousness . . .." They're saying if a person dies as a *person of good will,* not opposed to the Watchtower, and not a part of *Christendom,* she will be resurrected and given an opportunity to embrace *The Truth*—in other words, to become a Jehovah's Witness.

The hypothetical choice reminds me of a scene in the movie *The Godfather* in which the Godfather made someone "an offer he couldn't refuse". The offer was, "Do as I say, or die." Likewise, according to the Watchtower's plan for the post-Armageddon resurrection of non-JW's, those eligible for a second chance will be given a choice, "Become a Jehovah's Witness now, or be cast into the Lake of Fire."

The Society says, ". . . God looks at the heart. He sees accurately and judges mercifully. He has committed judgment into Jesus' hands, not ours."[13] Very true, but the Watchtower Society behaves just the opposite. Any JW knows how judgmental the Society is and how the elders lord it over people and sometimes even pronounce judgment, "You're going to die in Armageddon."

In reality, after all the verbal gymnastics the JW's do believe they are the only ones who will be saved. They just bounce around on the balance bars to avoid admitting it.

Jehovah's Witnesses' Typical Cult

If you look up *cult* in the dictionary, you'll find that it's just generic religion, or a group of people following a particular religious leader, such as Jesus Christ. However, in our growing and changing language, modern usage of *cult* now means a religion that is considered unorthodox or spurious. Some cults, though we may consider them so, are generally harmless. They are entitled to free practice of their religion, as we all are.

Some dangerous cults practice religious mesmerization, brainwashing, and total physical and emotional control of individuals. These cults sometimes take over mind, body, bank accounts, car titles, and property deeds. Sometimes they cause needless death. These we consider dangerous cults.

Some of the marks of the dangerous cult:

(1) They claim to have exclusive truth.

The cult says it has all the answers to every question—and has an exclusive communication with God. If you want the truth, you have to get it through members of the cult. You can't get it by just reading the Bible alone without their guidance.

Their claim of exclusive truth allows no dissension. The cult may challenge you to look at its teachings with an open mind and even to pray about them. However the cult doesn't allow this by its own members! They are told what they can read, listen to, and pray about.

Armed with belief of exclusive truth, the cult can make the most obscure and even outlandish interpretations of Scripture. An Old Testament passage that easily can be understood if read in context might be claimed as authority for the cult's beliefs or activities without even a remote connection. The cult member can't read the Bible and draw a conclusion. He must ask cult leaders what a passage of Scripture means.

(2) They claim authority.

As the exclusive purveyors of truth, the cult believes it has authority over its members. It may tell members who and when they can marry—or the cult even may order a divorce. For many years the Jehovah's Witnesses taught husbands and wives to inform on each another and to report to cult leaders about private sexual matters.

This authority in some cults is a threat to life. Members may be ordered to withhold medical treatment for a child. A group of JW elders ordered parents of a child to "let her die" rather than acccpt treatment. They claimed the child's death would honor God. In some groups this complete control extends to the property of its members. The Jim Jones cult took over all the assets of its members. Jim Jones told them what to do and when to do it. He ordered mothers to poison their children and then for all the adults to commit suicide. They obeyed; the cult self-destructed.

(3) Hidden teachings

Dangerous cults don't reveal all their strange doctrines when they try to recruit new members. For a JW to start his recruitment effort by saying, "Join us; if your child ever needs a blood transfusion, you'll have to let him die" or "Join us; our kids will have to give up sports and Christmas" would be a deal-breaker. Usually the JW's approach people with more orthodox teachings—beliefs that are shared with other religious groups. They offer comfort to the guilty by proclaiming, "There is no hell." They offer hope of eternal life on Paradise Earth. As the prospect becomes more interested and more committed to the cult, the leaders gradually introduce the more bizarre doctrines. The initiate is not allowed to know the inner secrets until he is fully indoctrinated.

(4) Exclusive association
The cult discourages or forbids camaraderie outside the group. The cult often trains adherents to believe "It's us against them" and to distrust anyone not in the cult. They consider alien even family members not indoctrinated into the cult.

How can you protect your family from a dangerous cult? The best defense against error is truth. You can depend on the Bible. If the Bible says one thing and some exotic guru, or a well-dressed couple with a child in tow, say something else, believe the Bible.

If people try to convince you to join their group and tell you everything you believe is wrong, that should raise in your mind red flags of danger. Use your common sense. If something sounds too strange to be true, it might not be. If everyone in the group thinks exactly the same, you might suspect that they have no intellectual freedom and that someone tells them what to think.

Some of the cults could have taught the communists a thing or two about brainwashing. Surrounded by caring people the prospect is love-bombed. Like Native American women who used to chew leather to make it soft and pliable, for the same reason cultists pay a lot of attention to prospects. The prospect is emotionally caressed, made soft and pliable, and led to believe these folks really care. Gradually everything he has believed gets washed out of his brain and replaced with the cult's doctrines. Soon he's afraid to form any opinion but rather trusts his handlers about what he should believe. Don't let the love-bombing numb your common sense. Seduction isn't real love.

While the handlers feed the novice small, sweet doses of Watchtower doctrine, he's like the proverbial frog in the saucepan of tepid water. You can heat the water so gradually that the frog doesn't notice. When it boils, it's too late.

Don't fall for the Hitler lie. Nazi dictator Adolph Hitler made outlandish claims that obviously were false. His tactic was to shout the lie louder and more often until people began to believe it. In the early years of World War II people didn't believe the holocaust was taking place. Such a gigantic cruelty was beyond their imagination. Nice looking, well-scrubbed, educated, and polite Germans repeated Hitler's lies, but that didn't make those lies true.

A lie is a lie even if it's loud and repeated. A lie still is a lie if it's repeated by kind and caring people.

People do commit unbelievable crimes. People do change the Bible to suit themselves. People do make up fantastic stories, begin to believe them, and then tell them for the truth.

The Bible contains the truth. Jesus Christ said, *I am the truth, the way and the life, no man comes to the Father, but by me.* Real truth is a person—Jesus Christ. You can get to know Him through the Bible, God's Word. This is the best protection against dangerous cults.

Protect your children. Children eventually must make up their own minds about what to believe. However, parents are responsible to teach children so those children can make informed decisions. Read the Bible to your little children. Tell them Bible stories. Take them to Sunday school and church. When they mature and are accountable, they will be protected from being drawn into a dangerous cult.

Having read thus far, you can recognize that Jehovah's Witnesses are a typical cult—and also are dangerous. They are typical because they have all the marks of a cult and dangerous because they cause death by withholding needed medical treatment. With one order Jim Jones killed more than 900 people. By their order to refuse blood transfusions Jehovah's Witnesses have killed many more than that.

Jehovah's Witnesses should have the freedom to believe and preach whatever they want, but they should not be allowed to cause death.

Chapter 4

Of What Is the Society Afraid?

Why did Paul and Pat Blizard get in trouble with the Society for reading the New American Standard Translation of the Bible? Of what was the Society afraid? How could private Bible study possibly harm an organization?

JW's are not allowed even to possess my book, *I Was Raised a Jehovah's Witness.* If a JW is caught with it or with Schnell's *Thirty Years a Watchtower Slave,* he will be disfellowshiped and declared an *apostate*. The Society also is afraid of what will happen if JW's read old Watchtower publications. In them the false prophecies and contradictory doctrines stand out and are exposed to the light. In them also the reader can see that the Watchtower Society claims to be a prophet of God. My stepfather once prided himself in his vast collection of old Watchtower books. Today he would be disfellowshiped for keeping them.

More than once atheists have studied the Bible to prove it wrong. In the process of that study, they changed their minds and became Christians. I have studied Watchtower books and literature to prove them wrong and never once have been close to being converted to the Society's way of thinking. Rather, the more I read the Society's literature, the more error I see in it and the more convinced I am that the Society is a false prophet.

Why don't Jehovah's Witnesses read books that expose the Watchtower, to prove them wrong in the same way atheists read the Bible? Remaining a Jehovah's Witness would be difficult after one read *Crisis of Conscience* by Raymond Franz or Bill and Joan Cetnar's story, "An Inside View of the Watchtower Society", in Edmond C. Gruss' book, *We Left Jehovah's Witnesses a Non-Prophet Organization.*

The Society doesn't want JW's to know what these books reveal. JW's say, "We have the truth and the truth has set us free." If they really were free, they could read anything they wanted. Like a walnut veneer over fiber board the Society displays some truth to cover its errors. JW's talk about the oneness of God, the hopeless condition of the world that can be set right only by God, and how human government and organized religion have failed to correct the problems. All true. However, those truths are used as a vehicle to transport error.

The Watchtower is afraid its errors will be exposed, so it forbids JW's to read certain things, the most important of which is a legitimate translation of the Bible, including the King James Version, Revised Standard Version, New American Standard Version, and the most popular version today—New International Version. But the Society says don't read those and many other good translations. It's not allowed.

The Society claims its NWT Bible is the best and most accurate translation. A second-year seminary student halfway through his studies in Greek and Hebrew knows more about biblical languages than does the entire translation committee of the Watchtower Society. The Society doesn't want JW's to know who translated the NWT. They claim only "a group of eminent Greek and Hebrew scholars". Other Bible translations make available translators' names and a list of their credentials. The Watchtower Society does not, because their "translators" were not qualified.

On several occasions Bill Cetnar witnessed the gathering of the NWT translation committee. He knew each member by name and by their qualifications. He watched them go into their conference room to work on the NWT. Bill told me that no member of the committee had training in Greek or Hebrew.

Of What is the Society Afraid?

Jehovah's Witnesses sometimes do risk exposure and read forbidden literature. Paul Blizard didn't leave the Watchtower immediately after reading a book opposed to the Watchtower or after reading a legitimate translation of the Bible. Paul hesitated, but later when he saw the crass disregard of his baby's life by JW elders, Paul began to put two and two together and escaped from the Watchtower.

When the Jehovah's Witnesses held their assemblies in Dallas or Fort Worth, I and other ex-JW's held picket signs and handed out gospel tracts as people entered the building. We cared about the people attending the assembly, because we once had been prisoners of the Watchtower; we hoped to see them escape the mind control and experience Christian liberty. Messages on the signs included:

"How Many Greek and Hebrew Scholars Translated the NWT? None."
"How Many False Prophecies Does it Take to Make a False Prophet?"
"Watchtower False Prophecies: 1914. 1925. 1945. 1975."
"Jesus Christ Loves You and Died For You."
"Did Christ Start Making Mistakes in 1914?"

Usually a man used a long-lens camera to take our pictures. Two or three men would approach each of us and ask us not to picket. We told them we had every right to picket on a public sidewalk.

On an especially hot summer day around 1980 I alone put out gospel tracts at the JW assembly at the coliseum in Dallas. In the parking lot I put a tract on each car; I stuck it under a windshield wiper or in a window that had been left open a crack in the 113-degree heat. A group of six men surrounded me. "We'd rather you didn't put tracts on these cars," one man said right in my face while the others stepped closer. Obviously they were trying to intimidate me.

"I'd rather do it," I said. "You guys put out literature and demand your First Amendment rights, yet you want to deny me the same right." Then I added a word I shouldn't have. "Hypocrites." I walked through their ranks and continued.

Near the front entrance I handed tracts to those entering. Some would not accept the tract. Others would accept the tract and start reading it. As they entered the building, a man standing at the door snatched it out of their hands. Some others would accept the tract and quickly stuck it in a pocket.

I received a phone call from a young man who told me that in about 1983, three years earlier, he had received one of my tracts. He quickly had hidden it in his pocket. He waited until he got home to read it. After he read it, he put it away. A year later he got the tract out and read it again.

The simple gospel tract explained that all have sinned, that Jesus loves us anyway, and that He died on the cross to pay the penalty for our sins. It stated that He asks us to believe in Him as LORD and Savior, repent of our sins, and ask His forgiveness. This all was contrary to what the young man as a Jehovah's Witness believed, but he was fascinated by the idea that salvation could be free. He wouldn't have to earn it. He could have forgiveness. He could have hope for an eternal home in heaven. But he put all that out of his mind as he had been trained to do.

As time passed, the little tract returned to his mind. He took it out and read it again. Then he decided to look up the Scriptures to which the tract referred. Then, with an open mind, he started reading the Bible; light penetrated the darkness. He realized that Jesus was LORD indeed. The young man found a copy of my book, *I Was Raised a Jehovah's Witness,* and read it.

He was so happy to be free of the Watchtower and to know he belonged to Jesus, he wanted to share it with me. So he looked up my phone number and called to tell me about the tract that three years earlier I had handed him.

The Society is afraid of truth. Little by little biblical truth penetrated this young man's mind. He had tested the mortar between stones of the Watchtower and found it weak. So he chipped it away. Soon the big stones moved; he was free.

Chapter 5

Watchtower Hierarchy

Throughout its history the Watchtower Society has railed against the Roman Catholic Church hierarchy and the catchall for all religious evil the Watchtower calls *The Clergy*. The Jehovah's Witnesses brag that they have no paid ministers, take up no offerings, and have nothing in common with the Catholic hierarchy.

Although the religious part of the Watchtower is well-organized and rather transparent, the business end is a maze. The *Governing Body* sets the Watchtower course theologically and sends instructions down a chain of command from the Brooklyn headquarters to the individual congregations. Most JW's would be at a loss to explain the property ownership and physical control.

The Society is comprised of 11 or more U.S. corporations that make up the Watchtower Society, including Watchtower Bible and Tract Society of New York; Watchtower Associates, Ltd.; Watchtower Foundation, Inc.; Watchtower Ventures, Inc.; and the Watch Tower Bible and Tract Society of Pennsylvania.[14] There are dozens of Watchtower corporations in other countries.

Don Alden Adams is regarded as the Watchtower Society president. He is in fact president of the Watch Tower Bible and Tract Society of Pennsylvania. Previous presidents of the Society,

Charles Taze Russell, Joseph Rutherford, Nathan Knorr, and Frederick Franz, ran the Society as a king runs a country with the Governing Body serving as advisers. Milton G. Henschel appears to have had less control and was the only Watchtower president thus far who did not die in office. In 2000 he stepped down and was replaced by Don Alden Adams.

The Society is one of the 40 largest revenue producers in New York, with an income of some $951 million annually, and is considered the largest publisher of literature in the world.

The Governing Body is made up of approximately 12 members who are of *The Elect*, those few survivors of the 144,000 *anointed ones* who believe they will go to heaven. (The rank-and-file hope for eternal life on earth if at the end they are found worthy.) The Governing Body functions as an executive committee that names branch representatives who liaison between the Society and Branch Committees in the 230 countries in which JW's are active.

Each country or area Branch is divided into Districts. Each District is divided into Circuits. A District Overseer is in charge of the Circuits. Each Circuit has about 20 congregations, all governed by a Circuit Overseer.[15]

The local congregation meets in a *Kingdom Hall* and has up to 200 members. (After a congregation reaches 200, it usually divides and starts a new congregation.) Each congregation is overseen by elders, one of whom is the Congregational Overseer, the equivalent of a church pastor. Elders have the authority to conduct judicial hearings involving members accused of *worldly activity* and any number of other transgressions.

Leadership responsibilities in the local congregation are shared by *servants*, equivalent to deacons. A *Territory Servant* coordinates the door-to-door activities in the congregation's area. A *Book Servant* dispenses literature. Other Servants manage the money and physical operation of the Kingdom Hall.

In 1986 a congregation in Bonham, TX, decided to break away from the Watchtower Society. The congregation, represented by trustees, owned the Kingdom Hall property. The Watchtower lawyers descended on Bonham and fought vigorously against the congregation's retaining ownership of the property. The escapees argued that the Jehovah's Witnesses were governed by the congregational form of church government, which means the congregation is the highest earthly authority. Therefore, they said the property belonged to them. The Watchtower lawyers argued that the Watchtower Society was an organized religion, hierarchal in nature as the Roman Catholic Church is, and governed from the top down. This argument was opposite to what the Watchtower has taught since its inception.

For most of its existence the Watchtower Society loudly denied being a religion. One of its most repeated pulpit-thumping statements was that it had no hierarchy but rather consisted of groups of Bible students with a congregational form of self-government. The escapees had to but show the Watchtower literature that claimed just the opposite of what the Watchtower lawyers claimed.

As usual, when the Society was forced to do an about-face, it claimed *new light* from Jehovah. That *new light* revealed that the Society indeed was a hierarchy.

The many new corporations formed in recent years demonstrate how the Society now covers its tracks to be sure no future congregation can break away and keep its property.

Contrary to 100 years of claims to the opposite, the Watchtower declared itself a hierarchy-governed religion and testified to it under oath in a court of law.

Control of the Roman Catholic Church never has been out of the hands of the Pope, although the number of cardinals who select the next Pope have multiplied over the centuries. For most of its history control of the Watchtower resided in its president. The first president, Charles Taze Russell, had an advisory committee of five men and two women, but he ran the show. When Russell died in 1916, Judge Joseph Rutherford took over and had an eight-man board of directors of the Watch Tower Corporations. Rutherford, however, was the Chief Executive Officer and made the decisions.

After Rutherford's death, Nathan H. Knorr took over as president. In the 1970s he allowed the seven-member board of directors to become the Governing Body and gradually increased its membership to 11. Chairmanship of the Governing Body began to rotate annually in alphabetical order. In 1976 Knorr put the Governing Body in charge of all operations of the Watchtower Society. Thereafter the Governing Body and Society became synonymous terms.

The number of members of the Governing Body diminished from the 11 to nine in 2007 and now varies from time to time.

Don Adams, the latest president of the Watchtower Society, seems to have lost much of the presidential authority. He is not a member of the Governing Body.[16]

Nevertheless, the Watchtower still is governed by a self-perpetuating hierarchy that controls from the top down.

Big-Money Organization

With annual revenue of more than $951 million,[17] the Watchtower has one of the largest cash incomes in New York and is one of the largest property-owners in Brooklyn. According to a May 14, 2007, article in the *New York Post,* "Watchtower owns 30 meticulously kept buildings and three lots in affluent Brooklyn Heights and DUMBO[18] worth hundreds of millions of dollars."

A broker estimated the Watchtower will get more than $60 million for just six sites. In 2004 when it relocated its Bible and magazine printing upstate to Wallkill, it sold its former book plant in Brooklyn for $205 million. The Watchtower ". . . also made hefty profits last year selling a 76-unit building on Livingston Street for $18.6 million and a 42-unit building on Hicks Street for $14 million," the article said.[19]

How does the Watchtower make so much money? The almost $1-billion annual income is from the sale of publications and does not include massive profits from real estate. You don't have to be an accountant to calculate high profits if most of your sales force works for nothing and pays its own expenses. Then the group has production workers—hundreds of them work for room and board and enough money to buy toothpaste.

When the time arrives for new construction, the Watchtower doesn't worry about high labor costs. JW's built a 27-building complex on a former dairy farm at Patterson, NY. It is designed to house and feed 1,600 people. The complex involves six apartment buildings, two- to five-stories high, a 450-car garage, a 144-room hotel, and a huge kitchen. Cost of construction was estimated at $50 million without labor costs. Volunteer Jehovah's Witnesses' labor saved the Society an estimated $130 million.

The Watch Tower Society of Pennsylvania in 1998 reported cash and short-term investments of $296 million, which with other receivables totaled $705 million in assets with only $71 million in liabilities.

The Canadian government requires a detailed report from nonprofit organizations. According to the Watchtower Society of Canada's report for the year 2000, it had cash on hand of more than $23 million and receivables of more than $24 million. At that time about 111,000 JW's lived in Canada and were dispersed in 1,300 congregations. If those figures were consistent annually, it would mean each Canadian JW's free labor is enriching the Society by $423 a year.

The Witnesses always have made a lot of noise about "no paid clergy". The Canadian report showed they had 302 employees paid between $1 and $29,999. That same year in Canada the Watchtower had 306 employees making between $90,000 and $109,999.[20] I found no such report for the U.S., so we don't know how many hundreds of JW leaders make more than $100,000 a year. So much for "no paid clergy"!

Local congregations raise most of the money and volunteer the labor to build their Kingdom Halls, but the Society retains ownership.

To where does all that money go? Not to buy groceries for the volunteer laborers. Watchtower farms, run by more volunteer workers, furnish the food.[21]

The Watchtower won't say to where all the money goes.

Arbitrary Authority

A just government goes by the rule of law, not of people who rule on whim. Likewise in an organization, those who have authority to make major decisions in your life should be consistent and have rules to follow. JW elders sometimes are inconsistent and make the rules as they go along.

We can see an example in the life of Timothy Campbell, a Canadian JW. His wife became delusional and believed she was Jesus Christ. She thought she had the authority to take another husband. She chose one of the elders in the local Kingdom Hall. The elder visited the Campbell home and explained to her that what she proposed was impossible. She decided if he wouldn't consent, she would marry another of the elders.

Her mental state continued to decline. She told Timothy she wanted no more to do with him or their children. She abandoned them and left their home.

Timothy conferred with the elders. Since his wife had abandoned them, Timothy wanted a divorce. The elders told him that under the circumstances, he could divorce her. A month before the divorce was final the elders changed their minds and said Timothy could not divorce his wife. Their reason: he was seeing another woman before he was divorced. The other woman was a fellow JW he had hired as a babysitter. He tried to explain to the elders that she was only a babysitter and that they were not romantically involved. It made no difference.

Timothy stood *on the carpet* at the Kingdom Hall, in which eight elders interrogated him; four were from his congregation and four from the babysitter's congregation. The next day one of the elders visited his home, told him he was being disfellowshiped, and walked away.

The babysitter resented the way he had been treated; later they did become close. Eventually they married and gave the elders ammunition for "I told you so." However, Timothy maintains his behavior throughout was *theocratic.* Then they disfellowshiped his new wife because she married him.

Two years later the elders reviewed Timothy's case. They decided he had been wrongly accused and reinstated him as a JW.

Even so, Timothy felt uneasy in that Kingdom Hall and searched in vain for another congregation away from those elders—one that would demonstrate Christian love. Duplicity of the Society concerned him, but if he dared to mention it, he would be disfellowshiped again. He had been warned. After a business failure and continued mental trauma about the contradictions and hypocrisy within the JW's, Timothy suffered a mental breakdown.

Timothy tried to take his own life but failed. For three weeks he went into a mental institution but still emerged depressed.

Later the elders called him on the carpet again for interrogation about his failed business venture. At the close they told him he once again would be disfellowshiped. The reason: he had demonstrated greed when he moved to another congregation. Later the elders denied that was the reason but gave no other. Timothy suffered a complete breakdown. He ran from the Kingdom Hall and screamed that he had no right to live. The elders brought him back in. He fell on the floor as he screamed and sobbed. The elders called the police, who took him away.

After Timothy settled down emotionally, he went home. Unable to work he went on welfare. His wife encouraged him to return to the Kingdom Hall. He did, but his faith in the Watchtower had been ground away. "I no longer believed that this organization had the approval of God," he said.

Timothy Campbell experienced an example of the arbitrary authority exercised by elders. They have the power to ruin lives. Their decisions are not consistent, based on reason, but are based on whim. They are dictators swollen with pride and jealously flaunt their authority.

Seeing his despair a friend recommended Timothy read *Crisis of Conscience,* an exposé of the innerworkings of the Society's Governing Body, by Raymond Franz. "Then it all came together. I was free," he said.

Timothy was rescued from the Watchtower. However, when the Society disfellowshiped him and Jehovah's Witnesses were told to shun him, his oldest daughter turned against him and convinced his 16-year-old son to run away from home. This sad story is an example of the cruel consequences of misplaced and misused arbitrary authority.

Timothy now enjoys faith in God and Jesus and understands the liberty spoken of in Scripture. His Christian ministry reaches out to Jehovah's Witnesses and encourages them to follow their conscience rather than to follow the Watchtower.

Greg Peterson, a former JW elder, also suffered as a victim of the arbitrary exercise of authority. Assembly leaders assigned him to count money at an annual assembly at which thousands of JW's gathered. The assembly organizers always needed more money. Greg kept account of the money. Around $30,000 was received during the morning and $25,000 to $30,000 in the afternoon, Greg said. The first day's total was more than $100,000, yet the overseer in charge, who drove an expensive Audi car, wasn't satisfied. When he complained to Greg that it wasn't enough, Greg asked, "How much does an Audi cost?"

That did it. "At the next assembly Greg was on a broom," his wife said. "They got rid of Greg because he asked too many questions."

What If Everyone Became a JW?

What would the world be like if everyone became a Jehovah's Witness? Dictators would tell people what they could think. Non-Watchtower books would be banned. No trial by jury would exist, nor would democratic elections or freedom of religion. Jehovah's Witnesses say theirs would be a perfect world, governed by Jehovah God. They demonstrate their "perfect" government now by claiming Jesus Christ returned invisibly in 1914 and now is reigning through the Watchtower Society. Look at the people governed by the Watchtower Society. They suffer thought control, absolute regimentation, and total control from above. The Watchtower Society's control includes meddling in a husband and wife's sex life by forbidding certain foreplay and prohibiting unbridled passion.

The Hierarchy Father Figure

Most social ills could be prevented if fathers functioned as they are supposed to. Gangs that roam the streets and prey on other people for the most part are made up of boys who have no fathers or whose fathers are ineffective and disrespected. Each unwed mother requires an unwed, irresponsible father. When the family unit disintegrates, the society around it sinks to a new low. Mothers rear children without support because fathers abandon their children. A home run by a grandmother rearing her grandchildren and in which men drop by only for overnight visits with her daughters is a monument to failed fathers.

The father is responsible to provide, protect, and lead his family. Every family needs a father.

If you have a father who loves you, he is your anchor when you need safety in a storm and your guide when you lose your way. An individual who doesn't have a father may function well, but he still is out of balance and has to compensate. He may serve as his own father. He may adopt one or more surrogate fathers. An organization might become his father.

As I drove through rural East Texas, I saw foot-high letters on a fence. The letters announced "Democrat". On his mail box a neighbor proclaimed in large letters: "Republican." Some men attend the Masonic Lodge faithfully and listen to the same ritual every week. These people may have had good fathers, but some people latch on to an organization, an authority figure, or a leader that can guide—something solid on which they can depend.

Individuals yearning for a father figure are easy prey for the cults. Lynette "Squeaky" Fromme found a father figure in Charles Manson, the man responsible for a gang of fanatic followers who killed eight people in 1969, including actress Sharon Tate and her unborn baby. Although Fromme was not present during the grisly killings, she was one of the demonstrators who demanded that Manson be freed. She had complete allegiance to Manson and still does. In 1975 she waved a pistol at President Gerald Ford—not to kill him but to publicize Manson's ideas, she said. She spent 34 years in prison for that and was released on parole August 14, 2009. She still is loyal to Manson.[22]

The adherent who adopts a father-cult doesn't have to worry about right or wrong. The cult makes those decisions. The father-cult definitely is in charge. It doesn't equivocate. It has all the answers. All opposition is false; no questions are allowed.

Those who grew up as Witnesses, like Paul Blizard and like I did, didn't know any better. They do as they are taught. The Society is their father.

If you have a family member under control of the Watchtower Society and you speak against the Society, the JW feels insulted just as if you had insulted her father. Proving the Watchtower wrong with Scripture doesn't convince her. How could her own father be wrong about those things?

If you can convince her that the Society has been lying to her, maybe she will *consider the possibility* that the Society is not her father after all. That consideration alone is enough to crumble the weak mortar holding the Watchtower stones together.

While I was pastor in Rowlett, TX, a 12-year-old boy suddenly went wild. I'll call him Bobby Smith and his parents Robert and June Smith (not their real names). Bobby sabotaged his home's electrical system and then tried to burn the house down. In rage he screamed at his father and then quietly tried to convince his mother to leave her husband. The parents approached me for help.

I listened. Bobby had been a normal kid until he started attending a Rowlett, TX, school. The family had lived in a rural area in which everybody knew everybody. The country school didn't follow strict rules that children must have birth certificates, but when in the larger city June took Bobby to school to enroll him, she learned that he couldn't be accepted without a birth certificate. She located it and took it back to the school.

In the school office the clerk read the certificate: "Bobby Lee Frankal." Bobby looked past his mother to the birth certificate and told the clerk, "That's wrong. I'm Bobby Smith." His mother assured him that the certificate was correct and said she would explain later. Bobby spent the day in confusion and, hoping for an explanation, hurried home.

His mother and father explained to him that June previously had been married to another man who was Bobby's biological father. The marriage broke up early. When Bobby was 3, June married Robert, the only father Bobby knew. Robert had intended to legally adopt Bobby and to get the boy's name changed but kept putting it off.

The revelation put Bobby into emotional turmoil. Like turning off a light in a dark cave, suddenly Bobby's love for his father turned to hate and distrust.

Robert and Bobby had been as close as any father and son. Bobby had been a well-adjusted, secure child. Now he hated Robert. "You're not my father," he screamed over and over. "You don't tell me what to do. You're not my father." The boy went from bad to worse, became increasingly violent, and tried to kill Robert.

I last saw Bobby when I helped his mother check him into a private psychiatric hospital.

I mentioned this unique situation to illustrate a point. When you learn that the person you thought was your father in reality is not and that the person has been lying to you, the bond is more easily broken. Bobby's stepfather was a good man with good intentions. Negligence and procrastination contributed to his family's breakup. (He and his wife soon divorced.) That by no means excused Bobby's bad choices.

When a JW realizes she has been lied to, she can consider the possibility that the Society is not an anchor or a leader worthy of allegiance. *Maybe the Society is not God's organization after all.* She may need to look elsewhere for her true father. In the Bible she can find Him—our Heavenly Father.

When she becomes an ex-JW and believes and trusts in the real Jesus Christ as the LORD, she has new family with a true father. That family reaches around the world.[23]

I have preached in many countries around the world. When I meet Christians, whether their language is Spanish, Portuguese, Russian, or English, I feel a kinship with them. We all are part of the Father's family. We weren't admitted to the family because we worked diligently but because we were born into it. To those who receive Jesus Christ, God gives the power to become the sons of God, . . . *Which were born, not of blood, nor of the will of the flesh, nor of the will of man, but of God."*[24]

When you were born into the human race, you didn't have to take an exam to qualify. You were a member without question. When you are born in the United States, you automatically are a citizen. The only way to enter the Kingdom of Heaven is to be born into it through the spiritual birth explained in John 3. Once a person has escaped from the Watchtower and committed his life to Christ, the new birth becomes clear like a dawning day.

Chapter 6

Jehovah's Witnesses' Mind Games

JW's Practice Group Paranoia

Many Jehovah's Witnesses are under the impression that men sit in plush chairs around shiny conference tables in corporate board rooms and congressional committee rooms and plot against Jehovah's Witnesses. All those plotters are part of the giant wicked entity known only as *They*.

They are in control of the medical profession whose only goal is to make money and kill people. *They* probably have a cure for cancer but won't let it be known because it would cut their income for cancer treatment. *They* put poison in white bread so people will get sick and spend more money on medical treatment.

I never saw these paranoid allegations in print, but over and over I have heard them.

JW's believe *They* are out to destroy them. JW's flatter themselves to think powerful people spend any amount of time thinking about Jehovah's Witnesses, good or bad.

Various levels of paranoia exist; some are more extreme than others. Paranoia among JW's seems to be contagious. An extreme example is a young man who, for his family's sake, I'll just call Gerald. Gerald's mother was a JW and his father a Baptist. For many years his parents had been divorced; for a while Gerald lived with one parent and then the other. I never met his mother, but I knew his father well. Gerald's mother told him demons were in possession of his father, a police officer. She convinced Gerald that *They* were out to get all JW's and that his father was part of the conspiracy.

Gerald and a young JW friend went into a variety store in Greenville, TX, in which Gerald got into an argument with a clerk. Later, outside the store, Gerald told his friend. "They'll try to get me now for that."

During one of Gerald's stays with his father, the 18-year-old became increasingly agitated. His father and stepmother were at work. Gerald's adult sister busied herself with housework. Gerald took several pills and drank six cans of beer while he shouted into a tape recorder. On the tape Gerald cursed his father and told him he knew his father planned to put marijuana in his car as planted evidence and to arrest him.

After about 30 minutes of cursing and railing in hate against his father, Gerald went into the kitchen. From outside on the back porch his sister watched him. When she saw him open a cabinet drawer in which their father kept a loaded pistol, she ran inside. Before she could reach Gerald, he blew his brains out.

After I started a mission church in our home in Richardson, TX, my mother, a devout Jehovah's Witness, visited us. To provide a place for the new congregation I had cleaned out the garage, put curtains over the door and carpet on the floor, and installed homemade pews and a pulpit. The large garage made a good auditorium for about 30 people.

"Here, Mama, I want to show you our auditorium," I said while I opened the door to the garage.

"Oh," she said and stepped through the door as she surveyed the transformed garage. Suddenly alarm covered her face. "Oh," she said again as if frightened and quickly stepped back into the kitchen. She closed the door behind her.

"You should have told me that was your church," she said. "I should not have set foot in there." Years later she expressed concern about it. She said if she set foot in a church, she would be committing a terrible sin. She asked whether I had deliberately tricked her into it.

Jehovah's Witnesses believe that if they set foot in a church, they will become demon-possessed.

While I served as pastor in Rowlett, TX, a female visitor told me her husband was a Jehovah's Witness and asked whether I would visit him. I visited him and found him to be rude, but I patiently reasoned with him. He didn't attend meetings or go door-to-door, but he still believed the Watchtower doctrines. Finally he agreed that he would visit our church.

Our mission church met in an elementary-school cafetorium. Every Sunday we hauled our sound equipment and piano keyboard into the building. We sometimes jokingly referred to our group as "The Gypsy Baptist Church."

A few minutes before time to start the morning service one of our ushers told me, "There's a couple just standing out in the hall." I went out to find the woman and her JW husband. She had an arm around him as she helped him remain upright.

"It's OK. They're just people in there. Let's go in," she said.

The man's voice trembled. "I just can't." His face was flushed. His hands shook. "I just can't," he said again.

His wife guided the trembling man outside.

Even though he was inactive, he still was convinced that if he set foot into a church, he would be demon-possessed. He was scared to death. The poor guy had no hope of eternal life on Paradise Earth because he did not measure up as a theocratic obedient JW. Does anyone wonder that the JW's have the highest rate of mental illness and suicide?

Does Believing a Fantasy Make It True?

Nonsense, you say. If you believe a lie is true, does your belief change it into truth? Nonsense. But some people actually think that if you believe diligently enough something is true, it will become true. I remember a book, *The Magic of Believing*, by Claude M. Bristol, that taught that premise. It was one of the early motivational books that encouraged positive thinking but went farther. The author taught that with your mind you actually could change things.

That kind of thinking is called *subjective thinking*. An example: A is convinced hell exists and people go there after death. B is convinced that no such thing or place exists. Each sincerely believes his premise is correct. So for A hell is a real place and condition; for B hell does not exist. Never mind that they contradict each other and that two opposite views can't both be true. Subjective theology and subjective thinking are irrational and require adherents to lie to themselves.

To make this closer to home, use the same kind of logic about the Internal Revenue Service (IRS), the income-tax bureau. Suppose A believes in his heart that IRS is an active entity with authority and means of enforcement. B believes in his heart that some cruel people made up the idea of the IRS to frighten the rest of us. "The tax man doesn't exist."

Can both be true? Of course not, B will find out when he has to pay hefty fines and late penalties. That kind of wishful thinking won't work on the IRS, people will admit. Why then do some think it will work with God who demands that sin be punished?

Some believe the Watchtower doctrines only *because they want to*. Some years ago I received a call from a young police officer who had read my book, *I Was Raised a Jehovah's Witness*, and wanted to meet me. He arrived at the church in Fate, TX, 20 miles east of Dallas, at which I was pastor. He told me he had been studying with the Jehovah's Witnesses. He read my book and changed his mind about becoming a JW. Just as a pastor long ago had helped me to pray and make a commitment to Christ, I helped this young man. The Watchtower error vacated his mind to be replaced with truth. He was worried, however, because his mother was about to be baptized a Jehovah's Witness.

He convinced her to visit me. In my office she was courteous and listened quietly to everything I had to say. I showed her in the Bible the truth about the deity of Jesus Christ—that He was

Immanuel, God in the flesh.[25] He was the *arm of the Lord* by whose stripes we would be healed.[26] I explained that when the LORD's arm did something, the LORD did it; Jesus was the LORD. I showed her in the New Testament how believers in Christ would be resurrected as He was resurrected and would live with Him eternally in heaven.[27]

After those and many other points I made, I asked her, "Do you understand?" She said, "Yes, I understand." As I talked to her, I pointed to the Scripture references for her to see. She said she understood.

After about an hour of her listening intently, with her son by her side, I asked her if she would make the same decision for Christ her son had made.

"No, I won't do that. I like the idea of eternal life on earth better than going to heaven, so I'll go ahead and be baptized a Jehovah's Witness," she said.

Over the years her son grew closer to God. Eventually he was called into the ministry, went to seminary, and became a U.S. Navy chaplain. The last I heard, his mother had drifted out of the Jehovah's Witnesses. She hadn't been able to keep up the pace.

If a JW joined the group because she picked out a religion like she would pick out a new dress, she is not facing objective truth.

Compartmentalized Thinking

A Jehovah's Witness in training must develop compartments in her mind to keep separate various Watchtower dogma that can't mix. The theory might be likened to her having several tanks of chemicals, each of which has some potency by itself but if mixed with contents of a neighboring tank either would be neutralized or blow up. She learns to think about only one doctrine at a time and not think about contradictions from other Watchtower doctrines. She doesn't allow the contents of one tank to leak into the next. She doesn't allow the Watchtower doctrine that Jesus is "a God" leak over into the doctrine of one true God and that all others are false. She doesn't allow the obvious duplicity, hypocrisy, and coddling of sexual abusers of children to leak over into her belief that the Watchtower is God's earthly organization and speaks with His authority.

The mind of the Jehovah's Witness also is like a labyrinth, with compartments isolated from each other; these compartments can be entered only through a narrow bottleneck that is under complete control of the Watchtower. Therefore, the fully disciplined JW won't allow any unauthorized thoughts to enter.

You can't at the same time be a Jehovah's Witness and be intellectually honest.

Fortunately real truth embedded deep in the JW's psyche aches to get out. I well remember people at the Kingdom Hall making fun of born-again Christians.

"I've been born again," one would sing out; the others would laugh.

But in my heart a memory worked its way to the surface: I could see myself as a little boy in Pyatt, AR, in which my father during the Depression had abandoned my mother and two siblings. A playmate had invited me to supper at his home. The entire family sat down at an oilcloth-covered table around a simple meal. I noticed that the family members sat with hands in their laps and looked expectantly at the father. He wore blue denim overalls; his tanned face was lined by labor in the sun. He surveyed his quiet family and bowed his head. They all bowed their heads, so I did too. The man began to talk to God as though he knew Him.

Perhaps I had heard people pray before and was just now big enough to understand it, but this was the first time I can remember hearing anyone pray. The man's family looked up to him and respected him. He talked to God with deep reverence. I felt as if I had, for the very first time in my life, entered into the very presence of God. Hearing the prayer and eating the food that had been blessed was the most spiritual experience of my young life.

I pushed the memory back down, but it continued to return. *How could that man have been evil and praying to Satan?* I had been taught by the Witnesses.

Another memory kept intruding into my disciplined brain—a quiet witness given me by the mother of one of my best buddies. Mrs. Atchley was a dedicated Christian and a member of a small Pentecostal church. She knew I was a Jehovah's Witness. I clearly saw that she didn't approve. But she showed no disapproval of me personally. She treated me with Christian kindness. I couldn't believe that Mrs. Atchley worshiped Satan, even though the Society said she did because she didn't pray to Jehovah by name. Like the man I first had heard pray, Mrs. Atchley apparently knew Jesus Christ personally. Both the man and Mrs. Atchley had a profound influence on my life. Neither person had the arrogant, self-righteous attitude engendered by training at the Kingdom Hall.

Deep in his mind the typical Jehovah's Witness buries Watchtower contradictions and real truths. They try to surface. When he begins to see the duplicity of the Society, he allows the thoughts to surface, begins to think objectively, and with an open mind begins to read the Bible in context. The building stones of the Watchtower begin to loosen and shift. The process of being rescued from the Watchtower has begun.

Chapter 7

Callous Cruelty

Earlier I mentioned Jan Groenveld, an Australian escapee from the Watchtower. I never met her personally, but before her death in 2002 I corresponded with her for several years. My grandson, Greg Edwards, who was in the U.S. Navy, visited her in Brisbane and found her to be kind and hospitable.

Although Jan had become a Christian, her husband continued to be a JW.

She told me of an incident at a JW funeral; the incident demonstrated callous cruelty by Jehovah's Witnesses.

Her best friend, whom we'll call Sue, had disassociated herself from the Jehovah's Witnesses. You'd think if an adherent wanted to resign from the organization, they would let her go and be done with it. But that is not the way the Watchtower Society works. You're either a friend or an enemy. If you resign and disassociate yourself, you must be hiding deep, rotten characteristics, or you would have stayed in the organization. The JW's lump the disassociated with the disfellowshiped and shun both.

Sue's husband, like Jan's, still was a loyal JW. He became ill with cancer and died. Jehovah's Witnesses flocked to the funeral. The JW in charge of the funeral service gave the standard, prescribed, Watchtower funeral sermon, which Jan described as "an infomercial".

At the close of the service, at her request, Sue stood to give a few words about her late husband. As soon as she stood behind the lectern, some 50 Jehovah's Witnesses refused to listen to "the apostate" and noisily stood and walked out of the building. Sue's family, neighbors, and co-workers looked aghast at the precisely-timed and coordinated exodus.

In Jan's own words, "And did they leave? No, they did not . . . they all stood outside the building and milled about as if waiting to be congratulated for that heinous act!"

Jan's husband stayed with her and greeted and hugged the bereaved widow. As Jan and her husband left the building, JW's in the throng outside reached past Jan to shake her husband's hand as if she were not there.

In another example of callous cruelty, an elder in Phoenix forbade parents to Homeschool their daughter on the grounds that the Watchtower had not sanctioned Homeschooling. The mild and respectful disagreement by the JW parents was considered by the elder to be a situation that was *troubling the conscience of the congregation*—sort of a catch-all rule like the old vagrancy laws some cities had that allowed them to arrest anybody for anything.

Other JW's were Homeschooling their children and had been harassed by the same elder. However, in other areas JW's were Homeschooling their children without criticism. The Watchtower had not published anything against Homeschooling.[28]

So why did the elder meddle and harass? No one knows. However, he did follow the pattern of many other elders swollen with authority. Most JW's know that if they complain about an elder to other elders, the whole bunch likely will gang up on the complainant. If she complains to the Circuit Servant, the next rung up in the hierarchy, chances are the complainant would be in deeper trouble and would be hauled up before the elders for a *judicial hearing.* The individual stands alone before five or six elders, who bombard her with questions. They are the prosecutor, the judges, and the jury. No attorney helps defend the accused.

Kind and Loving vs. Heartless

While I was pastor of a church in Rockwall County east of Dallas, a young couple visited the church from Lewisville, northwest of Dallas and about 40 miles from Rockwall. Ray and Lisa Ortiz had read my book, *I Was Raised a Jehovah's Witness*, and wanted to meet me. They recently had exited the Jehovah's Witnesses. They committed their lives to Christ; I baptized them.

To my surprise they continued to drive that long way to our church. I thought they would find a church closer to home, but instead they moved to nearby Rowlett and became some of our most active members.

Ray and Lisa were typical ex-JW's who now knew the real truth. They enjoyed freedom from the narrow Watchtower regimentation and freely shared their faith.

Several years after they united with our church, Ray phoned me from Wichita, KS, to say his brother had been in a four-wheeler accident on a dirt trail near Guymon, OK. An air ambulance took him, in critical condition, from a hospital in Liberal, KS, to Wesley Hospital Intensive Care Unit in Wichita.

Ray explained that his mother, a Jehovah's Witness, anxiously awaited word in a waiting area of the hospital and that the place was "full of Jehovah's Witnesses telling her not to allow a blood transfusion." Ray's voice reflected his emotional turmoil. His brother had lost so much blood that without a transfusion he would die.

I immediately drove to Wichita and to the hospital. In the ICU waiting room I met Ray's mother for the first time. She was distraught. She didn't want her son to die. She didn't want to violate the JW prohibition against blood transfusions. All day her friends from her Kingdom Hall had pressured to continue to refuse the doctor's request for a transfusion.

To my surprise she allowed me to pray for her. I told her I would try to talk to her son and see if he would make the decision. She seemed relieved at the prospect of the decision being taken out of her hands.

Ray and I talked to the doctor, who led us into the ICU room. The patient had been going in and out of lucidity. At that moment he recognized Ray and was able to speak. Ray and I talked to him for a few minutes. I explained the simple truth. Transfusing is not ingesting. In any case God would not want medical treatment that might save his life to be withheld.

The doctor asked him whether he would accept the treatment and sign a release.

In a few minutes the transfusion was started; the young man's condition improved rapidly.

When they saw me, all the JW's left. I had a long visit with Ray's mother. She said she was impressed by the difference between Ray's pastor and her JW friends. I wanted to save her son's life. Her JW friends' attitudes ranged from indifference to hostility.

She said she had not decided to leave the JW's, but she considered doing so when she saw how callous they were toward her and her son's life.

Ray kept in close contact with his mother, although she lived at Guymon in the Oklahoma Panhandle. About six months later Ray told me his mother had disassociated herself from Jehovah's Witnesses and had joined a Nazarene Church.

His brother slowly recovered his health. At the insistence of his wife, a JW, he got involved again at the Kingdom Hall.

Ray and Lisa moved to Guymon. I hear from them occasionally. They still are enjoying their Christian liberty and a deeper bond with Ray's mother now that she, too, is a Christian.

You can know God's people by their fruit. Unconditional love and genuine compassion reflect the love of Christ and are so different from the religiosity and self-righteous and heartless attitudes of the Pharisees and their modern counterparts.

Chapter 8

Still Anti-Education

For generations Jehovah's Witnesses have encouraged high-school students to drop out so they can spend more time in door-to-door witnessing. In recent years JW's told me they no longer discourage higher education. This is not surprising, since Watchtower doctrines change frequently.

However, what the Society says publicly to present a clean face isn't always so. A *talk* given by Edward A. Prince Jr. at a 2007 Jehovah's Witnesses District Convention demonstrated the duplicity.

Referring to John 7:15 in which learned men were amazed at Jesus' wisdom, Prince said, "Well, how did Jesus know? Who taught him? He was taught by Jehovah. Who teaches us? We have the greatest teacher. We are taught by Jehovah."

The speaker then went to great lengths to criticize higher education. He called Jehovah's Witnesses training "divine education" and said, "Yes, brothers, we are taught by Jehovah; divine education, it frees us from enslavement to false teachings. Think about what some are taught happens at death and how confused it can make them about Almighty God, Jehovah. But when we are taught by Jehovah we're freed from false teachings, superstitions, human philosophies."

Prince didn't spell out exactly how JW's get their "divine education". Obviously they get it from the Watchtower publications. They may call it *Bible study*, but it's little picked-out pieces of the Bible put together, according to the Watchtower blueprint.

When Prince said, "My brothers, aren't we grateful for the privilege of being taught by Jehovah?", the great gathering responded with thunderous applause.

How are Jehovah's Witnesses taught? They are required to attend five meetings a week to study Watchtower literature and to listen to men such as Prince. The literature is purported to be inspired by Jehovah through angels that guide the Watchtower writers. They also claim that in the Brooklyn headquarters Jesus Christ Himself resides after He returned invisibly in 1914 and that He rules through the Watchtower Society.

Prince did say JW's need a basic education so they can read and write. He said, "Well, what can a Christian youth . . . what can those of us who serve Jehovah expect if we were to pursue higher education? Here's some points to consider." Then he listed some disadvantages in higher education such as having to pay off student loans. Even with a scholarship a student would be advancing the "present system of things"; study can crowd out one's "spiritual activities".

Prince challenged 16- and 17-year olds about to finish school to ". . . trust Jehovah enough to put the kingdom first".

"Higher education exposes one to corrupting influences," Prince said. Then, to prove his point, he had two women testify about their college experiences. He was careful to explain that they had gone to college before they became Witnesses.

At length the speaker concluded with, "So brothers and sisters, may we follow our exemplar Jesus Christ closely, thus showing that we appreciate the superiority of being taught by Jehovah."

I inferred that he meant JW's were to continue discouraging higher education; the crowd agreed with enthusiastic applause. I also noticed something else important. Rather than calling Jesus Christ "Lord", he called Him "our exemplar", a serious demotion.

Still Anti-Education

Do Jehovah's Witnesses discourage higher education? Obviously they do. Do they admit it? This depends on the person to whom they are talking. (For more on this subject see Sound Bites for the Christian Witness, No. 11. *Anti-Education* in Appendix A.)

Chapter 9

Confront the Real Truth

The Truth about the Watchtower's Custom-Made Bible

Educators recognize Dr. Julius Mantey as one of the greatest Greek scholars of the 20th century. He co-authored the *Dana and Mantey Greek Grammar*, which was my second-year Greek textbook. It still is used in many universities and seminaries. He also was a consultant on the New International Version Translation Committee.

I met Dr. Mantey in 1983 at a convention of Ex-Jehovah's Witnesses. The convention was held at a Christian encampment in Pennsylvania. We both spoke at the meeting. His subject was "The Watchtower's New Testament".

Although Dr. Mantey was in his 80s, he was tall, slender, and stately—somewhat slowed physically but mentally sharp. He said, "The Watchtower's New Testament is not a translation at all. The Watchtower has taken the translations of other men and changed the words to fit their own doctrines."

After his speech I visited Dr. Mantey in his cabin and spent an hour interviewing him. He said the Watchtower had substituted synonyms and done minor rewording to avoid charges of outright plagiarism. Dr. Mantey brought the most serious charge, however, that JW's had changed Scripture that proved the deity of Jesus Christ. For example the Bible says Christ *made all things*. He always existed. *In the beginning was the Word. . ..* He was in existence in the beginning; through Him God made all things. The Watchtower maintains that Christ was a created being; after His creation, He created everything else. So the Watchtower *translators* inserted the word *other* to make it read, *. . . made all* other *things*. No grammatical justification for that and many other such changes in the Watchtower's Bible existed. Its translation committee blatantly and dishonestly made heretical changes to its Bible.

The Watchtower also took what Dr. Mantey had said out of context and misquoted him. The Watchtower claimed, in print by innuendo, that Dana and Mantey agreed with its translation of John 1:1, *. . . and the Word was a God.*

In their *The Kingdom Interlinear Translation of the Greek Scriptures* 1969, on Page 1158, the Society tries to justify this by quoting the *Dana and Mantey Greek Grammar*. Dana and Mantey said John 1:1 showed that Jesus was "divine". The Watchtower writers then explained that *divine* did not mean that Jesus was God but that He had godlike attributes. Dana and Mantey used the word *divine* in its literal meaning. *The Word was God!* From reading Dana and Mantey the Watchtower writers knew that the authors believed strongly in the deity of Jesus Christ.

Dr. Mantey wrote the Society several letters and asked it to stop misquoting him. The Society ignored him. Finally he threatened to sue. The Society stopped.[29]

"They knew what Dana and I believed, that we believed in the deity of Jesus Christ, yet they tried to make it look like we agreed with them," Dr. Mantey said.

Another Greek scholar, Dr. Randolph Yeager, author of the 18-volume "Renaissance New Testament", a detailed study of each word in the Greek New Testament, said, "The Watchtower's New Testament is intellectual harlotry."

The Watchtower also cites a *translator* who agreed with their "a God" rendition. They say Johannes Greaber's translation of the New Testament agrees with JW's. True, it does. But what is Johannes Greaber's translation? Greaber, a German defrocked Catholic priest, married a spiritist and fell in with her beliefs. He said he had a vision. Words passed in front of his eyes. He made notes of the passing words that became a new translation of the New Testament.

After ex-JW's such as Bill Cetnar blew the whistle and labeled Greaber for what he was, the Watchtower quit using him as a reference. But all along the Watchtower had known that Greaber was a fraud and used him anyway.

Any pastor who has been to seminary knows more Greek and Hebrew than those who claim to have translated the NWT. The Watchtower leadership knows its "translation committee" wasn't qualified. That's why it won't admit who translated the NWT. Ask any Jehovah's Witness. He will tell you, "Oh, we don't publish the names of our translation committee, because we don't want to give honor to men."

(For further information on the Watchtower's Bible, I recommend *The Jehovah's Witnesses' New Testament* by Robert H. Countess, Presbyterian and Reformed Publishing Co., Phillipsburg, NJ 08865. Countess has made a detailed, scholarly examination of the NWT's New Testament.) Although the NWT is a fraud, it still contains enough of the Word of God that some Jehovah's Witnesses, who diligently searched for the truth in it, realized that Jesus Christ is LORD, emerged from the cult, and became Christians.

The Truth About False Prophecies

Proving the Watchtower is a false prophet is easy. All you have to do is look at its old publications and see that the Watchtower Society claimed to be God's prophet on earth and that its prophecies didn't occur. The organization now forbids JW's to read old Watchtower literature.[30] Ex-JW's have made an extensive collection of old Watchtower publications, so the evidence is available.

After leaving the Jehovah's Witnesses a truth-seeker, without fear, can read the evidence.

Beginning in 1966 a current of excitement among Jehovah's Witnesses electrified them for the next nine years. Publications hinted that the 7,000 years since creation soon would expire. The time then would arrive for the Battle of Armageddon and the end of the wicked world. The Society was careful not to put the prophecy in print, but in Kingdom Halls around the world speakers talked about it; at JW mass assemblies it became the major theme of speakers. Speakers repeatedly told the prophecy; JW's believed it: The Battle of Armageddon would occur in 1975. Later as 1975 drew near, the prophecy was refined to "the autumn of 1975".

My mother believed the prediction and was excited. Since 1940 she had been expecting Armageddon. If she were found worthy, she would survive Armageddon and have eternal life on earth. Her worries would be over. The last time I visited her, she told me she was sure 1975 was it. The long-awaited culmination would be here.

From 1966 to 1975 the recurring subject of conversation among JW's was, "Nineteen-seventy-five". A Canadian ex-JW told me that in his Toronto congregation people who ordinarily planted a garden did not plant one in 1975. Another family whose home needed to be painted decided not to because no need would exist. They could choose any number of fine houses that would be vacated when *the wicked* were killed in Armageddon.

When my mother explained her excitement about 1975, I told her, "I'm not a prophet, but I'll tell you what will happen in the autumn of 1975. The Watchtower will have millions of books already printed that will explain that *they never really said Armageddon would occur in 1975.*" That's exactly what happened.

After 1975 the JW's didn't want to talk about it. In the 10 years after the failed prophecy a million people left the organization. Now JW's—even those who delayed medical treatment because after Armageddon they wouldn't need it—deny what they said about 1975.

Confront the Real Truth

The 1975 false prophecy culminated a long string of fictional claims that started nearly a century before. Early in its history the Watchtower Society became known for predicting the Battle of Armageddon and "The End". Those predictions got attention. Talking to people who believed it was exciting. The predictions helped the Society grow.

In 1886 Charles Taze Russell, founder of the Watchtower, claimed the preliminaries of the Battle of Armageddon had begun. He said, "The outward evidences are that the marshaling of the hosts for the battle of the great day of God Almighty is in progress while the skirmishing is commencing."[31]

In 1889 Russell said, "The battle of the great day of God Almighty (Rev. 16:14), which will end in A.D. 1914 with the complete overthrow of earth's present ruler ship, is already commenced."[32]

In 1894 he again said, "Skirmishing is already beginning . . . .."

In 1904 he said the "great time of trouble" would culminate in October 1914. The May 1, 1914, *Watchtower* said, "There is absolutely no ground for Bible students to question that the consummation of this gospel age is now even at the door . . . ."

Then, as the year of 1914 waned, Russell began to soft-pedal and prepare his people for a letdown. In the September 1, 1914, issue of the *Watchtower*, he said, "While it is possible that Armageddon may begin next spring, yet it is purely speculation to attempt to say just when. We see, however that there are parallels between the close of the Jewish age and this gospel age. These parallels seem to point to the year just before us—particularly the early months."

In 1915 he said World War I, then raging, would lead to the Battle of Armageddon, "which will be a great contest between right and wrong . . . and will signify the complete and everlasting overthrow of the wrong, and the permanent establishment of messiah's righteous kingdom . . . ."[33]

Why bring these things up now? Jehovah's Witnesses admit the Society made mistakes. After all, the JW's are only human, they say. To make ordinary human mistakes is not allowed in the prophet business. When an individual or an organization claims to be a prophet of God, he can't miss once. The Watchtower Society has in print on more than one occasion claimed that it is a prophet of God.[34]

In baseball you get three strikes and you're out. In prophecy you get one strike and you're out.[35] The Watchtower struck out at least once each generation. I suppose everything depends on people's short memory and disciplined followers who refuse to think about what they're ordered not to think about.

Russell died in 1916 without seeing his predictions fulfilled. My mother spoke in awe of Russell's death. She said he knew when he would die. He was aboard a train in Texas when he ordered preparation for this death. Russell had himself wrapped in a white sheet; shortly afterward he died. Mama believed the way he died indicated Russell's special contact with God. Whether she ever met Russell, I don't know. She did speak of "Pastor Russell" with reverence as if she knew him.

In 1920 Russell's successor, "Judge" Joseph Rutherford, published a book entitled *Millions Now Living Shall Never Die*, which said it contained *New Light*. Some of this *New Light* was a prediction of the end: "The old order of things, the old world, is passing away . . . 1925 shall mark the resurrection of the faithful worthies. . . . We are standing at the very portals of that blessed time!"[36]

Rutherford was so sure some Old Testament saints would be resurrected in 1925 that he bought a large home for them in San Diego. Pending their arrival, however, Rutherford occupied the home. *No sense in letting it go to waste*. The old false prophet lived there until his death in 1945.

In 1929 Rutherford said the time of "The End" was close because the Jews were returning to Palestine.[37] In 1930 he said, ". . . the great climax is at hand."[38] Russell started the recurring theme that the world as we know it soon would end. Rutherford continued; succeeding Society presidents have kept fueling the fire and spreading the alarm.

Answering a false alarm can be trouble. Police departments waste more time answering false alarms than they do responding

Confront the Real Truth

to real ones. In His parable of the Ten Virgins awaiting the bridegroom Jesus spoke of a false alarm.[39] The midnight cry, "The Bridegroom cometh," was a false alarm. The bridegroom didn't arrive until the five foolish virgins were absent. In view of Rutherford's 1920 prediction, "Millions Now Living Shall Never Die," most of the people who were old enough in 1920 to believe him now are dead. Certainly "millions" of them are not left.

In 1931 Rutherford stated positively, "His day of vengeance is here, and Armageddon is at hand and certain to fall upon Christendom, and that within an early date. God's judgment is upon Christendom, and must be shortly executed."[40] He kept on making prophecies that kept on failing.

I well remember my excitement in 1941 as a freshly baptized JW at the international convention of Jehovah's Witnesses in St. Louis, MO. Signs throughout the convention grounds proclaimed the theme of "Children". Each child received a free copy of the book, *Children,* bound in a dark blue cover. Judge Rutherford addressed many of his remarks to us children. He urged us not to marry. In just a few months Armageddon would occur. (In a few months I wouldn't be old enough to marry anyway.) Don't marry and bring children into this evil world, he said. Instead devote your time and energy to the field service.

Raymond Franz was 17, a few years older than I. He heard the same message. He obeyed and did not marry. He became a respected leader in the Society, an international missionary, and later a member of the governing body and author of Watchtower publications. Finally at age 36, with permission, he got married—too late for him and his wife to have children.

Later, he saw the innerworkings of the Watchtower Society, the hypocrisy and lying. Raymond Franz shook loose the mental conditioning and planned to leave the organization. However, before he could resign, a JW spied him having lunch with a former JW who had been disfellowshiped; Franz himself was disfellowshiped. In his book, *Crisis of Conscience,* he exposed the dishonest dealings of the Society.[41]

Back in 1939 I didn't understand what Germany's invasion of Poland meant, but I did perceive the electric tension transmitted from the adults to the children. People were fearful of war. I remember the adults talking about the young men who probably would have to go to war. We received news that my sister Naomi's husband, Walton Guynn, had fallen from the top of a windmill and would be crippled. "At least he won't have to go to war," my mother said.

Rutherford capitalized on 1939's war as had Russell in 1914. Rutherford proclaimed, "The time for the battle of the great day of God Almighty is very near . . . The disaster of Armageddon is just ahead."[42] The Jehovah's Witnesses went door-to-door and repeated Rutherford's warning. (Same song, next verse, with a new generation of singers, all of whom had short memories.)

In 1940 Rutherford said the work of preaching was about over. He alluded to Matthew 24:14, which every Witness could quote: *And this gospel of the kingdom shall be preached in all the world for a witness unto all nations; and then shall the end come.*[43] If the preaching was finished, the time for the end had arrived . . . again.

From that time to the present the Watchtower has proclaimed a midnight cry, "the time is at hand." The constant warning reminds me of a weathered banner sign on the front of a rural Louisiana restaurant, "Free Beer Tomorrow".

Jehovah's Witnesses hurry door-to-door to spread the alarm. *The world is in a mess, full of wars, civil upheaval, economic crisis, starvation, torture, corruption. It can't last much longer. "The time is at hand" for the culmination of this evil system of things.* They've been saying the same thing for more than 100 years. It's like the cute little redhead sang in the play, *Annie:* "Tomorrow, tomorrow, you're only a day away."

In New Guinea during World War II the natives watched with astonishment as United States Armed Forces unloaded onto their shores ships full of cargo. The cargo contained riches these little people of the remote jungle mountains and mist-shrouded valleys never had imagined. The people noticed peculiar things about the Americans who seemed awash in the riches of cargo. These Americans wore olive drab fatigues with "U.S." on them and marched down the road four abreast. They stayed in tents and used tables and chairs; sometimes they would set a vase of flowers on the table. All these activities by the Americans fascinated the New Guinea natives. They reasoned that the unusual activities by the Americans must have something to do with causing the cargo to arrive.

During the war the natives enjoyed the benefits of the cargo. From the vast amounts of cargo they received tools, weapons, good food, and clothing.

After the war the Americans departed and left much of their cargo behind. It soon ran out. The New Guineans longed for a return of the bounty of cargo. Leaders arose and started preaching the gospel of cargo. If the people would just act as the Americans had, the cargo would return. A picture in *National Geographic Magazine* showed a group dressed in fatigues with "U.S." on the back. Four abreast they close-order marched down the road. They shouldered sticks to look as though they were Americans marching with rifles. The cargo cult leaders assured the people that the cargo soon would arrive. They put tables in their homes with vases of flowers and looked anxiously for the cargo to get there.

The cargo never showed up, but the cargo cult leaders continued to promise: *It's coming soon. It's coming soon, maybe tomorrow. Just keep on doing the things we tell you. Believe your leaders.* Sounds familiar, doesn't it? For more than 100 years the Watchtower Society has been making predictions that failed.

Armageddon hasn't occurred as it has been promised since 1886. The Watchtower cult leaders continue saying, "It's coming soon. It's coming soon."

The excitement of Armageddon looming ahead constantly fills the minds of Jehovah's Witnesses. As I grew up, other kids would talk about the future and what they wanted to do with their lives. "I want to be a policeman. I want to be a nurse." Those expressions meant nothing to me because of the constant drums of impending destruction booming in my mind. I made no such plans. I thought no future would happen. Armageddon would occur before I had a chance for a life. I doubted that I had measured up as a JW. I wasn't as faithful in *witnessing* as I should be. I had bad thoughts. I wasn't as obedient to my parents as I should be. I dreaded to go to the Kingdom Hall, which I was supposed to do joyfully. The weekly Watchtower study was an endurance of boredom. For all those failings I felt guilty and feared I would be found unworthy and die an eternal death in Armageddon.

Do the past false prophecies bother JW's? Today if you visit a Kingdom Hall, you would have a tough time finding anyone who was an active JW in 1975. Those few who were active JW's in 1975 have effectively blotted the false prophecy from their memory as if the predictions never existed. But the false prophecies are there—recorded in history along with those of 1874, 1914, 1918, 1925, and 1945. The Watchtower tries to lock them up in a closet, but their bones rattle so loudly, you still can hear them.

Indictment of False Prophets

Jesus Christ warned us to beware of false prophets. What is a false prophet? A teen-ager might answer the question with a question, "Duh?" The word *duh* translates, "The answer is so obvious it makes the question stupid."

Obviously a false prophet makes false prophecies. It's too simple. Since its inception more than a century ago the Watchtower has made many false prophecies. According to Deuteronomy 18:20 to proclaim one failed prophecy makes the prophesier a false prophet.

To have any measure of success, a false prophet has to be believable at least to some people. He has to look good. Jesus said the false prophets are really wolves but look like sheep.[44]

Jesus also said you can identify a false prophet as you identify a fruit tree—by his fruit. In other words, look at the results of his prophecies. Have any of the prophecies of the Watchtower done any good to anyone? Well, Duh?

Two Ways of Prophesying

One can prophesy in two ways. A prophet may foretell the future by speaking in the name of the LORD. For example, the Prophet Jeremiah said, *This whole country will become a desolate wasteland, and these nations will serve the king of Babylon seventy years.*[45] The people of Judah went into captivity to Babylon and after 70 years were released. This proved Jeremiah was a prophet of God.

The Prophet Isaiah said, *Therefore the Lord Himself shall give you a sign; Behold, a virgin shall conceive, and bear a son, and shall call his name Immanuel.*[46] Christ was born of a virgin and was called *Immanuel*, God with us. This fulfilled the prophecy.

The second way of prophesying is to forth-tell the Word of God. The prophet will say or preach something God has said. Therefore, a person can have the gift of prophecy without ever foretelling future events. He simply states what God said. For example the LORD sent a prophet to remind Israel what He had done for them. *That the LORD sent a prophet unto the children of Israel, which said unto them, Thus saith the LORD God of Israel, I brought you up from Egypt, and brought you forth out of the house of bondage.*[47] The apostle Paul said we are to seek the gift of prophecy. Christian Sunday-school teachers and preachers are prophesying if they tell forth the word of God.

Obviously the Watchtower has struck out in the foretelling department, because its prophecies failed. What about the forth-telling department? When it says Jehovah said something, is it true? Did Jehovah really say it? When JW elders tell a woman to divorce her husband because of Jehovah's will, is it really His will? When a JW is accused of sexually abusing children and the elders tell the victim's parents, "Jehovah will work it out," is it really Jehovah's will to leave the child and other children at risk to the sexual predator? When a baby is at death's door and can be saved with a blood transfusion, is this really Jehovah's will expressed by JW elders that the child die? Are the changes made to the Bible that are contrary to rules of grammar and that have changed the meaning of Scripture expressions of Jehovah's will as claimed by the Watchtower?

The Watchtower has struck out in the forth-telling department of prophecy as well as in the foretelling department. So what did Jesus say about such false prophets? He said we are not to believe them.

Indictment Against Counterfeit Christians

Jesus said, *Many will say to me in that day, Lord, Lord, have we not prophesied in thy name? and in thy name have cast out devils? and in thy name done many wonderful works? And then will I profess unto them, I never knew you: depart from me, ye that work iniquity.*[48]

Although they are preoccupied with the presence of devils, as far as I know JW's have not tried exorcism. They believe devils inhabit objects such as crosses and flags. They are afraid to set foot inside a church building lest these individuals become inhabited by demons. Therefore, whether they lay claim to having cast out devils, I don't know. But I do know for sure they have prophesied and have claimed to do good works.

Jesus made a list of good works that are indicators of people who will enter the kingdom of heaven. These included 1. Feeding the hungry; 2. Giving drink to the thirsty; 3. Taking in a stranger; 4. Clothing the naked; 5. Visiting the sick; 6. Visiting the imprisoned. Doing these things demonstrates the difference between real Christians and counterfeit Christians.

Good works, JW's claim, are *field service*—distributing literature, book studies, and witnessing to people to recruit them into the ranks of the JW's. Compared to evangelical Christians, the Witnesses' benevolent work is as different as are a keyhole and a garage door. The JW's' benevolent work is miniscule and is restricted to those in the JW group.

The vast majority of good works spoken of by Jesus is done by Christians whom the JW's claim are demon-possessed.

Christians feed the hungry, give drink to the thirsty, and clothe people.

Sonny Stovall was an ordinary member of my church in Rockwall County, TX. He was a gentle giant whose hand was so big it enveloped mine, which is larger than most. Sonny wasn't a preacher, deacon, or holder of any office. He and a friend, Curtis Cosby, member of another church, on their own decided to help feed street people in Dallas. One evening each week they cooked several gallons of wieners and beans, made slaw and potato salad, and bought a stack of loaves of bread. They set up a serving line near the Farmer's Market and fed 150 or more people. On other days of the week other individual Christians or groups from churches did the same.

When a hurricane, flood, or major disaster strikes, usually the Texas Baptist Men, volunteers who pay their own way to feed the hungry and provide clean drinking water, arrive first on the scene.

The Red Cross and Salvation Army also arrive early on the scene of a disaster and provide food, clothing, and shelter. Compassionate, caring people—most of whom are Christians—fund these benevolences, but none of the benefactors are Jehovah's Witnesses. Indeed the Watchtower forbids JW's to give to the Red Cross or Salvation Army.

Illegal immigrants trudging through the Arizona desert in 110-degree heat often get lost, run out of food and water, and collapse on the hot ground and die. Others find plastic gallon jugs of water placed in the shade of a cactus plant or bush—left there by caring people, mostly Christians. These Christians had the same compassion Jesus had for the multitude.[49] They live up to Jesus' standard.

The church of which I served as pastor in Rowlett, TX, put up a booth in local craft fairs, patriotic fairs, and other events. The booth contained chairs in which people could sit and rest and contained coolers of ice water and cups. A sign on the booth announced, "Have a cup of cold water in the name of Jesus." We had Christian compassion on the tired and thirsty people. The JW's hold such acts in contempt and consider them *worldly*.

Compared to major benevolent acts, our effort was small, but it outmatched that of six-million JW's.

Christians Take in the Stranger

What once was a huge warehouse in Dallas has been transformed to a shelter for homeless people. Called "Dallas Life", the facility houses men and women in separate dormitories and families in small apartments. It's a place in which people can go and be fed, clothed, sheltered, and have an opportunity to get on their feet again. This benevolence is sponsored by First Baptist Church of Dallas and is another example of compassionate Christian giving.

Churches and other organizations such as the Salvation Army sponsor shelters in cities across the nation. Christians give most of the money that is necessary to operate those shelters. If a Jehovah's Witness contributes to any of those causes, he might be disfellowshiped and shunned.

Christian People Visit the Sick

When I started a new mission church in Richardson, TX, the city's population had grown to 24,000. The small Richardson hospital had no chaplain. On my first visit there to see one of my members I went from room to room and offered words of comfort and prayer. I offered these to each patient regardless of his or her religious affiliation or lack thereof. The patients seemed to appreciate my visit so much that I returned every week and made the rounds as if I were a staff chaplain.

Years later I took chaplain training at Baylor University Medical Center in Dallas. There I became acquainted with many men and women of God who dedicated their lives to visiting the sick. As did volunteers from other churches I served two days a month as chaplain at the local Rowlett hospital. Some were Baptists, some were Catholics, some were Presbyterians, some were

Methodists, and some were from other Christian denominations—but once again no Jehovah's Witnesses were involved.

Christians Visit the Prisoners

Lewis McClain retired as a missionary from Brazil and moved to his old hometown of Rockwall, TX. With great energy Lewis witnessed for Jesus; this retired missionary loved to share the gospel with people. He had compassion on the prisoners in the small Rockwall County jail that occupied the top floor of the old courthouse built in 1944. Every Sunday afternoon Lewis went to the jail and visited the prisoners. He used Scripture to comfort them and shared with them the good news of Jesus.

After several years Lewis decided to return to Brazil and resume his ministry there. He asked me to take over his jail ministry.

Soon after I took over, the county built a new jail—all on the ground floor. I was grateful that it was confined to one floor. I carried on as Lewis had and visited every Sunday afternoon. During my visit many of the prisoners wept. They said they were sorry for the messes they had made of their lives. (I believe some were just sorry they got caught, but that was not for me to judge.) Many believed and trusted in Jesus Christ, repented, and asked His forgiveness. Later after they got out of jail, some went back into criminal activity, while others whose lives were genuinely changed lived Christian lives.

As the community grew and the jail population expanded, I enlisted other churches to help. Soon I had so many churches taking turns to participate that I quit going to the jail personally and administered the ministry. Several Christian denominations comprised the jail ministry, but once again, no Jehovah's Witnesses volunteered or were involved.

After I started the new mission church in Rowlett, I asked one of our men, Larry Gener, to represent our church in the jail ministry. Larry was a career new-car salesman; he was accustomed to talking to people, but he was reluctant to tackle the jail ministry. His reluctance wasn't because he didn't want to do this.

He had the compassion and desire, but he believed he was inadequate. Once Larry saw the effect his witnessing had on the prisoners, he loved that ministry. He was good at it. I became convinced that the Holy Spirit had guided me to ask Larry to serve. He was such a gentle minister to the rough prisoners that you'd never guess he, as a kid, had been a heavy drinker and fighter on Chicago streets and later a tough Marine in and out of the brig. He not only served in the county-jail ministry for many years, he branched out into prison ministry in general. I have no doubt that God has used Larry's ministry to turn around hundreds of lives. His own life was an example of what God can do.

Larry and I are small examples of Christians who visit prisoners. Hundreds of men and women—compassionate Christians—minister to prisoners across the nation and the world.

Jehovah's Witnesses will visit fellow JW's in prison, but you won't find them in a compassionate ministry or contributing money to help those ministries. Indeed, if they do contribute money to these causes, they will violate Watchtower law.

In a parable Jesus spoke about a king and his subjects. Obviously the king represents Jesus. He said when people do those benevolent acts for others, they are doing them for Him. Jesus said to those who claim to serve Him, yet do not do those benevolent acts, *Depart from me, ye cursed, into everlasting fire, prepared for the devil and his angels.*[50]

Proof by Widows and Orphans

The apostle James said, *Pure religion and undefiled before God and the Father is this, to visit the fatherless and widows in their affliction, and to keep himself unspotted from the world.*[51]

Do Jehovah's Witnesses possess *pure religion and undefiled*? Do they visit *the fatherless and widows*? No doubt they visit those who are JW's, but what about the other widows and orphans whom Jesus loves? Has the Watchtower ever built an orphanage or a home for battered women?

Christians aren't perfect, but they are a galaxy closer to Christian ideals than JW's are.

Look at the thousands of orphanages that Christian churches have built across the nation. One example is Dallas' Buckner Children's Home that has taken in thousands of unwanted or abused children and reared them.

The ministry of the late Lester Roloff in Corpus Christi, TX, demonstrated what Christian care and discipline could do in the lives of children. Roloff accepted children whose parents no longer could control them; he also accepted orphans. More kids graduated from his home to become ministers than those who graduated and went into crime, a statistic far better than government programs achieve.

Adopt-a-child programs that help feed and clothe children in developing countries in Africa and South America are Christian ministries. Christians have compassion on the orphans.

Churches and Christian denominations subsidize many homes for the aged; these homes care mostly for widows.

What do Jehovah's Witnesses do for widows and orphans? JW's fail the test of *pure religion and undefiled* before God. That makes their religion impure and defiled.

Selfish Motives

But when he saw the multitudes, he was moved with compassion on them, because they fainted, and were scattered abroad, as sheep having no shepherd.[52]

Jesus had compassion on the hungry. He had compassion on people who were lost in sin. These included the harlots, crooked government officials, thieves, and self-righteous hypocrites. Because of that compassion Jesus preached the gospel and gave those people an opportunity to repent and believe in Him. Jesus expected His disciples to have the same compassion.

Out of compassion a Christian witnesses to other people. He has a personal relationship with Christ and wants to share the gospel with other people. He does this not so he can be saved from his sins, but because he is saved from his sins.

Jehovah's Witnesses rarely are moved by compassion. JW's I have known hold all non-JW's in contempt. And why not? The

Watchtower Society teaches them that non-JW's are *of the world* and are so detestable they will be subject to God's wrath and be destroyed in Armageddon. The Society teaches that all Christian churches are evil *Christendom* and serve Satan. JW's believe Catholics are especially wicked; they believe Catholics are part of the *Whore of Babylon*.

JW's witness to people not out of compassion but so they can go to the Kingdom Hall and turn in a report that shows they have put their time and distributed Watchtower literature. When you get through the rhetoric, you see that their basic motivation is selfish. They are trying to save their own hides by actively *witnessing*. They don't want to die in Armageddon, so they desperately work for their salvation.

The JW wants to convert you to become a disciple of the Watchtower—not to save your life but to save his own life.

Some Prayers Not Allowed by the Watchtower

Strange as this may seem, the Watchtower Society claims to be a Christian organization, yet it prohibits certain kinds of prayer.

Charles Trombley was a lifelong, active JW. His wife gave birth to a baby girl who had club feet. The parents firmly believed that Jehovah could do anything, including heal their baby's feet. So they prayed. Overnight the baby's feet became straight. The Tromblcys spread the joyful news. They had prayed to Jehovah; He had healed their baby girl.

Rather than rejoice with the Trombleys the JW's disfellowshiped and shunned them. Jehovah's Witnesses are not allowed to believe in any kind of divine healing. The Society teaches them that only the devil heals by miracle today. The Pharisees accused Jesus of the same thing.

JW's love to quote *Faith without works is dead.* They neglect James' other admonitions such as *Is any sick among you? let him call for the elders of the church; and let them pray over him, anointing him with oil in the name of the Lord.*[53]

The Witnesses act as if Jehovah has no interest in them as individuals. Their prayers are general—for the organization. The life of Christ demonstrates how God is interested in each of us as unique individuals. He wants us to have a personal relationship with Him.

JW's are not allowed to pray to Jesus. They believe He is not God in the Flesh but rather is an archangel who became flesh; therefore to pray to Jesus would be praying to another god.

They neglect the Bible that tells how the apostle Thomas doubted Jesus' resurrection and demanded proof. Thomas wanted to put his finger and hand into Jesus' wounds to prove He literally had been resurrected. Later, when Thomas saw Jesus, the Lord invited him, *Reach hither thy finger, and behold my hands; and reach hither thy hand, and thrust it into my side: and be not faithless, but believing. And Thomas answered and said unto him, My LORD and my God.*

Jesus didn't rebuke Thomas as JW's would rebuke one of their disciples for calling Jesus LORD and God. Rather Jesus said those who believe as Thomas did are blessed.[54]

JW's are not supposed to pray to God without calling Him *Jehovah*. They believe that to do so would cause Jehovah to bat their prayer down to Satan like a quick-reflexed ping-pong player.

JW's are not allowed to pray with non-Jehovah's Witnesses. Many times I have offered to pray for JW's; they have refused.

Point of Collapse

In 2008 an Interstate Highway 35 bridge in Minneapolis, MN, collapsed because a steel plate wasn't quite thick enough. Rush-hour traffic drove around several cement trucks and other heavy construction equipment that had been left on the bridge for the night. When the steel plate failed, it caused other plates to break. The bridge fell into the Mississippi River; with it, it dumped people, cars, and trucks.

On most bridges, if one component fails, only part of the bridge will be lost. I saw an example. Many years ago I was driving north on old U.S. Highway 81 toward Oklahoma City, OK, when a section of the bridge fell under the weight of a semi truck. The driver managed to stop on the steep incline of the fallen bridge just short of the river. Other sections of the bridge held.

The Watchtower Society is put together much like the Minneapolis bridge was, except that the Watchtower doesn't have just one weak component; it has many.

To be a Jehovah's Witness you must believe all the Watchtower teachings.

For example, if you believe all the Watchtower teachings except the prohibition against blood transfusions, you're out. The entire Watchtower structure is held together as though it is formed of stones built on top of each other. If the foundation stones get loose and crumble, all those above start tumbling down. That makes the Watchtower prison that confines JW's vulnerable. If you can convince a JW that one of the group's peculiar doctrines is in error, you can start the process of rescue.

Chapter 10

Replacing Error with Truth

The apostle Paul admonished the Philippian Christians not to be anxious and worried but to replace those negative attitudes with prayer and thanksgiving.[55] To remove a negativism or error from your mind is not enough. These must be replaced with something better.

After a Jehovah's Witness has realized the Watchtower possibly could be wrong and learns that she has been lied to, getting it out of her mind is not enough. The void must be filled with truth.

Jesus told a story of a man inhabited by a demon. The man got rid of the demon; his mind was left empty—"swept clean". The demon wandered around and decided he had things pretty good back there and returned. He brought with him seven other demons and left the poor guy worse off than he had been.[56]

After I escaped from the Watchtower, I tried to empty my mind of religion. I purposely went into spiritual limbo. I wasn't a Jehovah's Witness or a Christian or an atheist. I could best be described as a cynic who tried not to think about God.

Imagining a state of mind worse than being under the complete control of a cult, is difficult, but things can get worse. When I was a Jehovah's Witness, I had a strict moral standard. True, it allowed me to lie to *worldly* people. That moral standard had its faults but was better than none at all. I generally was law-abiding and sexually chaste and didn't get drunk. When I discarded the Watchtower false doctrines, I discarded the valid parts of its moral standards along with the false. I was like loose cannon in a gale as I rolled from one side of the ship to the other and knocked down everything in its path. That lack of moral standard, combined with youthful inexperience and immaturity, led me to do things for which I still am ashamed. Fortunately after a wild time of sexual promiscuity, drunkenness, and general hell-raising, a little maturity seeped into my mind; I regained my senses. I vowed to be a good person if not a religious one. Marrying my dream girl and the responsibility of taking care of her and rearing a family had a civilizing impact on me, although I still was in spiritual limbo.

Then at age 21 I became a Christian. The real truth purged from my mind the Watchtower false doctrines and replaced them with biblical reality. This happened when I had been out of the JW's for six years. For months my wife and in-laws gave me repeated invitations to church; their entreaties bordered on nagging. Finally, more to get them off my case than anything else, I visited their church. People in the church seemed more relaxed than the JW's had been. The atmosphere in the church was drastically different from the air of anxiety apparent in the Witnesses' Kingdom Hall. The people greeted me without suspicion as if they were genuinely glad I was there. I felt truly welcome. When a stranger visits a Kingdom Hall, the people warmly welcome him but at the same time are suspicious. Among the JW's the visitor becomes the main topic of conversation. People speculate about why he is there. "Maybe *they* sent him to spy on us," they speculate.

The church building at which my in-laws attended seated on simple wooden pews no more than 200 people. A colorful, patterned carpet covered the raised platform. Behind the pulpit a choir area accommodated 20 singers, an organ, and a piano. In front of the piano six musicians occupied a lower platform.

I loved the music. It was so different from the Catholic church and Lutheran church I had visited and was a world away from music in the Kingdom Hall. The JW's won't use any music that's not written by Jehovah's Witnesses. That eliminates all the beautiful old hymns and guarantees musical boredom. This little church congregation sang with gusto. As I listened, I felt uplifted.

The preacher got red in the face and yelled, but the effect on me was not the same as it had been when I was 4-years old and the preacher at the Oregon Flats Baptist Church near Bergman, AR, scared me to death. This time I could understand the words; the sermons interested me. The pastor preached about hell. He seemed to have genuine compassion for people who were going there. He wanted to see people "saved".

Saved was a new term to me. Preaching hell to me had no effect. My years of training as a Jehovah's Witness had calloused me to any fear of eternal hell. I didn't exactly disbelieve it nor did I believe it.

During the years since I had left the JW's, I rarely had let thoughts about God enter my mind, but when they did, I realized that I had no relationship with God. So I purposely didn't think about God. I could see that many of the folks in the church lived with the same personal relationship with God as the man I had first heard pray at that supper in Pyatt, AR.

I remembered an old woman in a rescue mission who years earlier had tried to tell me about Jesus. She seemed to have that same close relationship with Jesus Christ. Things she told me that I didn't understand began to fit together—not because of what she said or what the preacher said but because of the faith and love of God demonstrated by the Christian people.

That memory made me listen more attentively. As the pastor preached, scattered responses of "amen" and "hallelujah"—an almost musical exchange between pastor and people— occurred. At the end of the sermon the pastor pled for people to move forward to be "saved" or to "get right with God".

I continued to attend church services with my wife and in-laws. After the third church service I, along with the rest of the people, filed out of the building. The pastor, a tall, straight man in his early 30s, reached out and gripped my arm.

"Joe, don't you want to be saved?" he asked earnestly. His hand tightened on my arm; his eyes firmly held mine. They demanded an answer.

"Yes," I said simply, while in my heart I thought this would be impossible.

"Do you want me to show you how you can be saved?" he asked.

"Yes," I heard myself say, but still I thought I was without hope. And I really didn't think this man could show me.

The pastor guided me back to a pew, on which we sat down in the nearly empty church. "Jesus loves you," he began. The pastor opened his well-worn Bible to the 16th chapter of Acts. He read to me how Paul and Silas had been locked in stocks in a Philippian jail and how the Lord had shaken the prison with an earthquake so they were freed from their stocks. Thinking they had escaped, the jailor drew his sword to kill himself. But Paul cried for him to stop, *Do thyself no harm: for we are all here. The jailor fell down before Paul and Silas, and asked, Sirs, what must I do to be saved?*[57]

If I could have spoken face-to-face with Jesus Christ or the apostle Paul, I would have asked the same question. What must I do to be saved? *Beyond hope, probably*, I thought.

The pastor made me realize that the message was my answer too. *And they, (Paul and Silas) said, Believe on the Lord Jesus Christ, and thou shalt be saved and thy house.*[58]

For the first time I realized why Jesus Christ died on the cross. He died there to take the punishment for my sins. My sins were many, but still He loved me. Before I ever was born, He loved me. He suffered there, hanging on the cross, for every sin I ever had committed, to reconcile me to God. If I would believe and trust in Jesus Christ and commit myself to His eternal keeping, He would forgive my sins. Many times before I had read that passage of Scripture, but it never had soaked in. The answer to the greatest question of life now became crystal-clear to me. If I would repent and believe and trust in Jesus Christ, I, too, could be saved.

Replacing Error with Truth

There I sat in a church for which I had little respect and talked to a man in whom I had no confidence, but the Holy Spirit of God had penetrated my thick head and my calloused heart. I saw no blinding light. I felt no overwhelming emotional tug. But here before me was the answer in God's own Word: *Believe on the Lord Jesus Christ, and thou shalt be saved. Thou* meant me, Joe Hewitt, guilty of more sins than 10 men my age. Jesus would enter into my heart and forgive my sins and save me if I would believe and trust Him.

"Would you trust in Jesus Christ as your Lord and Savior?" the pastor asked.

"Yes." That word emerged immediately.

"Let's go down to the altar and pray," the pastor said. As we walked back down the aisle, part of me inwardly protested, *What are you getting yourself into?* But great relief soon engulfed that small protest. God would forgive my sins. I could be His son. I could have eternal life as a gift. I felt no anxiety about it and no fear—as I constantly had lived with as a JW—of failing to endure to the end; I was turning it all over to Christ.

We knelt at a mourners' bench covered in carpet remnants. The pastor helped me word a prayer that already was crying up to heaven. That prayer was being uttered in my heart in *groanings that cannot be uttered.*[59] I admitted to God that I was a sinner. I asked Him to forgive my sins and told Him I believed in Jesus Christ as my Lord and Savior. I asked Him to live in my heart and forgive all my sins. (I did not think about the doctrine of the Trinity, which the Jehovah's Witnesses had taught me to deny. I couldn't explain it, but to me at that point *God* and *Jesus* somehow were interchangeable terms.) I at last had replaced the Watchtower error with biblical truth.

My younger brother, Gordon, had a different story. From the age of 3 he grew up as a Witness. His friends had been Witnesses. Their bigotry and paranoia infected him. People looked on Gordon—the stepson and nephew of two of the most influential men in the Kingdom Hall—as a favorite and the opposite of his wild brother. The JW's had indoctrinated Gordon as thoroughly as they could any person. Yet when he grew up and left off the steady diet of Watchtower doctrine, he drifted away from it. (Charles Taze Russell, Watchtower founder, said that if anyone left off reading his Bible helps for any length of time, he would fall away and "go into darkness". He was right in that a JW must have a steady diet of the Watchtower doctrines. He has to be continually "pumped up" and excited. Otherwise, like a balloon with a hole in it, he deflates and quits the Watchtower discipline.)

After high school Gordon went to an airline school in Chicago and then to work for an airline. At first he rarely attended the Kingdom Hall meetings; then he quit altogether. He met and fell in love with a colleague who happened to be a Catholic. Much to the displeasure of our mother and stepfather Gordon and his wife joined the Catholic Church after they married. The Watchtower error that had filled Gordon's mind was replaced by Catholicism.

I well remember how Gordon, and his wife, Carol, were so happy in their personal relationship with Jesus Christ. They had gone to a Catholic Marriage Encounter and had made new commitments to each other and to Christ. My wife, Marilu, and I visited them in Chicago. We all gathered around the piano and sang the same songs of faith and assurance Marilu and I sang in our Baptist church. Gordon provided a much happier home for his children than the one from which we came. This contrast occurred not because he had not been loved but because of the *it's us against them* attitude that permeated every facet of life and the *touch not, taste not, handle not* hyper-legalistic laws upon laws with which he had to live. The Watchtower Society wasn't constantly around to nag his home with *publish-witness-hurry-hurry-Armageddon-is-just-around-the corner* and to pump fanatic adrenalin into their hearts daily.

Gordon didn't leave his formerly controlled brain empty and go off into spiritual limbo and immorality as I had done early on. He immediately replaced the Watchtower errors. That's what every ex-JW must do. Naturally I thought Gordon should have become a Baptist; he thought I should have become a Catholic, but we still are brothers in Christian faith as well as biological brothers who enjoy our freedom after rescue from the Watchtower.

Chapter 11

Corrections

When I did finally become a believer, I discovered that my upbringing as a JW adversely affected my own personal theology. The JW's use a lot of the same terminology as Christians—*gospel, kingdom, apostate,* etc. I had to first identify how my JW filter skewed my perception of these concepts. Then, I had to re-define them in the Christian context so I could apply them to my new life in Christ. In the next four chapters I'll look at a variety of these teachings and point out the contrast between what the JW's teach and what the Scriptures truly say about this concept.

What Is the Gospel of the Kingdom?

As a JW, early on I learned to quote Matthew 24:14, *And this gospel of the kingdom shall be preached in all the world for a witness unto all nations; and then shall the end come.*

The gospel of the kingdom, we were told, was the good news that Jehovah would have a kingdom on Paradise earth. He would rule righteous people who would live forever. It would be a *theocracy*—a new world, opposite to the present evil world that is full of disease, poverty, injustice, and wars.

Gospel means "good news." God wins. That's good news. According to the Bible an end to the present evil system of things will occur. This will mean an end to crime, injustice, poverty, wars, and death itself. But is the Society's idea of Paradise earth and disregarding heaven the same as that spoken of throughout the New Testament?

The Gospel of Mark starts with the words *the beginning of the Gospel of Jesus Christ*.[60] So the gospel is about Jesus Christ. What does Mark say about Jesus Christ? He lived a perfect life. He did miracles to prove He was the Son of God. He forgave sin. He allowed Himself to be nailed to a cross and died. He was resurrected from the dead. He ascended into heaven. That's the good news. The long-awaited Messiah has arrived. He brought salvation, forgives sin, and gives eternal life.

The gospel of the Kingdom is the good news about Jesus Christ's kingdom He will sit on the throne of His father David and will rule forever.[61]

Jesus said, *My kingdom is not of this world*.[62] His is a heavenly kingdom.

What a difference in interpretation of "gospel of the Kingdom". JW's say the kingdom of heaven is earthly. Jesus said the kingdom of *heaven* is *heavenly*. JW's rarely mention Jesus when they are talking about the gospel of the Kingdom. But the New Testament is all about Jesus. The Watchtower has taken one verse and built a body of theology around it to the neglect of the rest of the New Testament. Jesus said the meek shall inherit the earth.[63] I don't know when or for how long that will occur—but that doesn't mean we are to ignore the gospel of Jesus Christ, the gospel of His kingdom, and what the New Testament is all about.

The New Testament is all about the gospel; even to the casual reader this is obvious. It's about Jesus Christ. And the gospel of the Kingdom is about His heavenly kingdom. To be sure about this let us examine the way in which the apostle Paul explained the gospel.

1 Corinthians 15:1-4 says, *Moreover, brethren, I declare unto you the gospel which I preached unto you, which also ye have re-*

ceived, and wherein ye stand; By which also ye are saved, if ye keep in memory what I preached unto you, unless ye have believed in vain. For I delivered unto you first of all that which I also received, how that Christ died for our sins according to the scriptures; And that he was buried, and that he rose again the third day according to the scriptures.

This is the gospel Paul preached: the death, burial, and resurrection of Jesus Christ. Paul did not mention Paradise earth. Paul did, however, have much to say about heaven. The gospel of the kingdom is about Christ's heavenly kingdom.

Correcting Nonsense about God's Name

Jehovah's Witnesses believe that if you don't pray to Jehovah, God will re-route your prayers to Satan. You will, in effect, be worshiping Satan. The ex-JW has to replace that error with truth.

Imagine a father talking with his little 2-year-old son. The little son says to the father, "Da-da, wanna cookie." And the father says, "If you can't pronounce my name, 'Joseph', in Hebrew, I refuse to recognize you. I sure won't give you a cookie." It doesn't make a lot of sense, does it? God is not tricky. He doesn't require that we pronounce the right formula in a particular language. He won't re-route to Satan our call to Him!

We are to follow Jesus' example in prayer. Throughout the gospels He prayed to the Father. We are to pray in Jesus' name and by His authority. If we pray to the Father as Jesus did, how could the Father re-route our prayers to Satan?

God understands us whether we address Him in English, Spanish, Russian, Hebrew, Swahili, or in any other earthly language. To say we must use the name *Jehovah* so we can be heard is attributing to God a narrow-mindedness that is insulting to His majesty and omniscience.

How the Name *Jehovah* Originated

The ancient Hebrews believed the name of God to be so holy, they did not try to pronounce it. The name was written in the Hebrew Scriptures as the equivalent of *YHVH*, called the *Tetragrammaton.* When the reader read the Scriptures aloud and arrived at the word *YHVH,* the Hebrew reader felt unworthy to try to pronounce the name of God, so he substituted the Hebrew word for Lord—*Adonai.*

Imagine what difficulty one would have if our language had no vowels. If you read the word *bd,* you wouldn't know whether it meant *bad, bed, bud,* or *bid.* In the Old Testament days the Hebrew language had no vowels—only consonants. By listening to the Bible read aloud people learned to pronounce the words. Later vowel signs were added so the reader would know how to pronounce the words without being taught audibly. In about 250 B.C. The Old Testament had been translated into Greek, so a written record of how the words were to be pronounced existed. When the Hebrew scribes who copied the Scriptures used the newer Hebrew that included the vowel signs and they arrived at the Tetragrammaton, *YHVH,* they wrote in the vowel signs for *Adonai.* So the end product was the consonants for *YHVH* and the vowels for *Adonai.* That was OK, because the readers always pronounced the word *Adonai* anyway. This would be similar to circumstance in which the Tetragrammaton was included in our English translation and we simply substituted the word *LORD*.

Centuries later the English translators didn't know about that history, so they put together a word using vowels for *Adonai* and consonants for *YHVH* and arrived at the word *Jehovah.*

In most English translations the *YHVH* is translated *LORD.* That is a good translation for the true meaning of the Tetragrammaton; *YHVH* is the *I AM, the Self-Existent One, the One Without a Beginning and Without an End, the Creator of All Things.*

When you see the word *Lord,* it may mean the LORD God, or it may mean just a human lord. *Adonai* is a generic word for *lord* and in Scripture is translated *lord* or *Lord*. The word *LORD* in all capital letters is a translation of *YHVH*, or what we commonly call *Jehovah* or *Yahweh*.

Therefore, the name *Jehovah* is a hybrid name that translators put together from two other words. Do you suppose God was offended by our ignorance when we used this strange word to call on Him? If we used Watchtower logic, we'd say he bounced our prayers back to Satan because we used a made-up word, *Jehovah*.

God is love; God is long-suffering and merciful. Before we pray, He knows what we are about to say; He knows to whom we intend to speak. We don't have to speak to God in Hebrew. He understands English just as well. From Hebrew we have translated many words whose meaning was a little fuzzy to us—and the correct pronunciation even more so. God understands our intentions. So if in English we pray to Him and use the name *Jehovah*, a name that has become part of the English language, He knows about it, hears our prayer, and answers our prayer. If from our hearts we address our prayer to God—to the Great Creator of all things—the same is true.

While the dogma about the name *Jehovah* arises out of one side of the Watchtower's mouth, the other side of the mouth uses other names for God for publications aimed at non-JW's. In a tract, *Life in a Peaceful New World*, published in 1987, the Watchtower uses the following names for God:

God, 21 times; *Creator,* three times; *Father,* one time; *Jehovah,* zero times.

In the New Testament how did Jesus address God the Father? He called Him *Father*. If addressing the Almighty God as *Jehovah* was so important, why did Jesus not do it?

Do JW's Properly Worship Jehovah?

Another glaring difference between Christians and Jehovah's Witnesses is in worship. What is worship? How do we worship Almighty God? The Bible tells us we are to worship Him and that we are to worship Him only.[64] But how?

One way to worship is through praise. To praise God is to ascribe to Him those attributes to which He is entitled. If we say to an ugly woman, "You are beautiful," that is not praise but flattery and could be understood as mockery. If we call a beautiful woman *beautiful,* that is praise. because it ascribes to her an attribute to which she is entitled. If we call God the *Creator,* that is praise. If we call Him *mighty, everlasting, all knowing, merciful, loving, faithful*, and *compassionate*, that too is praise. That is worship.

In worship we are to be reverent.[65] We are to worship the one true God and none other. As did the Magi and the Apostles, we are to worship Jesus.[66] Throughout the New Testament Jesus' disciples worshiped Him.[67] Jesus never discouraged worship of Himself. If we believe, as Jesus said, that Jesus and the Father are One, no contradiction exists if we worship the Father and the Son as only one God. The writer of the Book of Hebrews tells us that all the angels are to worship Christ.[68] The apostles and early disciples were right to worship Jesus. The angels were right to worship Him; so are we.

Compare the difference in how Christians and Jehovah's Witnesses praise Jehovah. Christians gather and sing hymns of praise. If we mean the words we sing, we are praising God and worshiping Him. We also praise God in prayers. When in our prayers we say, "Almighty God, creator of all things", we are ascribing to Him the attributes of omnipotence, deity, and creation—to all of which He is entitled. Throughout the Bible we see people praise God in that way.

Throughout the Old Testament God's people used music in worship.[69] Psalm 150 tells us we are to praise God with all kinds of musical instruments and dance. Musicians set the psalms to music; in the temple choirs sang them as praise to God.

More than even the Watchtower study, Watchtower hymns bored me. The music seriously lacks melody and beauty. JW's are stuck with it. They are not allowed to listen to traditional or modern Christian hymns. Michael J. Manley, the music director in our church in Rockwall, TX, uses a mixture of old hymns and newer songs. One of those is *There Is No God Like Jehovah.* With enthusiastic praise the congregation usually stands and sings it. Jehovah's Witnesses would not object to one word in that song, but they couldn't use it. A JW didn't write it. The Watchtower didn't publish it. If a JW used the song, she might be disfellowshiped.

Many Christian song lyrics include "praise His name", a phrase that means different things to JW's and Christians. To the JW, God's name is *Jehovah*. JW's praise those put-together letters, "J-e-h-o-v-a-h". To the Christian, God's name is *Jehovah*, which means I AM, the self-existent one, the first cause of all things, the Almighty God. All those are included in His name, His person, His attributes, His office, and His authority—not just a set of letters. We praise the *name* of the LORD, not the *names*. We praise His name in the same way in which we baptize in the *name* of the Father and of the Son and of the Holy Spirit. Notice that Jesus did not say "in the *names* of".

For no purpose are we to use God's name in vain.[70] Earlier I used the example of buying something in your employer's name under his authority. If my employer gives me an American Express credit card to use to buy airline tickets for use in company business, I shouldn't flash it around to show it off or use it foolishly or for unauthorized buying. Neither should a JW elder tell a child, "Jehovah doesn't want you to play sports, because you would be mixing with worldly people." Nor should a JW elder call a woman on the carpet and question her about her private sex life with her husband. The elder should not tell her "Jehovah doesn't approve" of certain foreplay. Is this not using God's name in vain? The Watchtower encourages blaming all its rules on Jehovah. Speaking presumptuously and using the office of God without authorization is using God's name in vain and is being a false prophet.

Christians meet to worship. JW's meet to study and train.

The Truth About The Truth

Truth is truth, whether anyone believes it. Jesus said, *"I am the way, the truth and the life, no man cometh unto the Father but by me."*[71]

The Watchtower claims its teachings are *The Truth*. Jesus said He is The Truth.

Christians say, "I'm a Christian." Jehovah's Witnesses say, "I'm in The Truth." When a JW drops out or quits, they say, "He's out of The Truth."

Christians get together and ask, "How long have you been a Christian?" Jehovah's Witnesses ask, "How long have you been in The Truth." The Watchtower has removed the true meaning for The Truth from the JW's' minds and replaced it with something that means, "Watchtower doctrines and discipline".

When a JW finally gets free of the Watchtower, she must reprogram her mind to the real meaning of The Truth. Truth is free of error and is not something the Watchtower manipulates and changes each generation.

Who Are the Apostates?

Jehovah's Witnesses use the term *apostate* for anyone who has left their organization. Tom Walker, a member of my church in Richardson, TX, worked with a smart-aleck JW who bragged that one of the elders in his Kingdom Hall would debate anyone any time.

Tom told him, "My pastor will debate your elder."

When the guy found out who Tom's pastor was, he said, "We don't debate apostates."

For them not to debate ex-JW's who know most about the Watchtower Society is highly convenient.

The Bible has this to say about apostates also known as *antichrists: Dear children, this is the last hour; and as you have heard that the antichrist is coming, even now many antichrists have come. This is how we know it is the last hour. They went out from us, but they did not really belong to us. For if they had be-*

longed to us, they would have remained with us; but their going showed that none of them belonged to us.[72]

According to the apostle John people who claimed to be Christians and then turned against Christianity never were Christians. To paraphrase 1 John 2:19: *They left the fellowship of Christians, but they never really belonged with us, because if they had really belonged, they would have remained, but their leaving and turning against us showed that they never really belonged.*

However, John wants to assure those real believers in Christ: *But you have an anointing from the Holy One, and all of you know the truth. I do not write to you because you do not know the truth, but because you do know it and because no lie comes from the truth. Who is the liar? It is the man who denies that Jesus is the Christ. Such a man is the antichrist—he denies the Father and the Son.*[73]

How does one deny that Jesus is the Christ?

Christ is not Jesus' last name but is His title. The word means "Anointed One". The Hebrew word is *Messiah*, which means the same thing, "Anointed One". In Old Testament times a person set apart to rule was anointed with fragrant oil. Oil literally was poured on his head. This act seems a little more messy than the way European kings and queens were crowned, but it meant the same thing. Anointing symbolized commissioning a person with special authority.

The high priests of Israel were anointed.[74] In the Old Testament, in which the word *Messiah* is used, *Messiah* clearly is God in the Flesh. In Genesis 49:10 *Messiah* is the same as *Shiloh* (the peace bringer, or the one to whom the scepter belongs). *Messiah* is the Redeemer-God that Job could see with his eyes (Job 19:25-27). In Isaiah 7:14 *Messiah* is Immanuel (God with us) and in Isaiah 9:6 is the Child born, the Son given, the great Governor, Wonderful Counselor, Mighty God, Everlasting Father, Prince of Peace. In Isaiah 53 *Messiah* is *the arm of the Lord*.

If someone denies that Jesus is Messiah, he denies that Jesus is the Christ. If you deny that Jesus is Immanuel, you are denying that Jesus is the Christ. When Jesus Himself asserted that *before Abraham was I AM,* He claimed to be God in the flesh. The Jews took up stones to stone Him. When a Christian asserts to a JW that Jesus existed before Abraham and is the I AM, the JW's react with a similar attitude. The Jewish leaders denied that Jesus was the Christ. Modern Jehovah's Witnesses claim to believe Jesus is the Christ but deny Him Christ's attributes—that He is God in the Flesh, the everlasting father, and the mighty God described by Isaiah.

Whoever denies that Jesus is one with Jehovah denies that Jesus is the Christ or is calling Jesus a liar. According to John's definition the Watchtower Society qualifies as an *antichrist.*

JW's Changes Called *Inspired*

Jehovah's Witnesses ignore Jesus' instructions that we are to baptize disciples in the name of the Father and of the Son and of the Holy Spirit.[75] Instead the JW's change the baptismal formula. The candidate for JW baptism must take a test and answer 80 questions; then just before he is immersed, usually in a swimming pool, the JW performing the baptism asks him,

1) On the basis of the sacrifice of Jesus Christ, have you repented of your sins and dedicated yourself to Jehovah to do his will?
2) Do you understand that your dedication and baptism identify you as one of Jehovah's Witnesses in association with God's spirit-directed organization?[76]

This represents such a difference in what many pastors, during baptism, say: "Upon your confession of faith in our Lord and Savior Jesus Christ, I baptize you, my sister, in the name of the Father and of the Son and of the Holy Spirit. Buried in the likeness of his death, and raised in the likeness of his resurrection to walk in newness of life."

Which of these baptismal formulas faithfully follows Scripture is obvious. One glorifies an organization, while the other honors Jesus Christ.

I have not seen a Watchtower statement in print that says the Watchtower has the authority to change the Bible, but in practice it does that. The JW baptismal formula is an example. Another is the NWT Bible. Wherever a verse emphasizes the deity of Jesus Christ, the NWT "translators" changed it.

Bill Cetnar related a conversation he had with Nathan H. Knorr, Watchtower president. Bill asked, "Since the *Watchtower* and *Awake* magazines and the Watchtower books carry the authority of Jehovah, when do the words become inspired?" Bill Cetnar worked at the *Service Desk,* an important position at *Bethel.* His job included answering theological questions addressed to the Watchtower. (I have written to the Watchtower with questions. The returned reply was signed with a rubber stamp, "The Watchtower.") At the time Cetnar didn't doubt that the Watchtower words were inspired. He just wanted to know when inspiration went into effect. Did this happen when the writer wrote the article? (Bill himself wrote articles for *Awake.)* Was it when the type was set? Was it when the printing was finished?

"It's inspired when it leaves the Sixth Floor," Knorr told him. The Sixth Floor was the place in which the finished printing products emerged to be shipped.

Years later Bill Cetnar tested the mortar holding the stones in the Watchtower. The mortar crumbled; the stones shifted, and the prison collapsed around him. He learned about the free gift of salvation through Jesus Christ and escaped from the Watchtower.

The 144,000 Male Jewish Virgins

Going door-to-door to visit people with whom I hoped to share the gospel, I encountered a man who said he had been "studying with Jehovah's Witnesses".

"What do you think about what they teach?" I asked.

"Some of it is quite different," he said, "but they back it up with the Bible. Whatever they say in their books, they have Scripture references right there to back it up."

That was the impression the Society wanted to leave.

I can remember "witnessing" to people when I was a Witness. I challenged them to look up the references. Most people never bother, especially when they are challenged to do so. The abundance of references had impressed the man I visited. However, he hadn't bothered to look up any of those biblical references.

A Watchtower book, *The Truth that Leads to Eternal Life,* makes this assertion, "Did you know that only 144,000 chosen from among humanity over the past nineteen centuries would gain heavenly life? And did you know then that the Bible holds out hope of eternal life under righteous conditions here on earth for all others who would become faithful servants of God? (Ps. 37:10, 11, 29, 36:10, 11, 29)"[77]

The reader erroneously assumed that the references would back up the statements. Let's look more closely at these references. Psalm 37:10, 11, 29 reads, *For yet a little while, and the wicked shall not be: yea, thou shalt diligently consider his place, and it shall not be. But the meek shall inherit the earth; and shall delight themselves in the abundance of peace . . .. The righteous shall inherit the land, and dwell therein for ever.* Does this prove that only 144,000 will go to heaven and that the rest of the saved will have no hope of heaven but instead will live on the earth? No. Not by any stretch of the imagination. People who are conditioned to believe everything the Watchtower Society says will believe it—not because it makes sense but because of blind obedience to the Society.

Other references such as Revelation 7:4, 14:1-3 don't say it either. Obviously 144,000 male Jewish virgins (12,000 out of each of the 12 tribes of Israel) are different from 144,000 Jehovah's Witnesses (married and unmarried male and female Gentiles). The Bible also doesn't say the 144,000 Jews are the only ones who go to heaven either.

On page 33 in the Watchtower book *Man's Salvation out of World Distress at Hand* the Watchtower decided to explain this more fully. Following the list of the tribes this explanation is given:

"The number of those sealed Israelites is certainly an ideal number that is to say, twelve times twelve thousand, or one hundred and forty-four thousand, a perfectly balanced number. But what makes them an 'ideal' Israel is not entirely their number, but, rather, their moral, religious qualities."

Who besides the Watchtower is to say that 144,000 is a "perfectly balanced number"? The number 12 is pretty well balanced as well; so are lots of other numbers. If 144,000 is "balanced", so what? That doesn't say a thing about a bunch of Gentiles having exclusive rights to go to heaven. The Society calls the 144,000 "ideal Israel". So since 12 times 12,000 is an "ideal number" that "proves" these are the Ideal Israel or Spiritual Israel. By now the reader says, "Oh, well. This is too confusing for me. I guess they know what they're talking about." Or, a reader might say, "Oh, well. None of this makes any sense to me. I think they're nuts."

What would Watchtower logic make a dozen eggs? A perfectly balanced number, 144,000 eggs become chickens, so we're not really talking about eggs at all but instead chickens. Little chickens turn into big chickens; big chickens grow into turkeys. Turkeys fly, so the 144,000 will fly up to heaven.

"Wait a minute," you might say. "That's ridiculous. Chickens don't become turkeys." But if you disagree with someone who makes up all the rules and can prove anything he wants with his circular and confusing illogic, what chance do you have of winning an argument? That's the dilemma that engulfs the poor JW.

Then on page 35 of the book the Watchtower goes deeper in "proving" its 144,000 doctrine.

"Natural, fleshly Israel was founded upon the twelve sons of the patriarch Jacob, but it is the spiritual Israel, the Christian Israel, that is founded on the twelve apostles of the Lamb Jesus Christ (Eph. 2:20). So, without question, it is this spiritual Israel that is 'the ideal Israel'."

Can you see how this really IS working up to proof that only 144,000 will go to heaven? No? Neither can anyone else who has control of his own intellect.

The Watchtower admits the 144,000 are fleshly Israel—literal descendants of the sons of Jacob—but then the Watchtower says "spiritual Israel makes up the 144,000 who go to heaven".

The round-and-round illogic of the Watchtower Society is enough to make one dizzy; I suppose that is by design. The average, intellectually honest person who reads the Watchtower reasoning might laugh it off. But the convinced JW's number in the millions and believe whatever the Watchtower says. If the Watchtower said so, they would believe eggs didn't mean eggs at all but high-flying turkeys.

These are people who had in their hearts an empty place in which Jesus Christ would have fit perfectly. But partly because of the failure of Christians to reach out and share the gospel with these people, the JW's emerged and offered them a substitute: faith in the Society's Paradise New World. The people were hungry. The JW's fed them. The label said *food,* but the people were fed plastic. People were filled but not nourished. What seems comedy is tragedy.

How many people do you suppose have already gone to heaven? Old Testament saints already are in heaven.[78] Jesus said many would arrive from the east and the west and would sit down with Abraham, Isaac, and Jacob in the kingdom of heaven. New Testament saints have gone to heaven. In 2 Corinthians 5:8 the apostle Paul spoke of being absent from the body and being present with the Lord. Where is the Lord? In heaven. And so when a Christian dies, he is separated from his body and is present with the Lord immediately in heaven. How many millions of people do you suppose already arrived in heaven *before* the Watchtower decided on the gross number?

We also find that the saints who still are living when Jesus Christ returns will go to heaven.[79] The Bible tells us that when the Lord Jesus Christ returns, the dead in Christ will be resurrected. *Then we which are alive and remain shall be caught up together with them in the clouds, to meet the Lord in the air: and so shall we ever be with the Lord.*

The Bible says what it means and means what it says. We don't need a hierarchy to tell us it means the opposite to what it says. The meaning is obvious. Believers in Christ go to heaven. The exact number is not important.

Chapter 12

The Truth about Blood

Jehovah's Witnesses possibly are best-known for their refusal to accept blood transfusions and for their attitudes about taking in blood in any form. This chapter looks at some of these practices and studies whether they are or are not based on Scripture.

Why Not Accept a Blood Transfusion?

Before the Watchtower Society officially disfellowshiped me and before my mother, a JW, was forbidden to speak to me, she and I had a conversation in which we discussed accidents and blood transfusions. She removed a card from her purse and held it up for her other children and me to see. She said, "If I'm ever in an accident and can't speak for myself, don't ever let *them* give me a blood transfusion. This card says it's against my religion." My sisters, Naomi, Wanda, and Rose, and I looked on incredulously. *Was she really serious? Would she rather die than accept a blood transfusion?*

"Yes," she said, "I would rather die than violate the command of Jehovah not to eat blood." We tried to convince her that a blood transfusion was not the same as eating blood. She was a thoroughly disciplined Jehovah's Witness, so arguing with her about this issue was the same thing as trying to reason with a fence post.

"If I'm around and you have an accident and can't answer for yourself," I said indignantly, "the first thing I'll do is take that thing out of your purse and throw it away."

She said my attitude hurt her. She assured us that she wanted to die rather than accept a blood transfusion. She said we should honor her choice.

In spring 1970 doctors told Mr. and Mrs. Robert Johnson of Athol, MA, their 5-year-old son, Terry, needed open-heart surgery. They said a congenital heart defect caused him always to be short of breath and exhausted. The doctors said without the surgery he probably would not live many more years. The doctors were 90-percent sure that the operation would make Terry well. Nevertheless his parents refused to allow the surgery, because blood transfusions would be necessary—and as Jehovah's Witnesses the transfusions would be a violation of their religious beliefs.

The doctors suggested that they remove some of Terry's own blood over a period of time and use it during the surgery, but the parents refused. The doctors explained that these transfusions only would replace some of the boy's own blood. He would not be eating blood. Following the Watchtower instructions the parents refused. The doctors considered seeking a court order, but the parents said that if the transfusions were performed, they would not take Terry back into their home.

Because of the ingenuity of the doctors, the surgery was performed successfully without blood transfusions. The boy survived, but he had to live with the reality that his parents had been willing to sacrifice him in order to maintain their religious beliefs.

Why would people be willing to die rather than to accept a blood transfusion? Why, if they had a means to stop it, would parents be willing to let their own child die? Why would parents be more willing to abandon their child rather than to accept him back into their home after having been given a blood transfusion?

JW's are willing to kill a child by neglect; they claim obedience to an Old Testament law they have chosen to obey while they ignore dozens of others.

Members of the Masai tribe in Africa feed cow's blood to sick children. Many people today, especially in Europe, eat blood sausage and blood pudding and think nothing of it because they believe the Old Testament dietary laws no longer are in effect. They believe these have been fulfilled by Christ. Even if the Old Testament dietary law still were in effect, it would not prohibit blood transfusions.

To make the law mean a prohibition of blood transfusions makes much less sense than does the modern Orthodox Jew's refusal to eat meat and dairy products at the same meal or even from the same plate at different meals.

The Orthodox Jewish doctrine is based on the commands in Exodus 23:19, *Thou shalt not seethe a kid in his mother's milk.*[80] The pagans would boil a baby sheep or goat in its mother's milk and to promote fertility would sprinkle the broth over the flocks and fields. God's people were not to participate.

Those Hebrews who delighted in adding to the Law decided that they would be better off not boiling a kid in any milk, lest perchance it be the mother's. The next step was not to eat any meat at the same meal at which milk was served, lest the kid and milk somehow get mixed in the stomach. Later that was expanded to include any dairy product and meat. The law continued to be added to until a piece of cheese or any dairy product could not be placed on the same plate on which meat had been eaten, lest the commandment be violated. For the strict Orthodox Jewish family this hyper-legalism necessitates two complete sets of dishes. But the Orthodox Jewish belief doesn't hurt anyone. No children are killed by neglect. No one starves to death for the prohibition to be obeyed. Indeed if an Orthodox Jew eats a cheeseburger while he drinks a glass of milk, he will not be ostracized by his family—criticized maybe but certainly not shunned and declared as one dead and consigned to eternal damnation.

The Watchtower Society similarly has added to the prohibition against eating blood to the point that it refuses to take an inoculation again disease if that inoculation involves blood serum.

At one of the Ex-Jehovah's Witnesses for Jesus conventions, Bill Cetnar told a story of how the Society learned what actually was involved in making smallpox vaccine. As a writer for the *Awake* magazine, Bill took a tour of a pharmaceutical facility in which smallpox vaccine was made. Jehovah's Witnesses were forbidden to take smallpox vaccinations because they thought the manufacturers used blood to make it. JW doctors furnished forged certificates for JW missionaries going overseas and JW children to take to schools.[81] In the vaccine facility Bill looked at a great number of eggs used to produce the vaccine and asked, "Where's the blood?"

"There is no blood," the guide replied.

"I know there's blood in that vaccine. Where is it?" Bill demanded.

"There is no blood—just unfertilized eggs," the guide insisted.

Back at Watchtower headquarters Bill broke the news to president Nathan Knorr, who was taken aback. Over and over he quizzed Bill to be sure he was correct. "There was no blood."

Gradually word went out; first it went to the JW missionaries going overseas. They were required to be inoculated for smallpox. They no longer had to carry forged vaccination certificates but now could take the inoculations. JW children no longer had to take forged vaccination certificates to school.

Many JW men were locked up in federal prison for violating the draft laws. Those prisoners had refused to be inoculated for smallpox because of the blood prohibition and had been severely punished. Now the Society quietly got word to them that they should take the vaccine. The men who by going to prison had suffered for the Watchtower and then in prison suffered punishment for obeying Watchtower rules reacted with indignation.

Some of the prisoners continued to refuse to accept the inoculation and were disfellowshiped for disobeying the Society.

Christians long have been accused of having a preoccupation with blood. In the early days pagans who did not understand the Lord's Supper accused Christians of being cannibals. Today Christians who preach the atonement of Christ stress His shed blood. They cite such examples as: *. . .which he hath purchased with his own blood . . . .*[82] *In whom we have redemption through his blood, the forgiveness of sins, according to the riches of his grace.*[83]

How much more shall the blood of Christ, who through the eternal Spirit offered Himself without spot to God, purge your conscience from dead works to serve the living God?[84]

The blood of Jesus Christ being shed for us is an essential part of the gospel story.

Some other cults emphasize blood but not the blood of Christ. For example the Mormons believe that man's shedding his own blood can atone for his sins. That's why the State of Utah allows a condemned criminal to choose his method of execution. He can choose the shedding of blood—death by firing squad. The Watchtower Society is preoccupied with blood generally but not with Christ's shed blood. In the Watchtower book, *Life Everlasting in Freedom of the Sons of God,* which contains the chart indicating that Armageddon would occur in the autumn of 1975, Watchtower includes several odd references to blood. They note such "milestones" of history as:

"1492 Pope Innocent VIII dies after blood transfusion.
"1918 First use of stored blood.
"1937 First blood bank on a large scale established at Cook County Hospital.
"1945 Watchtower exposes blood transfusion, Psalm 16:4.
"1963 Pope John XIII dies . . . despite blood transfusions."

Did the Watchtower just then in 1945 discover Psalm 16:4? In that psalm David said, *Their sorrows shall be multiplied that hasten after another god: their drink offerings of blood will I not offer, nor take up their names into my lips.*

This is another example of how the Society took a verse of Scripture out of context and put a different meaning on it to suit the Watchtower's own purposes.

The Pharisees sought to kill Jesus because they believed He violated the Sabbath when on that day He healed the sick. The same reasoning would cause a parent to kill his or her own child rather than violate a Pharisaical doctrine made by human beings.

A website secretly sponsored by people who still are affiliated with Jehovah's Witnesses lists names of people who have died needlessly because they denied blood transfusions.[85]

The website states: "The Names listed in this Memorial constitute only a small sampling of the victims who should be included, according to published statistics. Relatively few cases are brought to the attention of the news media unless doctors ask courts to intervene. When adult JW's are admitted privately to hospitals and sign legal release papers, their deaths because of refusing blood are generally recorded only in confidential patient files. Published obituaries usually omit such details. Names are listed on the website if reported in the public news media or if submitted by relatives, friends, or other knowledgeable individuals who vouch for the information."

The sponsors, called Associated Jehovah's Witnesses for Reform on Blood (AJWRB), say, "Blood (in the Watchtower proof text, Genesis 9:4-7) is used for life. Its use is symbolic not literal. Additionally, the entire discussion of blood takes place in the context of killing, either animals or humans. This is an important point because blood transfusion does not involve killing. Quite to contrary, such blood is used for the purpose of preserving life.

"This brings up another important point, and that is, which is greater, the symbol or the reality, blood or that which it represents—life? Consider this: Which is greater Jesus' shed blood or the red wine, which symbolizes his blood? Clearly the blood of Jesus is greater since the Bible teaches that his shed blood was able to provide for the forgiveness of sin. Based upon this, isn't it reasonable to conclude that God would put a higher value on human life than he puts on blood, which is a symbol of life?

"This illustration may be helpful to consider: If you were robbed and a thief demanded your wedding ring, would you refuse to give it if he threatened to kill your spouse? Would you reason: 'This ring represents my marriage to my spouse and that's more important than my spouse's life.' Such reasoning is seriously flawed, yet this is the exact reasoning used by the WTS to support its ban on certain types of blood transfusions. Yes blood is a symbol of life, but the life is certainly more valuable than the symbol."

The website contains many heartbreaking stories of parents whose children died because the parents obeyed the Watchtower. One mother said, ". . . if the Bible says nothing about transfusions, how can the Governing Body say with certainty that blood transfusions are wrong in Jehovah's eyes? How could I forgive those men for my son's death? In my opinion, the men of the Governing Body have the blood of many innocents on their hands. They who taught us falsely in God's name are accountable to him."[86]

The AJWRB traces to an H. G. Wells 1898 novel, *War of the Worlds,* the history of the Watchtower's understanding of blood. The novel says, "They did not eat, much less digest. Instead they took the fresh living blood of other creatures and injected it into their own veins." They refer to a 1945 *Watchtower* that quotes a 1929 *Americana Encyclopedia.* This book describes a 17th-century understanding of blood ". . . as the blood is the principal medium by which the body is nourished, transfusion, therefore, is a quicker and shorter road to feed an ill-nourished body than eating food which turns to blood after several changes . . .."

In my mind a picture emerges of Watchtower Society leaders reading the 1945 *Watchtower* magazine without fully understanding that the 17th-century idea about blood was faulty. In their minds blood was food as it had been for the fictional Martians and the ignorant 17th-century physicians.

In a news release dated September 28, 2000, the JWARB said, "The policy on hemoglobin and other blood fractions was changed in the June 15, 2000, issue of The Watchtower. This latest change may in fact cause further confusion for many Witnesses since products like Hemopure® are derived from large quantities of stored animal blood. Numerous witnesses have questioned the logic of such inconsistent dogma. Some believe that the governing body of Jehovah's Witnesses is simply changing its long-standing doctrine gradually to avoid legal problems from anticipated with an overt change to a policy that has resulted in so many deaths over the years."

Like other JW dogma the blood rules keep changing. Before 1945 a JW could take a blood transfusion without penalty. Then the Society would not allow JW's to take blood transfusions period. Then they were allowed to take certain portions. Now they are allowed to take portions from animal blood. The dogma is supposed to be based on Scripture, but the JW's don't offer proof texts for the changes.

I pray that these people, who are brave enough to oppose a Watchtower rule, albeit in secret, will continue to be open for truth and see that some of the other teachings are in error as well. Usually when a JW learns that one of the Watchtower doctrines is false, the rest of their peculiar beliefs collapse on each other as though they were crushed stones.

Obviously the Old Testament law forbade the Israelites to eat blood.[87] They were not to drink it. They were not to eat the flesh of an animal that had been strangled, because the blood was still in it. They couldn't eat pork.[88] They were not to eat shellfish or fish that had no scales. They were not to wear a garment that was woven with two different kinds of fabric such as wool and linen.[89] Out of those and many other prohibitions The Watchtower chose one to observe and ignored the rest.

Jesus fulfilled the law.[90] Believers today are under grace, not the law. But the blood law was carried over into the New Testament, the JW's say, and cite the council at Jerusalem recorded in Acts Chapter 15. Some Jewish Christians had told the Gentiles that they had to obey the law of Moses and be circumcised *before* they could become Christians. The apostle Paul confronted them and insisted that salvation was entirely by grace—the free, unmerited favor of God. The disciples brought the question before the church at Jerusalem. James, the pastor of the church, wrote a letter to the Gentile believers in Antioch, Syria, and Cilicia. That letter said:

. . . certain which went out from us have troubled you with words, subverting your souls, saying, Ye must be circumcised, and keep the law: to whom we gave no such commandment: . . .. For it seemed good to the Holy Ghost, and to us, to lay upon you no greater burden than these necessary things; That ye abstain from meats offered to idols, and from blood, and from things strangled, and from fornication: from which if ye keep yourselves, ye shall do well. Fare ye well.[91]

The letter gives the reason: *For Moses of old time hath in every city them that preach him, being read in the synagogues every Sabbath Day.* James did not enumerate conditions of salvation. He gave instructions to avoid offending the Jews and for the new Christians to *do well.* The apostle Paul made clear the fact that eating meat that had been sacrificed to idols was not wrong *per se,* but if it caused offense to a brother, Christians shouldn't do it.[92]

The pagan Gentiles considered fornication morally acceptable and customary. A man had a wife to bear children and had concubines for cohabitation. Jesus clearly stated that fornication was sin. Therefore it couldn't be classified as a fulfilled Old Testament Law.

The Gentiles ate meat that had been strangled; it meant nothing to them. However, when these people became Christians and continued to eat this meat, the Jewish believers were offended.

The new Gentile believers were to be careful. They were instructed not do anything to cause other believers to stumble or be offended. These were not conditions of salvation. The condition for salvation is believing in, trusting in, and relying on Jesus Christ as Lord and Savior.[93] During the council at Jerusalem Peter said, *But we believe that through the grace of the LORD Jesus Christ we shall be saved, even as they.*[94]

Chapter 13

The Soul, the Spirit, and the Afterlife

Many differences exist between the Jehovah's Witnesses understanding and the biblical concept of the soul, the spirit, and life after death. In this chapter these will be explored.

What Is a Soul?

The Watchtower has difficulty understanding the difference between a person and a body. To the Watchtower a person is a body and a soul is life that dies when the body dies. The Watchtower Society says "animals as well as humans are called souls." True. The Bible says animals have souls. I find nothing in the Bible that says an animal's soul lives on after death of its body. Because of that we assume an animal's soul does not continue in existence after death of its body. But because people are spoken of as living after they die, I believe the human soul lives on. For example, Abraham, Isaac, and Jacob—long dead—are spoken of as living.[95]

Adam became a living soul.[96] Like Adam, you are a soul. Obviously you are body. You also are a spirit or have a spirit just as you have a body and a soul. Let's examine the soul. Just what is it?

Whether soul means *self, life,* or *personality* depends on the context. *My soul thirsteth for God, for the living God. . .*. Obviously this is *self* or *personality*. *For thou hast delivered my soul from death . . .*.[98] Here the Bible talks about *life*.

My soul longeth, yea, even fainteth for the courts of the LORD. . . .[99] What can this be but *self* or *personality? . . . every living soul died in the sea.*[100] What can this be but *life*?

. . . as her soul was in departing, (for she died) that she called his name Benoni: but his father called him Benjamin.[101] This was Rachel's *personality,* or *life,* departing her body. She died. Her life was departing. Her personality was departing. *. . . that soul shall be cut off from Israel.*[102] Here the word *soul* is synonymous with *personality* or *person*. The Old Testament is full of references to the soul—meaning *life, personality,* or *self*.

In the New Testament also we find many verses in which soul means *life,* or *self,* or *personality,* but it also means something that survives after death of the body. Jesus said, *And fear not them which kill the body, but are not able to kill the soul: but rather fear him which is able to destroy both soul and body in hell.*[103] Therefore, soul and body are different.

After death of the body, what about a person lives on? The Bible says the soul. Atheists say, "Nothing."

When Lazarus's body died, which part of him went to the place in which Abraham greeted him? When the Rich Man, who mistreated Lazarus, died, what part of him went to hades in which he begged for water? Surely their personalities made the trip. Therefore, your personality lives on after death of your body, just like Abraham's, Lazarus's, and the Rich Man's did.[104]

The Watchtower tries to explain this Scripture away as a parable with no real meaning. The Scripture is about *"a certain"* Rich Man and *"a certain"* beggar. This is not the account of a parable but of real people with real events. If you want to be amused, ask a JW to explain Luke 16. The person's explanation is so silly that it serves as an example that a JW will swallow a camel because the Watchtower told him it'll go down easy like a gnat.

The facts are: The Rich Man died. *He* was buried. So who was *he?* His body was buried. *He* went to Hades. So who was *he?* The he was his soul that went to Hades. The Rich Man was body and soul, yet he was one person. The personality inhabits the body. The arrangement is similar to that of a computer. You can't see the software. It's in there somewhere as it operates the computer. You can see the hardware—the computer itself. The human soul or personality is like the software. The human body is like the computer hardware.

Lazarus died. He was carried away by angels to the place in which Abraham greeted him in Paradise. Did Lazarus' diseased body go to Paradise? No. It was *him*—his personality, his soul. So what happened to Lazarus' body? The Bible doesn't say. Most likely, since Lazarus had no one to care for him, his dead body was taken off to Gehenna, the Jerusalem dump, and burned. That made no difference to Lazarus. He was through with it anyway. For the believer in Christ, *To be absent from the body is to be present with the Lord.*[105]

The soul involves emotions. The souls of David and Jonathan were knit; Jonathan loved him as his own soul.[106] David's soul hated the enemy.[107] Job said . . . *his soul within him shall mourn.*[108]

Uninformed people have assumed that "animals don't have souls because they can't love." Dogs love their masters. The lioness loves her cubs. In grief a pet cat may refuse to eat. Animals have souls and emotions.

The soul feels sorrow. Jesus in the Garden of Gethsemane said, *My soul is exceeding sorrowful unto death.*[109] The soul suffers: *Their soul is melted because of trouble.*[110]

The aged Simeon said to Mary, *Yea, a sword shall pierce through thy own soul also.*[111]

The soul clearly does not go into a grave and rot. At death the soul and body are separated. In Zarephath, Zidon, the son of the widow who had fed Elijah, died. Elijah *stretched himself upon the child three times, and cried unto the LORD, and said, O LORD, my God, I pray thee, let this child's soul return unto him again. And the LORD heard the voice of Elijah; and the soul of the child came into him again, and he revived.*[112] Obviously the boy's soul was separated from his body. By a miracle the soul then returned to his body.

Humanity is not able to destroy the soul. A person may kill the body and cause the soul to be separated, but only God can destroy the soul, which does not necessitate annihilation of that soul. *And fear not them which kill the body, but are not able to kill the soul: but rather fear him which is able to destroy both soul and body in hell [Gehenna].*[113] The words *soul* and *person* are interchangeable, as are the words *body* and *person*, and *spirit* and *person*. I am body. I am soul. I am spirit. And so are you.

According to the Book of Revelation[114] unregenerate humanity will be resurrected, judged, and cast into the Lake of Fire to be destroyed eternally. These people do not cease to exist but are cast into the Lake of Fire in which the Beast and False Prophet already will have been for 1,000 years. If the Lake of Fire meant annihilation rather than everlasting destruction, the Beast and False Prophet would not last 1,000 years in its flame.

The soul—the person—is conscious after death. *Whether we wake or sleep, we should live together with him.*[115] The apostle Paul said we would be . . . *absent from the body, and present with the Lord.* [116] These Scriptures suggest a conscious existence; this point is further strengthened by Paul in Philippians 1:23: *For I am in a strait betwixt two, having a desire to depart, and to be with Christ; which is far better.*

Souls under the altar in heaven speak; therefore they are conscious.[117]

The Watchtower claims such promises given in the Bible to all believers only are for the 144,000. Believers go to heaven—not their old diseased bodies but their souls go. In heaven a believer gets a new, heavenly body.[118]

The Sadducees, who denied the resurrection, asked Jesus about a man who died leaving no heirs and whose widow married his seven brothers each in succession. They asked whose wife she would be in the resurrection. Jesus said no marriage union would exist in heaven, but people would be like the angels. Are the angels not conscious?

The Watchtower tries to disprove these truths with Bible verses taken out of context and with tricky verbal gymnastics. For the Society's claims to be true the Bible would have to contradict itself.

If the Watchtower is correct—that a person is a body with a soul that is life without intellect and a spirit that is like an electrical current without intelligence—how can a believer still exist with the Lord while the person is absent from the body? This is similar to someone who added one plus one plus one and said it equals one. It doesn't add up. But to the JW's that's OK. What the Watchtower says doesn't have to add up because it's *Jehovah's earthly organization.* How does the JW know these facts? Because the Watchtower Society said so.

The Rastafarians use the same circular logic. They believe Ras Tafari Haile Selassie was Christ because he was the *King of Kings and Lord of Lords and the Lion of the Tribe of Judah.* How do the Rastafarians know that? Because Haile Selassie himself said so. As *King of Kings and Lord of Lords and the Lion of the Tribe of Judah* he certainly had the authority to say so. This cult, mostly on the island of Jamaica, claims that a righteous Rastafarian never will die. But they keep on dying, just like the Watchtower's prophecies keep on failing. But cult members regardless of their group keep on believing the lies.

What Is a Spirit?

The Watchtower claims the spirit is just energy—like an electrical force or inanimate oxygen—and that the Holy Spirit is an impersonal energy field.

How could an impersonal energy field or the body's oxygen be held responsible for anything? How could such a *spirit* be held blameless? The apostle Paul said, . . . *I pray God your whole spirit and soul and body be preserved blameless unto the coming of our Lord Jesus Christ.*[119] Paul addressed as *you* the Christians at

Thessalonica and indicated they possessed *spirit* as well as *soul* and *body*.

The Society suggests that the spirit of people is oxygen.[120] The Watchtower explains, "Whereas the human soul is the living person himself, the spirit is simply the life force that enables that person to be alive. The spirit has no personality, nor can it do the things a person can do. It cannot think, speak, hear, see, or feel. In that respect, it might be likened to the electric current of a car's battery." The Society says humans and animals have this same *life force* or *spirit*.

I think Society members are close to the truth when they say the soul is the living person, but remember, they can't tell a *person* from a *body*. But to call our *spirit*, created in the image of God, just electricity is a tenuous position. *So God created man in his own image, in the image of God created he him; male and female created he them.*[121]

In what way did God create people in His image? Does we look like God? No. Man was created a spirit being. In that respect we are created in the image of God. *God is a Spirit.*[122] God is not just oxygen nor is He non-thinking electrical current—and neither is the spirit of human beings.

Our spirits are born again when they are regenerated. Jesus said, *That which is born of the flesh is flesh; and that which is born of the Spirit is spirit. Marvel not that I said unto thee, Ye must be born again.*[123]

The spirit of man is the candle of the LORD, searching all the inward parts.[124] Can something impersonal search?

Our spirits have intelligence. *For what man knoweth the thing of a man, save the spirit of man which is in him?*[125] Oxygen or electricity isn't intelligent or emotional. Our spirits have emotions. *When Jesus therefore saw her weeping, and the Jews also weeping which came with her, he groaned in the spirit, and was troubled.*[126]

No Bible evidence exists that indicates that animals have spirits, although they do have oxygen and a life force. So according to Watchtower logic, animals as well as people would have spirits.

What Is Resurrection?

In its book *Aid to Bible Understanding* (ABU) the Watchtower Society devotes six-and-a-half pages to the subject of "resurrection".

Elsewhere the Society denies eternality of the human soul, but its explanation of the resurrection approaches admitting that the human soul lives on after death. The book states, ". . . how easy for the great Universal Sovereign and Creator to resurrect a person by re-patterning the same personality in a newly formed body."[127] Later the book states, "It is the soul, the person, that is resurrected with a body to suit the environment into which God resurrects him." Here *personality, soul, person,* all are synonymous. Apparently the Society agrees with the usual interpretation of the Greek word *psyche*. Depending on the context, it can mean any of the three.

In the beginning of its section on resurrection the Society considers resurrection both literal and physical.

How can the Society say the human soul is not eternal, yet the personality, or soul, survives death, is given a new body in the resurrection, and has eternal life?

The Society teaches that for obedient Jehovah's Witnesses resurrection is literal and physical and that non-JW's *of good will* who physically arc rcsurrcctcd will have another shot at becoming Witnesses. If they refuse their second chance, they are to be cast into the Lake of Fire. Both these resurrections are literal and physical, but the Society denies that Jesus literally and physically was resurrected.

The ABU makes a flat statement that Christ's resurrection was ". . . in the spirit" to life in heaven. To back it up the ABU cites 1 Peter 3:18, *For Christ also hath once suffered for sins, the just for the unjust, that he might bring us to God, being put to death in the flesh, but quickened by the Spirit.* The NIV says . . . *made alive by the Spirit.* The NASV says . . . *in the spirit.* Whether Peter meant Christ was resurrected by the Holy Spirit or that Christ's spirit was made alive is arguable. That by no means negates a great body of Scripture that proves that literally and physically He was resurrected.

In an apparent effort to bolster its teaching that Christ's resurrection only was spiritual, the ABU says, "He was granted immortality and incorruption, which no creature in the flesh can have. . .."[128] Here we see one of many contradictions in Watchtower teachings. The Watchtower promises obedient JW's that they, in fleshly bodies, will be immortal on earth, but they deny it for Christ.

The resurrection of Jesus Christ is one of the most attested-to facts of human history. More documentation of it exists than about whether Julius Caesar ever lived. Many secular records of the resurrection including writings of Flavius Josephus and Pliny the Younger exist.

The resurrection is a vital part of the gospel. If no resurrection occurred, then Christ lived and died a lie and the gospel writers—Matthew, Mark, Luke, and John—testified to a lie.

The ABU says Christ appeared in "various fleshly bodies . . . for the purpose of proving visibly that he had been resurrected." So God perpetuated a ruse to fool people into thinking Christ was literally and physically resurrected when he wasn't?

The ABU says, "His resurrection, so well attested furnishes a guarantee to all humanity in that [God] has resurrected him from the dead." The statement cites Acts 17:31, . . . *whereof he hath given assurance unto all men, in that he hath raised him from the dead.* The Society lists many Scriptures that back up the resurrection; all these imply a literal and physical resurrection—against which a simply "spiritual" resurrection would be meaningless.

You may have heard people speak of a dead loved one this way: "He is still with us in spirit." If a woman's husband dies, fond memories may remain in her heart, but he won't keep her physically warm on a cold night or guard the door against intruders.

In further attempts to justify the false doctrine of a spiritual-only resurrection the Society offers the same kind of resurrection for the 144,000, *the called and chosen and faithful* and *spiritually begotten.* So they are just spiritually resurrected until they get a heavenly body, ". . . a body to suit the environment into which God resurrects them."[129] So the 144,000 get a new spiritual body, but Jesus doesn't? So far anyway, the Society denies Jesus a body of any kind, because it says He now is ruling and reigning invisibly through the Watchtower Society in Brooklyn, NY.

Not a shred of evidence that only 144,000 have a hope of heaven exists, but bushels of evidence indicate that all believers do have that hope. Paul said, *For our conversation is in heaven; from whence also we look for the Saviour, the Lord Jesus Christ: Who shall change our vile body, that it may be fashioned like unto his glorious body . . . .*

Our citizenship is in heaven; Paul said Christ will change our bodies to be like His.

First Thessalonians 4:13-18 is one of the great passages on the resurrection that the Watchtower almost ignores and then makes a puny effort to negate its truth. During my mother's funeral in Wichita, KS, in 1975, the JW preacher explained that she, a lifelong, loyal Jehovah's Witness, would have no conscious existence until the resurrection. Then he read the passage from the NWT—a cumbersome paraphrase. An example is verse 14, *For if our faith is that Jesus died and rose again, so, too, those who have fallen asleep [in death] through Jesus Christ will God bring with him.*

The JW's agree that those asleep meant those who had died. The KJV says, *For if we believe that Jesus died and rose again, even so them also which sleep in Jesus will God bring with him.*

In both versions Paul speaks of believers in Christ's resurrection. The KJV continues, *For the Lord Himself shall descend from heaven with a shout, with the voice of the archangel, and with the trump of God: and the dead in Christ shall rise first: Then we which are alive and remain shall be caught up together with them in the clouds, to meet the Lord in the air: and so shall we ever be with the Lord.*

Inspired Scripture gives these comforting words to all believers, not just to the 144,000.

The Lord Himself will descend from heaven. Is that someone invisible?

Jesus will return with the sounds of the archangel's voice and the trumpet of God. Are these sounds marking the descent of an invisible Jesus? (Were these sounds heard by anyone when an invisible Jesus allegedly descended on Watchtower Headquarters in Brooklyn?)

Then those believers who still are alive at His return will be caught up together with the resurrected believers to meet the Lord in the air. Oops! Did that happen when the JW's say Jesus returned invisibly in 1914? That did not happen! Russell said the great meeting in the air had been postponed until 1918. That didn't happen then either!

Still the JW's insist that Jesus quietly and invisibly returned in 1914 and now is ruling and reigning through the Watchtower Society.

JW's explain away the resurrection of believers and their trip up in the air to meet Jesus as something that happens at the believer's death. They stop before the promise that we will ever be with the Lord. Either the Society contradicts itself that ordinary believers won't go to heaven, or the promised trip up in the air to meet Jesus is only for the 144,000. If so, what bearing did it have on my mother, who was of the Jonadab class, the *other sheep* group who are not eligible for heaven?

You can spiritualize anything to death or just call it "figurative" or "true in a sense". The Watchtower Society is expert at that. It can make anything mean whatever the Society wants it to—even opposite to what the Bible says. JW's believe the Society has that authority, so they accept it.

So believers didn't ascend up to meet Jesus in 1914, according to the Society, and they won't do it in the future either, so those events will just "figuratively" happen to people when they die and Jesus was just "spiritually" resurrected from the grave. All this makes sense if you have traded your ability to reason for blind obedience.

One of my seminary classmates, Louis McGarity, had a favorite statement he used to end a theological argument. He sim-

The Soul, the Spirit, and the Afterlife

ply would say, "Remember what Paul said," and walk away. This would leave his opponent to wonder. Paul said something about most theological questions, so that should have covered it. About the physical and literal resurrection, one might say, "Remember what Matthew, Mark, Luke, and John said." They all had a lot to say about the resurrection of Christ, the central truth of Christianity.

In 1 Corinthians 15 the apostle Paul defends the doctrine of the resurrection.

First, Christ died as prophesied in Scripture. And He died for our sins. He was buried and also rose again the third day as Scripture had foretold. No suggestion exists whatsoever that His resurrection was invisible and only spiritual.

Eyewitnesses to the resurrection included Peter, then all the Apostles, and then more than 500 believers at once, of whom most were still alive when Paul wrote about it.

Paul says for believers the resurrection of Jesus proves a literal resurrection:

Now if Christ be preached that he rose from the dead, how say some among you that there is no resurrection of the dead? But if there be no resurrection of the dead, then is Christ not risen: And if Christ be not risen, then is our preaching (in) vain, and your faith is also (in) vain. Yea, and we are found false witnesses of God; because we have testified of God that he raised up Christ: whom he raised not up, if so be that the dead rise not. For if the dead rise not, then is not Christ raised: And if Christ be not raised, your faith is (in) vain; ye are yet in your sins. Then they also which are fallen asleep in Christ are perished. If in this life only we have hope in Christ, we are of all humanity most miserable. But now is Christ risen from the dead, and become the first fruits of them that slept.[130]

Christ was resurrected—literally and physically. The disciples saw Him, touched Him, and ate with Him. Jesus promised that believers would be resurrected as He was. The only reason anyone would have to deny the literal and physical resurrection of Christ would be to prop up a failed false prophecy that has been teetering since 1914.

What the Bible Teaches about Hell

Before we begin a discussion, let's agree on standards of authority. If we use different standards, like surveyors who use different lengths for feet, we never will arrive at an understanding. Would you agree?

1. The Bible, as originally given in the original languages, is our authority.
2. The Bible does not contradict itself.
3. Whatever Scripture is not clear to us must be interpreted by that which is.

In its book, *Reasoning from the Scriptures*, the Watchtower gives an erroneous meaning to the Hebrew word *sheol* and the Greek word *hades*. It says they "refer . . . to the common grave of dead humanity."

Sheol in the Old Testament and *hades* in the New Testament mean "the realm of the dead", according to *Theological Dictionary of the New Testament*.[131] Simply put, *hades* is the place to which dead people go. They go to the grave, as the Rich Man in Luke 16 did. Or they may not be buried at all but abandoned like road kill. The Watchtower is correct in saying *hades* is the grave, but it's much more. After the Rich Man died and was buried, he awoke in *hades*. He had a conscious existence. His *psyche*, translated variously *life, self,* or *soul,* was conscious in the bad part of *hades* while his body rotted in another (Luke 16:24). Lazarus's *psyche* was conscious in the good part of *hades*, while his body rotted in the grave or the dump, another part of *hades*.

The word *hades*, in common usage among the Pharisees of Jesus' day, was understood by them to mean a place in which both the souls of the righteous and souls of the wicked went after death, according to the Jewish Historian Flavius Josephus.[132] Greek pagans, as well as the Jews, used *hades* to mean "the realm of the dead" to which dead people, including the body and the *psyche,* go.

None of the writers of the New Testament found that they needed to modify the common meaning and common understanding of the word *hades*. Therefore, we safely can assume that the understood meaning was correct.

The Watchtower book also refers to Ecclesiastes 9:5: *For the living know that they will die, but the dead know nothing; they have no further reward, and even the memory of them is forgotten.*

This may look like contradiction in Scripture.

1. The dead certainly do know something. The Rich Man did. Lazarus did. Abraham, Isaac, and Jacob, though they were dead, lived.

    I am the God of Abraham, the God of Isaac, and the God of Jacob? He is not the God of the dead but of the living.[133]

    Therefore we are always confident and know that as long as we are at home in the body we are away from the Lord. We are confident, I say, and willing rather to be absent from the body, and to be present with the Lord.[134]

2. The dead do have a further reward.

    Just as man is destined to die once, and after that to face judgment.[135]

    Behold, I am coming soon! My reward is with me, and I will give to everyone according to what he has done.[136]

3. The memory of them is not forgotten.

    I will perpetuate your memory through all generations; therefore the nations will praise you for ever and ever.[137]

Does the passage in Ecclesiastes mean the Bible contradicts itself? No. The Book of Ecclesiastes in context speaks of wisdom *under the sun*—the wisdom of people and not of God. Many scholars believe Solomon, the wisest man in the world, wrote Ecclesiastes. Often the wisdom of humanity agrees with the wisdom of God, but other times it does not.

Ecclesiastes is valuable to compare the wisdom of people with the wisdom of God. Finally the writer of Ecclesiastes admits, *Now all has been heard; here is the conclusion of the matter: Fear God and keep his commandments, for this is the whole* [duty] *of man* (Eccl. 12:13).

The Bible does not contradict itself. Although Solomon didn't understand it at the time he wrote Ecclesiastes, (1) the dead do know something; they are conscious although separated from their earthly bodies. People of God, separated from their bodies, are with the Lord and certainly are not in a senseless state. (2) The dead do have a further reward. Those who depart their bodies with unforgiven sin go to the bad part of *hades,* in which they get the same kind of reward as did the wicked Rich Man of Luke 16. Those who depart their bodies with all their sins forgiven go to the good part of *hades;* there they get the same kind of reward as did poor Lazarus, who had begged at the Rich Man's gate.

The Watchtower also refers to Psalm 146:4-5, *Do not put your trust in princes, in mortal men, who cannot save. When their spirit departs, they return to the ground; on that very day their plans turn to nothing. Blessed is he whose help is the God of Jacob, whose hope is in the LORD his God.*

Read these verses in context. They don't uphold the Watchtower position at all.

When their spirit departs indicates a separation at the time of death. A person is not just a body! Certainly their plans for earthly life are nothing.

Blessed is he . . . blessings are in store for people who trust in the LORD though they die. Life after death exists. We have conscious existence after death. These truths are taught in both the Old and New Testaments.

Jesus believed in hell.

But I tell you that anyone who is angry with his brother will be subject to judgment. Again, anyone who says to his brother, Raca, is answerable to the Sanhedrin. But anyone who says, You fool! will be in danger of the fire of hell.[138]

Jesus said a person is better off losing an eye or a hand or a foot than to be thrown into hell.[139]

Peter believed in hell.

Peter said for angels who sinned, God sent them to hell into gloomy dungeons to be held for judgment.[140] Peter used a different word from *gehenna* and *hades*. He used *tartaras*, the deepest abyss of *hades*.

The Greeks used the word *tartaras* as an equivalent to the Hebrew *gehenna*. According to the *Renaissance New Testament*, "*Tartarus* is the name of a subterranean region, doleful and dark, regarded by the ancient Greeks as the abode of the wicked dead, in which they suffer punishment for their evil deeds; it answers to *gehenna* of the Jews."[141]

The Watchtower book[142] argues that *gehenna* means what it meant when first used and nothing else. Originally the name was "the Valley of the Sons of Hinnom", a place outside Jerusalem in which refuse was burned. If you say "Valley of the Sons of Hinnom" quickly a few thousand times, it gets shortened to *gehenna*. People understood it to mean the place in which refuse, including dead bodies of animals and paupers, were burned along with other trash. That kind of trash doesn't make good fuel, so it burns slowly and puts out a lot of smoke. The smoke always ends there. It smelled bad and constantly rose up from *gehenna*.

Like today's English, the Hebrew language was a living language. New, expanded meanings sprang from old words. Since *gehenna* was such a bad place, its name also acquired the meaning of a place of eternal punishment. Those in the New Testament times clearly knew what *gehenna* meant; it wasn't only the Jerusalem city dump. Read in context the above words of Jesus. Could he have meant just being thrown into the Jerusalem city dump? Continuing the metaphor of the dump, Jesus said, . . . *Where their worm dieth not, and the fire is not quenched.*[143] Jesus makes a point that a person is better off going with Him after he or she leaves the body than to go to the other place He calls *hell.*

When you're dead, what's the difference where they dump your body? The Rich Man of Luke 16 might have been buried in a silk-lined casket, but this meant no more to him than did the Jerusalem city dump. He was dead. Where his self—his personality, his soul—went is what mattered.

If we took every word back to its etymological origin, few things would mean what we intend. For example the word *pneuma* meant *breath, wind,* and *spirit.* Originally the word meant *breath.* So if we changed all the New Testament uses of *pneuma* to *breath,* it would change the meaning of many verses. No such thing as a spirit and no such thing as wind as we know it would exist.

. . . Just then a man in their synagogue who was possessed by an evil "breath" cried out . . . wouldn't make any sense, nor would, *And Jesus returned in the power of the Breath into Galilee:*[144] Determined by the context *pneuma* means breath, wind, and spirit. You easily can read the verse and determine which of the three meanings to apply.

The word *gehenna* meant the Valley of the Sons of Hinnom, the Jerusalem dump on fire, and it also meant a place of punishment so bad it would be better for you to sacrifice an arm or eye than to go there after death.

[145]The Watchtower book appeals to logic, "Is eternal torment of the wicked compatible with God's personality?" (Some Watchtower writer might have been called into account there for writing *God* instead of *Jehovah.*)

The Watchtower equates punishment of wicked people after death with the pagans who sacrificed their infant children to Molech. Is that a fair comparison? The Watchtower also uses an illustration of holding a child's hand over a fire to punish the child. *Gehenna* is not for innocent children; it's for wicked people who sinned against God and died in their sins.

Let us also appeal to logic.

1. Does total justice exist in the world today?

    No. People are robbed, cheated, starved, tortured, and killed. All their lives many of their tormentors get away with murder. That's not justice.

    Good people sometimes suffer terrible deaths. Some die an inch at a time from cancer, while some very wicked people die painlessly in their sleep. Where's the justice in that?

    Adolph Hitler was responsible for the deaths of 50-million people. Could he possibly have been punished sufficiently on this earth? Hitler was so afraid of suffering that he shot himself to guarantee a quick and painless death and then bit down on a cyanide capsule just in case. Mao Zedong murdered 25 million Chinese when he ascended to power in 1949 and millions more afterward. Josef Stalin murdered 30 million Ukrainians by starvation; this was in addition to millions more who were shot, worked to death, or frozen to death. Both Mao and Stalin died peaceful deaths. If they had been arrested and punished as much as we could punish them, how could justice possibly be done to these men? That is impossible in this life but not in the next life. Total justice does not exist in this life.

2. God is just.

    He will judge your people in righteousness, your afflicted ones with justice.[146]

    Righteousness and justice are the foundation of your throne; love and faithfulness go before you.[147]

    The LORD works righteousness and justice for all the oppressed.[148]

    But the LORD Almighty will be exalted by his justice, and the holy God will show Himself holy by his righteousness.[149]

> *And will not God bring about justice for his chosen ones, who cry out to him day and night? Will he keep putting them off? I tell you, he will see that they get justice, and quickly . . . However, when the Son of Man returns, will he find faith on the earth?* [150]

3. When will justice be done?

   Justice is not done in this life, so it must be *after* this life. How many lifetimes would be necessary to punish Hitler for 50-million deaths? Stalin for another 50 million? Mao Zedong for another 50 million?

   Logically, if justice will be done, it will be after this life. That fits with the biblical doctrine of hell and of proportionate punishment for the wicked and proportionate reward for the righteous.

Chapter 14

God's Chosen People

Are the Witnesses really chosen by Jehovah? Is the organization truly a Christian one? How do the JW's regard Christ's relationship to the Father? This chapter examines other aspects of the organization's teachings and these tenets' comparison to Scripture.

Why Are They Called *Witnesses*?

As a JW one of the first things I was taught was to explain to people that we were like the early Christians who went door-to-door bringing good news—that we were "witnesses". We were the only people who went door-to-door as Jesus and His disciples did.

If anyone asked why we were called *witnesses*, I quoted Isaiah 43:10, *Ye are my witnesses, saith Jehovah, and my servant whom I have chosen.*

That was us—witnesses, chosen by Jehovah; I really thought that verse proved it. But the Watchtower Society had taken the verse out of context.

To whom was the LORD speaking? To Israel. So the people of Israel were His witnesses.

They were witnesses of what? A witness is one who has observed something. What had Israel observed? We must read the rest of the verse.

Ye are my witnesses, saith the LORD, and my servant whom I have chosen: that ye may know and believe me, and understand that I am he: before me there was no God formed, neither shall there be after me.

Israel was to bear witness that the LORD is the I AM. No God was formed before Him. No God would be formed after Him. At this point the JW who reads this far has to close off the partition to another compartment in his mind that says "Jesus is a God" but not "The God".

That's not all. The next verse tells us something else to which Israel was a witness: *I, even I, am the LORD; and beside me there is no saviour.* Once again the trained JW has to close off a partition to the compartment in his mind that says Jesus is our Savior.

Therefore, Israel was the witness—that only the LORD is God, the I AM and that He is our only Savior.

Isaiah 43:10-11 is a classic example of how the Society takes Scripture out of context and misapplies it. Once a JW reads these verses in context, with a mind open enough to want to know their true meaning, the mortar joints in the Watchtower crumble and the big stones begin crashing down. This leaves only a cloud of dust that hovers over a pile of rubble.

Who Are the Real Witnesses?

After his eyes are opened, the former JW can see that millions of Christians around the world reach out to share the gospel—the good news of Jesus Christ—with others. These people are witnesses of what Jesus Christ can do—that He forgives sins, and gives the gift of eternal life. They share the joy of knowing to Whom they belong and know about the place to which they are going. These Christian witnesses testify to what they have experienced. They attend classes on how to more effectively share their faith. Then they share their faith—not to turn in a report but out of love and compassion.

The JW's make a lot of fuss about the differences in the many Christian denominations; they exaggerate those differences. Differences do exist, but these Christian groups have much more in common than they have differences.

One of the great examples of Christian witnessing is the worldwide effort to distribute "The Jesus Film". The full-length motion picture with professional actors and sets simply portrays the gospel of Luke.

In 1996 I preached in Muravlenko, Russia, a city of 40,000 situated 1,650 miles east-northeast of Moscow at 64 degrees north latitude in Siberia. The typical Russian city of precast concrete apartment buildings five-stories high with no elevators sat on 600 feet of permafrost. I thought I indeed had gone to the "*uttermost parts of the earth*". I have been to many countries and many isolated places, but this was the first time I ever had gone beyond the Coca-Cola™ signs. Muravlenko was hundreds of miles beyond them but was not beyond The Jesus Film. One evening the church in which I preached showed the film as it used a 16-millimeter projector. A Jewish school teacher I had invited sat next to me. When she saw the portrayal of Jesus on the cross, she wept.

At that time The Jesus Film had been translated into more than 500 languages. The one I saw in Siberia was in Russian.

When I served as pastor in Rowlett, TX, several churches of different denominations divided the city; each took a portion to distribute The Jesus Film video tapes to every home in the city. A group of Churches of Christ took on the project of getting a Jesus Film tape into every home in Alabama. Across America and around the world The Jesus Film has been financed and distributed by individual Christians and churches.

Besides preaching at the local church, I preached in four out of five schools in Muravlenko. English is a required subject there; the teachers welcomed me to speak to their students.

Accompanied by a translator and members of the local church I visited many homes and found another surprise. In each home I asked, "Do you have a Bible?"

The answer was almost always, "Yes." And the Bible almost always had the "Gideon" seal. Gideon Bibles had gone far beyond the Coca-Cola™ signs and had been given away to Russian people.

Gideons are Christian businessmen of different denominations who give their time and money to buy Bibles for free distribution in schools and to people around the world. The Bible you find in a hotel or motel room was put there by the Gideons.

The Gideons are real Christian witnesses. The Watchtower says the Gideons, the Christians who go door-to-door sharing their faith, and the Christians who distribute The Jesus Film all serve Satan and will die in Armageddon. After a JW has breathed the dust of a collapsed Watchtower and then the free air of Christian liberty, he can see the Society's blatant hypocrisy.

Is Jesus a Lesser God?

The central doctrine of Christianity is Christ, the Messiah, God in the Flesh, Who died for our sins and was resurrected. All of this the Jehovah's Witnesses deny, yet they claim to be Christians.

The apostle Paul said, *Who is a liar but he that denieth that Jesus is the Christ? IIe is antichrist, that denieth the Father and the Son.*[151]

JW's will protest that they don't deny that Jesus is the Christ. They use the word *Christ* like another name but don't understand its meaning.

Christ from the Greek language is the same as *Messiah* in the Hebrew language. *Christ* and *Messiah* mean "the Anointed One" Whom God promised to be our Savior, to be Immanuel, which means "God with us" or "God in the flesh". Christ claimed to be that promised Messiah.[152] He said He was one with the Father.[153] Yet the Watchtower Society says Jesus Christ is a created being—an angel.[154] They deny that Christ is eternal—without beginning and without end.

That makes the Watchtower religion not a Christian religion.

Early on Almighty God taught His people Israel that He is One God and that He would tolerate no other gods before or besides Himself.[155]

When the Old Testament prophets speak of God or the LORD, they speak of Yahweh or Jehovah, the Self-Existent One, the Lord of creation, the Great First Cause of all things.

Examine Isaiah 9:6, a prophecy of Christ: *For unto us a child is born, unto us a son is given: and the government shall be upon his shoulder: and his name shall be called Wonderful, Counselor, The mighty God, The everlasting Father, The Prince of Peace.* (Even the NWT "translators" didn't dare water down this verse, although they did paraphrase it.)

More than 700 years before the birth of Christ, the prophet Isaiah spoke of Christ Who would be born, Who would be a son, and Who would receive the government. He would be the Wonderful Counselor with Whom we could have a personal relationship; He would be one and the same Everlasting Father and be one and the same Prince of Peace. This is a description of Jesus Christ, the eternal Son of God, the Messiah.

Part of that prophecy has been fulfilled: Christ was born in Bethlehem. He, the Son of God, was given as a sacrifice for our sins. According to Bible prophecy the government shall be on His shoulder when He returns to earth to rule and reign in righteousness. To those who know Him personally, He now is the Wonderful Counselor. He will rule from the throne of David in Jerusalem; He is <u>the</u> mighty God, not <u>a</u> god. He is the everlasting Father; He is the Prince of Peace.

The same prophet in Isaiah 7:14 said, *Therefore the LORD Himself shall give you a sign; Behold, a virgin shall conceive, and bear a son, and shall call his name Immanuel.*

In Matthew 1:22-23 the angel of the Lord proclaimed the birth of Jesus to be the fulfillment of that prophecy: *Now all this was done, that it might be fulfilled which was spoken of the Lord by the prophet, saying, Behold, a virgin shall be with child, and shall bring forth a son, and they shall call his name Emmanuel, which being interpreted is, God with us.*

Jesus Christ, born of the virgin Mary, was Emmanuel, God with us, and God in the flesh: Remember that the *LORD he is God; there is none else beside him.*[156]

The prophet Micah, a contemporary of Isaiah, made another prophecy about Christ. He said Christ would be born in Bethlehem, that He would be ruler in Israel, and that He was from everlasting.[157]

Michael the archangel, whom the JW's say became the Christ, had a beginning. Michael did not exist from everlasting. Only the Lord is eternal and without a beginning. The Bible makes plain the fact that only Jehovah God the LORD is our Savior: *I, even I, am the LORD; and beside me there is no savior.*[158] The Witnesses call Jesus Christ our "Lord and Savior". If the Society's teachings were true, they would insult Jehovah by calling Jesus "Savior".

The virgin Mary praised God and rejoiced in "*God my Saviour*".[159] John said Christ was the Savior of the world.[160]

Throughout the Old Testament, God's Word teaches that only the LORD (Yahweh or Jehovah) is the Savior.[161] In the New Testament the Lord Jesus Christ and God are called *Savior.* Belief in a secondary, lesser god as Savior would be in direct contradiction to Scripture. The only way the Old Testament and New Testament harmonize is that the Lord Jehovah and Lord Jesus Christ are One.

If we do not accept the Bible for what it says, "Jehovah is our only Savior" conflicts with "Jesus is our only Savior". The LORD is one God. He appears to us in more than one person, yet He cannot be divided. This is not the only thing about God that is difficult for us to understand, but we trust Him and His Word. The JW's trust the Watchtower Society and its word in direct contradiction to Scripture.

The Old Testament says every knee shall bow to God.[162] The New Testament says every knee shall bow to Jesus Christ.[163]

In his letter to the Philippians the apostle Paul said of Jesus, *Wherefore God also hath highly exalted him, and given him a name which is above every name: That at the name of Jesus every knee should bow, of things in heaven, and things in earth, and things under the earth; And that every tongue should confess that Jesus Christ is Lord, to the glory of God the Father.*[164]

In that verse the word *Lord* is a translation of the Greek word *kurios,* same word the Watchtower in Romans 14:11 KJV translates *Jehovah: For it is written, As I live, saith the Lord, every knee shall bow to me, and every tongue shall confess to God.* The NWT says, *For it is written: "As I live," says Jehovah, "to me every knee will bend down, and every tongue will make open acknowledgment to God."*

Bad Grammar, Bad Theology

In Romans 10:13 Paul is talking about the Lord Jesus Christ, *For whosoever shall call upon the name of the Lord [kurios] shall be saved.* This is a quotation from the Old Testament. The Watchtower Society's Bible says, *"For everyone who calls on the name of Jehovah will be saved."* The subject is Jesus Christ the Lord. If you believe that Jesus is the Lord *(kurios),* you'll be saved. And if you call on the Lord *(kurios),* you'll be saved. But there the Watchtower inconsistently inserts in its English translation the word *Jehovah* to fit the Watchtower's inconsistent doctrine.

In Revelation 1:8 Jesus said, *I am Alpha and Omega, the beginning and the ending, saith the Lord [kurios].* But the Watchtower Society translates it *"'I am the Alpha and the Omega,' says Jehovah God, the One who is and who was and who is coming, the Almighty."* Arbitrarily they change the speaker from Jesus to Jehovah. That's all right with me, because Jesus is Jehovah. He is God. But the Society's grammar is incorrect.

In the Old Testament the LORD states emphatically that he is Saviour and Redeemer.[165]

Job, who probably lived before Abraham and the Mosaic Law, said, *For I know that my Redeemer liveth, and that he shall stand at the latter day upon the earth.*[166]

Who stood on the earth? Jesus Christ. Who will return and again stand on the earth? Jesus Christ, our *Redeemer.*

The New Testament proclaims Jesus Christ as Savior. The herald angel said, *For unto you is born this day in the city of David a Saviour, which is Christ the Lord.*[167] In Acts, Luke said, *Him hath God exalted with his right hand to be a Prince and a Saviour, for to give repentance to Israel and forgiveness of sins.*[168] Only God can forgive sins.

Many other Scriptures throughout the New Testament say that Jesus is our Savior.[169]

The apostle John, who in John 1:1-3 so clearly stated that Christ was the eternal God without beginning, in 1 John 4:14 said, *And we have seen and do testify that the Father sent the Son to be the Saviour of the world.*

The human mind finds the concept of how at the same time God could reign in heaven in the person of the Father and be on earth in the humble person of the Son to be difficult to understand. Many times I have seen two or three Jehovah's Witnesses brag to each other about how they got the best of some *goat* in an argument by asking, "Who ran the universe for three days and nights while Jesus was in the grave?", whereupon his admiring audience would laugh. Ridicule of non-Witnesses is an integral part of the Watchtower culture.

The Watchtower book, *Let God Be True,* asks that question, "Who ran the universe during the three days that Jesus was in the grave, or, for that matter, during the thirty-three-and-one-half years on the earth while he was made a *'little lower than the angels'*?"

Colossians 1:16-17 says Jesus created all things and *by him all things consist.* He holds the universe together. The Society's idea of God is not big enough for One Who could be in heaven as the Father, on both earth and in heaven as the Holy Spirit, and incarnate and in humility on earth as the Son all at the same time and yet be One God. God is omnipresent— everywhere present at the same time. He is omnipotent and has all power. To doubt that God could hold things together and be in many places at the same time, even as different persons, is to put limits on God that don't exist. We can't judge God by our own limitations. Jehovah God has no limits.

God's Chosen People

Christ has many names and titles; among these is the *Word*. The Watchtower people agree with all Bible scholars that the *Word* spoken of in John 1:1 is Christ: *In the beginning was the Word, and the Word was with God, and the Word was God. The same was in the beginning with God. All things were made by him; and without him was not any thing made that was made.*[170] You don't have to have a Ph.D. to understand what the Word of God plainly says that Christ already existed in the beginning. In the beginning, whenever that was, Christ was with God. That shows that He had a different personality from God. Then John plainly said that Christ was God. That's really the only way it all adds up. Jesus Christ and Jehovah God are one and always were. To make sure we don't misunderstand, the apostle John repeated, *The same was in the beginning with God.*

Christ made everything that was made. He did not make Himself. These and other Scriptures that so plainly refute the Watchtower doctrines became such a problem to the Society that it produced its own Bible, the NWT. In the Society's Bible in John 1:1, the Watchtower inserted the article *a* before *God* and made it to read, *In the beginning the Word was, and the Word was with God, and the Word was a god.*

One lie leads to another. This made JW's believe in two Gods, Jehovah and Jesus. This is a violation of God's clear command, *"Thou shalt have no other gods before me"*,[171] a clear contradiction to Deuteronomy 6:4, *Hear, O Israel: The LORD our God is one LORD.* But the disciplined Witness doesn't allow these Scriptures to cross over the partition in his cleanly swept mind to the compartment that claims Christ is another god. To do so would cause a neurological short-circuit.

Jesus either was the promised Messiah—the promised God in the Flesh—or He lied when in John 4:26 he said, . . . *I that speak unto thee am he* [the Messiah].

Almighty God, in proclaiming His Name to Moses said, *I AM.*[172] Jesus proclaimed Himself to be the *I AM*. When the Pharisees tried to accuse Jesus of being illegitimate, Jesus said unto them, *Verily, verily, I say unto you, Before Abraham was, I am.*[173] To say "*I am*" in Koine Greek, the language spoken then and the language of the New Testament, all you had to say was *aime.* If you wanted to emphasize the statement, you would use the first person article *ego,* which literally meant "I. I am." Jesus was emphasizing that he was the I AM. The NWT changed it to say, "*I have been*", a totally inaccurate translation.

The Jews took up stones to stone Him. Why? Because Jesus had proclaimed Himself to be the I AM, the Lord, Jehovah, the Self-Existent One.

On the basis of rationalism the Watchtower Society denies Jehovah's ability to be one God—manifest to us in more than one person at the same time. The same rationale should apply to Luke 2:51, which says Jesus as a child was subject to Mary and Joseph: *And he went down with them, and came to Nazareth, and was subject unto them: . . . And Jesus increased in wisdom and stature and in favour with God and man.*[174]

If a created, lesser god could lay aside the free exercise of his power, humble himself, be obedient to earthly parents, grow physically and in wisdom, and then later reclaim his power and glory, why couldn't the Almighty God do the same thing?

If Jesus had arrived on earth in all His glory and power, His admonitions to us to pray, to have faith, and to completely trust God would have been without personal example. When Jesus told His disciples to pray, He personally demonstrated prayer and faith. He had left the free exercise of His power in heaven and trusted in the Father and the Holy Spirit to empower Him as He went about His earthly ministry.

In John 10:27-30 we find an example of this humility before the Father, *My sheep hear my voice, and I know them, and they follow me: And I give unto them eternal life; and they shall never perish, neither shall any man pluck them out of my hand. My Father, which gave them me, is greater than all; and no man is able to pluck them out of my Father's hand. I and my Father are one.*

I have heard His voice and followed Jesus. He has given to me eternal life. He holds me in His hand; no one can pluck me out of His hand. The Father also holds me in His hand. Wait a minute. Only one of me exists. Am I in Jesus' hand or in the Father's hand? If Jesus and the Father are not one, I would have to become two persons—one of me in the Son's hand and the other of me in the Father's. If we believe the Bible, no problem exists: the Father and Son are one.

Hebrews 1:3 likens Christ's relationship to the Father to the sun and light emanating from it. They are inseparable. This verse also tells us that after Christ had purged sin by His sacrificial death for the sinner, He regained His heavenly glory. Much of the Book of Hebrews is devoted to explaining the greatness of Christ in eternity past and eternity future.

Christ had to humble Himself and become a human being to be the propitiation, or sacrificial offering, for our sins. The Watchtower Society denies that Jehovah could humble himself to that degree.

Believers in New Testament times ascribed the same glory to Christ as God. For example Peter wrote to the Christians in Pontus and Bithynia, . . . *To him be glory both now and for ever. Amen.*[175] Pliny the Younger (Gaius Plinius Caecilius Secundus), proconsul of Pontus and Bithynia and persecutor of the Christians there, wrote to the Roman Emperor, Trajan, and told him the Christians were wont to address hymns to Christ as to God. This secular record backs up the scriptural record.

Hymns, prayers, and doxologies address God and Christ as one: Christ is called *King of Kings and Lord of Lords, the beginning and the end, the first and the last.*[176]

If Jesus were not one with the Father, He could not be *the only Potentate, King of kings, and Lord of lords.*

A mischievous little boy inadvertently gave an example that helps understand the unity of God in three persons. In the Sunday-school class the little boy habitually kicked other children.

"Did you kick that little girl?" his mother asked.

"No, I didn't. My leg kicked her," the little boy answered.

Needless to say, that excuse didn't wash with his mother. If his leg did it, he did it.

Isaiah 53 often is called "The Gospel According to Isaiah." The Prophet Isaiah called the Messiah *the arm of the Lord.* In Chapter 53 we can see the prophecies about Christ's being sent to earth and about His suffering for our sins. For example, *But he was wounded for our transgressions, he was bruised for our iniquities: the chastisement of our peace was upon him; and with his stripes we are healed. All we like sheep have gone astray; we have turned every one to his own way; and the LORD hath laid on him the iniquity of us all.*

When the *arm of the Lord* does something, the LORD does it.

Jesus Christ is God, not another god but one with the Father, as He said.

Chapter 15

Repair the Reflexes

JW's Are Trained to Obey without Thinking

When a recruit enters military service, an important part of his training involves marching to the commands of a gruff drill sergeant. When the sergeant orders "Fall in", every person in the company hurries to his assigned place in the formation and holds out an arm to measure the proper distance to the next person. The entire group stands frozen as statues in four neat, straight rows. They say nothing and look straight ahead. When the drill sergeant commands "Right face", like slats on a venetian blind the group turns in unison. When the sergeant orders "Forward, march", at the same time each soldier puts his left foot forward. Forty or more soldiers move as one.

Why all that training? Without question soldiers and marines instantly must obey. Drilling hones their reflexes. For them obedience is automatic. Discipline is the difference between an army and a mob. In combat instant obedience without question can save their lives and win a battle.

During peacetime what do experienced soldiers and marines do? Over and over they train to maintain their skills and sharpen their discipline.

Jehovah's Witnesses refuse military service, but they use some of the same effective methods as military trainers do. JW's are like recruits on the parade grounds—marching in order and being taught to obey without question. For the soldier some of the seemingly inconsequential maneuvers such as "About face" and "parade rest" are for Jehovah's Witnesses like the Watchtower's list of 78 forbidden.

I won't bore you with all 78, but here are some things JW's are forbidden to do:

- Wearing or owning a religious emblem such as a cross
- Use of wind chimes
- Any involvement in another religion, or connection with one. Such involvements include church yard sales, bingo, weddings, baptisms, or funerals.
- Birthday celebrations
- Bonfires
- Toasting at weddings and parties, etc.
- Voting
- Employment in defense industries
- Wearing beards or mustaches that go below the crease of the mouth
- Celebrating Christmas, Easter, Valentine's Day, and all other holidays
- Not to sing worldly songs or songs from other religions
- Reading books and literature from false religions. This includes any other than those published by the Watchtower
- Youth clubs and camps
- Subscribing to worldly magazines
- Hunting or fishing
- Watching soap operas
- Joining the Girl or Boy Scouts, Brownies or Cub Scouts, or similar organizations
- Attending school dances and sports events.
- Wearing mourning clothing

Repair the Reflexes

- Becoming an officer in a union or any other involvement in trade unions. These involvements would include voting and picketing.
- Throwing rice or flowers at weddings
- Giving money or goods to the Red Cross, Salvation Army, or any other charity
- Giving free rein to "unbridled passion" with one's marriage partner
- Involving one's self in extracurricular school activities
- Serving on a jury
- Selling (while on the job) Christmas or other holiday items
- Seeing a psychiatrist or psychologist
- Playing chess, cards, checkers, and similar games
- Working overtime
- Making friends with one's next-door neighbors, classmates, work associates, etc., unless this is done with the intention of witnessing to them
- Questioning the Watchtower Society
- Reading non-Witness publications and outdated Watchtower Society publications

"Silly," you say. To the JW this is not. If he disobeys any of these rules, his leaders will bring down on him wrath that is greater than that of a harsh drill sergeant. The indoctrinated JW believes if he gets out of step, the Society has the authority to forfeit any possibility he has for eternal life.

The JW is in constant training. While Christians attend a worship service, sing praises to God, and pray, the JW is busy doing drill exercises. She learns, without thinking, to quote Bible verses just as quickly as a soldier obeys a drill command. While the Christian is in Bible study, the JW is role-playing Bible ping pong, as she, verse after verse, fires back and forth.

The military functions on the belief that soldiers who aren't in constant action or training become lax and that their discipline deteriorates. If a regiment had nothing to do, soldiers were not assigned to guard duty, and the military base became wide open, the soldiers would venture out into the countryside as they looked for alcohol and entertainment. They might wander off and disappear—never to return. The same principles apply to Jehovah's Witnesses. The Watchtower believes JW's constantly have to be pumped up, excited, and motivated, or they might wander off.

Indoctrinated to React Automatically

At Dallas Theological Seminary I participated in a panel discussion about cults. Other participants were Pastor Rene Lopez, a theologian once had recently published a commentary on the Book of Romans and who had once studied with Jehovah's Witnesses, and James Walker, a former Mormon and president of Watchman Fellowship, an organization dedicated to telling the truth about cults. One of the students asked the panel how people become Jehovah's Witnesses.

James Walker said, "If you drop a ton of Bibles on a desert island, some of the people there will become Christians, but none will become Jehovah's Witnesses." Pastor Lopez and I agree; we did so based on our own experience dealing with Jehovah's Witnesses.

Some people to whom I have talked, or about whose experiences I have read, have read the Bible alone—without any coaching from anyone—and decided the closest churches to the New Testament are Catholic, Presbyterian, Methodist, Baptist, Pentecostal, Church of Christ, or others of that type. Without being coached by a JW, none have decided the Watchtower is correct.

The only way a person can become a Jehovah's Witness is to be indoctrinated by Jehovah's Witnesses. And the only way a person can remain a Witness is to consume a steady diet of the Society's doctrines. Russell recognized that fact and wrote about it. He said, "Furthermore, not only do we find that people cannot see the divine plan in studying the Bible by itself, but we see, also, that if anyone lays the Scripture Studies (Russell's writings) aside, even after he has used them, after he has become familiar with them, after he had read them for ten years—if he then lays them aside and ignores them and goes to the Bible alone, though he has understood this Bible for ten years—our experience shows that within two years he goes into darkness. On the other hand if he had merely read the Scripture Studies (Russell's Watchtower writings) with their references and had not read a page of the Bible as such, he would be in the light at the end of two years, because he would have the light of the Scriptures."[177]

Russell's instructions still are obeyed by modern JW's. They are encouraged to read the Watchtower literature primarily and to use the Bible to check proof texts. The Watchtower calls it *Rightly dividing the word of Truth.*

The Bible is not to be read like any other book, according to the Watchtower Society. Rather, the Watchtower tells the JW to read a piece here and a piece there. Then the Watchtower will re-organize the passages and put them together according to the Society's pattern to back up its peculiar doctrines.

JW's talk a great deal about "Bible studies". They invite prospects to host a "Bible study" in their own homes; the study would be conducted by Jehovah's Witnesses. These Bible studies in prospects' homes involves studying a Watchtower-published book and looking up the Scripture references, which the Jehovah's Witness study leader explains. As the study progresses, the students look up fewer Scripture references until they quit looking them up altogether.

Here is an example of how the Watchtower references don't prove what they're supposed to prove. They say you should pray only to Jehovah. They then list as proof John 14:6, 13-14 and 1 Timothy 2:5:

Jesus saith unto him, I am the way, the truth, and the life: no man cometh unto the Father, but by me (John 14:6). And whatsoever ye shall ask in my name, that will I do, that the Father may be glorified in the Son. If ye shall ask any thing in my name, I will do it (John 14:13-14). For there is one God, and one mediator between God and men, the man Christ Jesus (1 Tim. 2:5).

These Scripture verses have nothing do with naming only Jehovah in prayer. They have nothing to do with God sending your prayers to Satan. To get those meanings you would have to be coached; you also would have to be gullible.

Many of the references at the bottom of the page of Watchtower publications represent bluffs that have nothing to do with what the Watchtower purports to prove.

Mind-Control Process

When Jehovah's Witnesses arrive at your door, they want only to discuss current events and the terrible state of the world and to leave you some literature. But by the way, they say, maybe you'd like to have a free Bible study in your home. The JW's tell you they will be glad to visit you once a week and conduct the Bible study.

They are clean-cut, friendly people and really seem to know their Bible, so the prospect invites them to drop by for a Bible study. The prospect now is considered a *person of good will*—an interested party. The alleged Bible study really is the beginning of the mind-control process.

Usually two JW's conduct the study. One is experienced; the other is a learner.

If you have invited the JW's into your home, whatever you say is wrong. You may say, "I believe Jesus died on the cross."

"No. No," the JW will tell the prospect. "Jesus didn't die on a cross. A cross is a pagan symbol. Jesus died on a torture stake."

Being firmly corrected, the prospect will stay quiet a while. Then the prospect perhaps later may mention something such as "I really hope to go to heaven when I die." With all four feet the study conductors jump on him. They tell him that for us ordinary people no hope of heaven. They tell him heaven is only for the 144,000—and nearly all of them already are there. "So forget heaven. You can hope for eternal life on Paradise earth, if you're found worthy."

Repair the Reflexes

Soon the prospect is afraid to open his mouth. The Bible-study team corrects him and quotes Scripture. He feels as though he is a fool, so he just keeps quiet.

This process of mind control is like the process of making Maraschino cherries. First the natural color of the cherries is bleached out; then the bright red color is added. The Watchtower representatives bleach out the proselyte's beliefs. But they don't leave his mind empty. Just as quickly they refill it with the Watchtower doctrines.

This process sometimes is called "thought reform" or "brainwashing".

The controllers instill fear. *The world is in turmoil and can't last much longer. Jehovah will bring sudden destruction on all evil doers. The only way you can avoid being classified as* an evil doer *is to be part of God's earthly organization, the Watchtower Society.* After a short time the prospect is afraid Armageddon will occur so quickly, he won't have time to qualify.

After a while, when the prospect is far enough along in the studies to decide he'll never accept a blood transfusion, vote, celebrate Christmas, or salute the flag, he's invited to the Kingdom Hall. There he gets a combination punch. He is made to feel guilty and anxious about his standing with God. At the same time he is covered with love and friendship by the JW's.

Whatever he believed earlier has been removed and replaced by Watchtower teachings. He believes that he is enlightened. He belongs to a group that has exclusive communication with Jehovah God. He is *in the Truth*. He has entered a new and exciting life. Often the prospect has undergone such a personality change that his family barely recognizes him.

As the prospect becomes more entrenched in the social structure of JW's, he is too busy to do much else. He constantly is surrounded by JW's who demand all his emotional and physical strength. When he's not physically doing something within the JW environment, he's reading Watchtower literature. The controllers use fatigue. The prospect runs out of energy and becomes increasingly pliable. The handlers keep him so busy in *theocratic* activities that he has little time or energy to think about anything else.

The prospect loses contact with old friends and family, because the JW's have convinced him these associations are *worldly*. The JW's tell him he should avoid contact with old friends and family members except to witness to them. Otherwise their worldliness will rub off on him. JW's lead him to understand that the worst thing he can do is to lose contact with *God's earthly organization* and become *worldly*. If he does, he will be destroyed in Armageddon, which can occur at any moment.

The JW's convince the prospect that the Watchtower has all the answers. He sees how cocky the experienced JW's are, how they delight in arguing with people who claim some Bible knowledge, and how they even like to tangle with preachers and pastors who know little about the Jehovah's Witnesses. They laugh at preachers who answer a question with "I don't know." The Watchtower does know, he believes, and has the answer to any and all theological questions.

When the prospect is thoroughly indoctrinated and has had experience going door-to-door with seasoned JW's, she is ready for baptism. Kingdom Halls have no baptistery in them. Rather, baptisms are conducted at district conventions. Usually this happens in a swimming pool. First the prospect must answer 80 questions. Then she is baptized. The Bible's baptismal formula says the person is to be baptized in the name of the Father, the Son, and the Holy Spirit; the Watchtower changes that formula. Rather than using the name of the Holy Spirit, *Jehovah's earthly organization* replaces the Holy Spirit.

The United States constitution guarantees freedom of assembly. Obviously this is to prevent a totalitarian government from taking over and having dictatorial power. Denial of freedom of assembly indicates totalitarian control.

Freedom of assembly is exercised in many venues, including in churches. Within the churches themselves, small groups assemble. Some of these groups are church-sanctioned; others are serendipitous, informal get-togethers. Churches and other religious organizations pride themselves in having independent

Repair the Reflexes

Bible studies and discussion groups. They don't ask permission; they just do it. Not so with Jehovah's Witnesses. No gatherings are allowed except those sponsored or approved by the Society. No freedom of assembly exists within the discipline of the Watchtower Society.

Many Jehovah's Witnesses have been disfellowshiped for having unauthorized Bible studies.

One of the five weekly meetings every JW is required to attend is the *Watchtower Study*. When I was growing up as a JW, I dreaded this meeting because I found it to be a time of utter boredom. In the *Watchtower Study* footnotes, at the bottom of each page are questions. Answers are hidden in the text. No other answers are permitted. One who had not studied the lesson arrives with a clean, unmarked Watchtower magazine, which clearly indicates she has not studied the lesson. The studious ones arrive at the Watchtower study with their answers already underlined in red. They display their marked Watchtowers as badges of pride.

The weekly Watchtower study is a good example of thought control in the Jehovah's Witnesses' entire environment. No independent thought is tolerated. The Society prescribes the questions and provides the answers.

What churches would call a *sermon*, the JW's call a *talk*. The Society furnishes the outline for the week's talk. Individual speakers have little latitude in what they can say. The same is true for weddings and funerals. The funeral speaker takes a canned talk out of the Watchtower cupboard and spoon-feeds it to the faithful JW's and to the *worldly* people among them at the wedding or funeral.

Another form of control is the *weekly report*. Each active JW is classified as a publisher. Each week he is required to fill out a publisher's report form and to submit it at the Kingdom Hall. If she fails to do so, the JW loses her publisher's status, which is the first step of decline that leads to being consigned to death at Armageddon.

In the witness work each publisher is required to put in at least 10 hours a month. Like an attorney keeping track of billable hours, diligent JW's keep a log of every eligible minute. If she writes a letter including some Watchtower doctrine, she writes down the time. If she witnesses to someone on the phone, she makes a note of the minutes spent. The majority of the witness time of the JW is spent going door-to-door. Sunday is a big day for that. This is when JW's catch at home people who are not in church. The JW records and reports all that work as well as a list of all literature distributed.

The Jehovah's Witnesses' favorite occupation is that of self-employed building custodian. It frees up time to go door-to-door during the day. The Watchtower Society requires that the *witness work* take precedent over vocation and family. Recreation time is not even considered. When I was growing up, the closest thing our family had to a vacation was driving cross-country to a Watchtower convention or assembly.

As a youth I corresponded with a young JW in Henderson, TX. This individual wanted to be a lawyer (*bad thoughts, worldly ambition*). When he mentioned to members of his congregation's leadership about his career goal, they lambasted him so severely that their ignorant reaction broke through his mind-control shield and caused him to do some independent thinking. He left the Jehovah's Witness organization and went to law school.

Another tool of Watchtower mind control is the information network. Simply put, witnesses spy on each other and inform on each other.

The JW remembers Rule Number 1—that the *Watchtower Society is Jehovah God's organization and speaks for Him*; therefore, the JW approves of anything the Society says or does. The JW learns to play the system by being careful not to put himself in danger of rebuke by the elders. He goes to great lengths to demonstrate his abject loyalty to the Society and informs on friends who have confided sinful thoughts or doubts about the Society. He has been taught to believe that if he is aware of another person's sin, he must report it to the elders or be as guilty as the other person is.

A big deal is made of confession. The JW is instructed to tell the brethren about his own *evil thoughts* and to demonstrate repentance. Confession, however, has become a vehicle for accusation. A JW can include in his confession information about the person that influenced him to sin and can name others who are committing worse sins.

A comment we often hear about Jehovah's Witnesses is, "They are so sincere." The appearance of sincerity is cultivated. The Watchtower Society demands not only that the JW be sincere in believing all the Society's doctrines but be willing to change when *new light* is received from God (through the Society). Absolute sincerity also is required in believing the new doctrines that contradict the old ones. Sometimes the believer is required to deny that the original belief ever was held. Along with sincerity at all times the JW must appear to be well-adjusted, happy, and full of enthusiasm.

Correcting the "Cross" Reflex

The Society seeks documentation from literature—and in so doing lifts sentences and paragraphs to prove its position. It even quotes works that are opposed to the Watchtower doctrines. It takes these statements out of context and implies that they mean the opposite of what the writer intended.

For instance the Watchtower denies that Romans crucified on crosses tens of thousands of people. That kind of cross they used often is called a *Roman cross*. The Bible teaches that Roman soldiers nailed Jesus to a cross. According to unquestionable historic accounts from many sources this cross was shaped just as the traditional *Roman cross* was.

For every ounce of obscure opinions the Society uses to purport that Jesus died on a stake without a cross-piece, a ton of documentation proves the cross was a cross.

A senseless attack on something as insignificant as the design of the cross has the same psychological purpose to the Society that arguments over the shape of the conference table had to the Vietnamese communists at the Paris Peace Talks to end the Vietnam War. Neither the Society nor the Communist Party is stupid; members are wily. To get an advantage they harass and distract.

When I witness to a JW, I avoid using the word *cross,* because doing so triggers an automatic response from the Witness. This response derails her mind. If, however, she brings up the cross for the purpose of denying it, I feel obligated to tell her the truth. When a JW escapes the Watchtower, she must repair her reflexes by putting facts in place of the error she has believed.

In a Jehovah's Witness *Bible Study* the study leaders explain that the cross is a pagan symbol. They say *Jesus died on a torture stake.* They explain that the Greek word *stauros* is an upright post. (*Strong's Concordance* says *stauros* means stake, post, pole, or cross.) Therefore, we have to examine the word's use in context.

The Society strains at a gnat to try to prove that Jesus was not put to death on a cross. It cites Acts 5:30 and 10:39, in which the cross is called a *tree.* It cites obscure writers who supposed that Jesus died on an upright pole without a cross-member. What's the difference? The shape of the cross has no bearing on Christ's sacrificial death.

Those Christians prone to idolatry would have venerated a single pole, a hangman's noose, or an electric chair, because they need a symbol. The Society implies that *Christendom,* the one apostate pot into which they dump all professing Christians, has a paganistic, mystic attachment to the shape of the cross.

The JW Bible study-leader works diligently to convince the prospect that the cross is pagan—even a smutty phallic symbol. (How the shape of a cross is more like a phallus than it is an upright stake is beyond me.) The JW leader teaches the prospect to react without thinking. When someone mentions *cross,* by reflex action she is to deny that Jesus died on one and to state positively that He died on a torture stake.

The Greek word translated *cross* meant one of the sharpened palisade stakes in the walls of a temporary Roman legion fort. It meant a *fence post*. It meant a *sharpened stake in the ground*; on that stake a man could be impaled. The word also meant *cross* in the traditional sense. As with any word with many meanings the reader must put it into context.

The Watchtower's use of *torture stake* instead of *cross* is not inaccurate *per se.* Neither would *post* or *pole* or *tree* have been inaccurate. The Watchtower translation is misleading and dishonest—another of its many attempts in any way possible to discredit orthodox Christianity.

No matter how the Watchtower plays tricks with words, truth is truth. Jesus died on a <u>cross</u>.

The Compulsion to Follow

After Hurricane Katrina ravaged New Orleans, Kimberly Butler with her four children moved to a Dallas suburb and settled into an apartment. After they lived there almost three years, disaster struck the family again. On March 30, 2008, while Mrs. Butler was in the bathroom, one of her children sat on the sofa, lit a candle, and set the sofa on fire.

Mrs. Butler grabbed 7-year-old Joshua and 2-year-old Jamerie and took them through the smoke-filled apartment to safety outside. She told them to stay there and ran back inside for the other two children—Joshay, also 7, and Jeremiah, 4. She didn't realize that 2-year-old Jamerie followed her back into the burning apartment.

Back outside with the other two, Mrs. Butler realized the 2-year-old was gone and dashed back in. She couldn't find Jamerie. Unable to breathe in the thick smoke and scorched by the flames, Mrs. Butler ran back out. Later firefighters found Jamerie's body in the master bedroom.[178]

The 2-year-old child couldn't make decisions for herself. She knew instinctively to follow her mother. She didn't assess the situation, calculate consequences of various options, and make a decision of whether to stay or to follow her mother. Rather the toddler followed her mother just as a baby chick would follow its mother.

The 7-year-old child was old enough to weigh his options and decided to stay as his mother had told him.

When a person becomes a Jehovah's Witness, she has been trained volitionally to turn off her decision-making ability and blindly to follow the Watchtower Society. If her child has been injured and only a blood transfusion will save the child's life, the JW follows the Watchtower dictum and lets the child die. The JW doesn't weigh her options and make a rational decision; rather she follows the Watchtower Society like a toddler following her mother back into a burning building would.

In rare instances in which the JW returns to his senses and shakes off the Watchtower brainwashing long enough to give permission for the blood transfusion, among family and friends who shun him he suddenly becomes a *persona non grata*. They declare him *an apostate* and consign him to destruction in Armageddon.

Of course the compulsion to follow is not altogether bad. It depends on whom you follow. Jesus called his followers *disciples*, which means "disciplined ones". Following Him is the safest course.

The Bad Boy, Organized Religion

Charles Taze Russell grew up in a Congregational church, but at an early age he rejected the idea of hell and *organized religion*. At age 18 in Pittsburgh, PA, he organized a Bible class. Six years later in 1876 that class elected him *Pastor*. The title stuck. Today Jehovah's Witnesses still affectionately refer to him as *Pastor Russell*, although they reject the title for others. They call their equivalent the *congregational servant* and later the *congregational overseer*.

Russell's successor, Judge Joseph Rutherford, railed that "religion is a snare and a racket." He denied that the Watchtower Society was a religion. Obviously Jehovah's Witnesses clearly are very religious people. Their claim not to be part of a *religion* soon became an embarrassment to the Society. When the Society needed for the government to give it tax-exempt status on the basis that it was a religious organization, the organization quickly expedited *new light* from heaven. The disciplined followers promptly erased from their minds the catchphrase "religion is a snare and a racket."

However, they still labeled *organized religion* as a bad boy. One of the main selling points the JW's use is that organized religion has failed. As an example they point to wars, political corruption, genocide, and lawlessness. Organized religion has failed to straighten out the evils of the world. The prospect to whom the JW's witness usually has unresolved spiritual issues. Organized religion has failed him, too. The Society lumps all other religions—Judaism, Islam, Hinduism, Buddhism, Catholicism, Presbyterianism, Methodism, Episcopalianism, the Southern Baptist Convention, and all other Christian denominations—into the same mold and labels all of them *organized religion* and *failed*.

An important part of the prospect's indoctrination is to disbelieve anything *organized religion* claims. After all *organized religion* has failed. The prospect does not realize that she is being taken into one of the most organized religions on the face of the earth. She is aligning herself with the ranks of some of the most disciplined and regimented religious followers anywhere.

Sound Bites for the Christian Witness

I attended an annual convention for Ex-Jehovah's Witnesses for Jesus when it met at the Blue Mountain Christian Retreat near New Ringgold, PA. There I learned that some ex-JW's were witnessing via a telephone ministry. When I returned home, I started writing short messages for Jehovah's Witnesses.

I bought a telephone answering machine with a three-minute tape, got a separate telephone line for it, and ran a classified ad in *The Dallas Morning News,* "Jehovah's Witnesses, call 555-5555 (not the actual number) for a recorded message." All hours of the day and night JW's called the line to hear a three-minute message that I changed weekly.

During a Watchtower assembly at the Coliseum in Fair Park, Dallas, the message on my picket sign read, "JW's Call 555-5555." *The Dallas Morning News* ran my picture on page one; the photo showed the sign and phone number. That day and night my answering machine recorded 154.

JW's could call that phone number in private without anyone else knowing. After the caller listened to the message, for further information he or she could leave an address or phone number. If callers asked for further information, I mailed gospel tracts or visited them personally. Usually after the message ended, the caller hung up without saying a word. Sometimes the caller cursed me, told me I was serving Satan, or told me that I was damned to die in Armageddon.

For many years I continued that ministry. Even then I continued to work with other ex-JW's across the country. At no cost I furnished them with cassette tapes of my brief messages.

In Appendix A I have included some of the messages I used with Jehovah's Witnesses. I hope these will help you rescue slaves of the Watchtower and help those rescued repair their reflexes.

Chapter 16

Enjoy Christian Freedom

Released Prisoners

My wife and I arrived early for one of the annual conventions of Ex-Jehovah's Witnesses for Jesus, to be held in the Pennsylvania Pocono Mountains. We settled into our cabin and at dusk went outside to enjoy the cool autumn air. We met two women conference attendees who also were early arrivals.

"The cafeteria isn't open yet. Want to ride with us into town to get something to eat?" I asked the two women. They agreed and climbed into the back seat of our car. We exchanged names and hometowns.

"How long have you been out?" one of the women asked me.

We all laughed, because we were talking as though we were people who had been in prison. One of the women had been out of the Watchtower for only two years; the other had been out for five years. We actually were slaves of the Watchtower and had been freed. We were as full of joy as inmates released from a physical prison might have been.

More than 250 people attended the convention that amounted to a celebration of Christian freedom. The ex-JW's I met there all were Christian witnesses. They shared their faith without hesitation. Their motivation had changed. Previously as JW's they had tried to win people to the Watchtower way because they had to. They worked because they were afraid if they didn't, they'd die in Armageddon. Their hearts had been filled with anxiety because they feared that despite all their efforts, they would fail to measure up.

The ex-JW's at the meeting represented six different Christian denominations. All delighted in God's grace—His free, unmerited favor. We basked in the light of eternal security of the believer, because we knew for sure that we had a home in heaven. We shared the good news because we wanted to. We worked for Jesus because we were saved—not to become saved.

Our attitudes reminded me of the example the apostle Paul gave about believers no longer slaves being but being sons and heirs.[179] The JW in bondage to the Watchtower is like a slave. She works because she has to. The Christian is like the son or daughter and heir. She has a place in the master's house because of who she is, not because of what she does.

I have seen new Christians full of joy because God's grace had pulled them out of addiction or immorality, but I never have seen joy any greater than that of ex-Jehovah's Witnesses who have become born-again Christians.

(By the way, Ex-Jehovah's Witnesses for Jesus is not an organization. It simply is, as the name implies, people who are ex-Jehovah's Witnesses and who now are followers of Jesus Christ. No other membership requirement exists. The group has no officers and no organization except the same, loose fellowship that exists between all Christians. Just as any person who is a born-again Christian can use the name *Christian*, any ex-Jehovah's Witnesses who are born-again Christians may use the name *Ex-Jehovah's Witnesses for Jesus*. The name was originated by Bill Cetnar, who now is with the Lord. In Kunkletown, PA, his wife, Joan, continues their ministry. (Their testimony is included in *We Left Jehovah's Witnesses: A Non-Prophet Organization*, by Edmond C. Gruss, Presbyterian and Reformed, Phillipsburg, N.J., 1974.)

Assurance of a Heavenly Home

My stepfather, Ray Alexander, was the most diligent-working Witness I knew. For many years he *pioneered*. He was a homebuilder, but he always put the *witness work* first. He spent much more time working for the Watchtower than he did making a living. After I became a Christian, on one of the rare occasions when we were together, I asked Ray why he drove himself so arduously as he went door-to-door daily and put out *The Watchtower* on the street corners. I knew he was getting old and needed to start letting up. I also knew keeping up the pace was difficult for him.

"I have to remain faithful to the end," he said.

"Surely if anyone could earn his salvation, you could have done it in over 30 years of working for it. Ray, suppose you quit witnessing and then die. Would all your work have been for nothing?" I asked.

"Yes," he answered solemnly.

Ray's life was filled with anxiety. He was like the hired hand who worked diligently for just enough to live day to day. If he stopped working, he would starve. But I, as a member of God's family, had a secure livelihood and retirement by inheritance. I had peace of mind. I witnessed for Jesus—not so I could become part of God's family, but because I was part of God's family.

Peace is a benefit of a personal relationship with Jesus Christ. While the obedient Christian has the assurance of knowing where she is going, the JW's life is filled with anxiety.

I believe anxiety killed my mother. For years she suffered with painful shingles. She didn't trust doctors, so she didn't receive treatment early enough. Back then the cause of shingles was not understood, but the disease could be treated if it was started in time. She didn't. So the last six years of her life were torturous. She was afraid she couldn't endure faithfully to the end, so she prayed to hurry the end and to die.

When JW elders in the Richardson, TX, Kingdom Hall officially disfellowshiped me, my mother treated me as dead, so during the last four years of her life I saw little of her. Because she was near death, the elders gave her special permission to see me. They allowed us two visits. On one of those times she asked, "Joe B., would it be wrong for me to pray for death?"

I was shocked that my opinion would be worth anything to her. "No, Mama, it wouldn't be wrong. People in the Old Testament prayed for death."

Then I asked, "Won't you trust in Jesus Christ as your Lord and Savior instead of the Watchtower Society?"

"I do trust in Jesus Christ," she said.

Further conversation convinced me that she still believed in the Watchtower error. I was afraid she was trusting in who she thought Jesus was—Michael the Archangel—rather than the LORD. But I am not her judge. I just hope that in her heart, she trusted in the Lord Jesus Christ.

We're all sinners. Every group with which I am familiar except the Rastafarians admits that.[180] So how is a sinner saved? A sinner is saved, the JW's say, exclusively through their organization. You can't make it to heaven anyway, because almost all of the 144,000 seats already are taken, but you might have eternal life on earth if you earn it, they believe. But the Bible says differently. Salvation is a gift of God to those who believe.[181]

After I had been a Christian for several years and had drifted out of church, my conscience began bothering me. My wife did her part also. At night in bed after the kids were asleep, my wife and I had some serious conversations. One Saturday night we vowed to each other that the next morning we would go to church.

The feisty little pastor, Benny Smith, preached on. Ephesians 2:8-9, *For by grace are ye saved through faith; and that not of yourselves: it is the gift of God: Not of works, lest any man should boast.* All the years I was growing up as a slave of the Watchtower Society, I never heard that verse preached, nor had I ever read about it in any of the Watchtower literature.

Listening to Benny Smith, I was reassured: Salvation is a gift. I could have it by the grace of God. In Romans 11:6 the apostle Paul made this clear, *And if by grace, then is it no more of works:*

otherwise grace is no more grace. But if it be of works, then is it no more grace: otherwise work is no more work.

The choice is clear: either one or the other—grace or works. If anything is added to grace, it no longer is grace anymore.

I knew that if I was saved, this had to occur by grace. I knew I was too far gone to be good enough to be saved. I had been out of God's will so long that I did not have assurance of my salvation. However, as I became involved in church and Bible study, I gained assurance.

After we moved to Arlington, TX, we remained faithfully in church. My assurance of my salvation grew. My pastor there, Rayburn Blair, once said, "I know that I know that I know that I'm saved."

JW's believe that if a person has that attitude about assurance of salvation, he is being presumptuous. Nevertheless I know Christian assurance is not based on the Christian's goodness or worthiness but on the perfect promises of Christ.

The Witnesses believe that when a person dies, she has no conscious existence until the resurrection. Then she goes on trial. Jehovah decides whether she is to live eternally on the earth or is to die the second death and be cast into the Lake of Fire to be consumed and end her existence.

But what does the Bible say? The Bible says the believer goes to heaven. Jesus said,

But lay up for yourselves treasures in heaven, where neither moth nor rust doth corrupt, and where thieves do not break through nor steal.[182] The believer can have *treasures in heaven.*

Jesus also said that our names *are written in heaven. Notwithstanding in this rejoice not, that the spirits are subject unto you; but rather rejoice, because your names are written in heaven.*[183]

The believer has an eternal home in heaven. The apostle Paul said, *For we know that if our earthly house of this tabernacle were dissolved, we have a building of God, an house not made with hands, eternal in the heavens.*[184]

The Society says these Scriptures refer only to the elect, whom the Society numbers at 144,000 only. But the Bible doesn't teach class distinctions about salvation. Rather, all believers are members of the elect. The Society, not the Bible, divides believers into two classes: the elect and the non-elect.

The heavenly Jerusalem is in heaven, not on earth; as John saw in his vision it travels down from heaven.[185] The Scripture does not say it actually rests on the earth, nor does the Scripture say whether it will rise again into heaven. The writer of the Book of Hebrews says, *But ye are come unto mount Zion, and unto the city of the living God, the heavenly Jerusalem, and to an innumerable company of angels.*[186]

Witnesses think they will be resurrected and will populate the earth. The Bible says the children of the resurrection do not marry. Jesus said, *But they which shall be accounted worthy to obtain that world and the resurrection from the dead, neither marry, nor are given in marriage: Neither can they die any more: for they are equal unto the angels; and are the children of God, being the children of the resurrection.*[187] Resurrected believers go to heaven.

Jehovah's Witnesses expect to be resurrected and then bear children to populate a new world—a contradiction to what Jesus said.

Believers will be resurrected as Jesus was resurrected. The JW's have a problem with that. They deny that Jesus' resurrection was physical and literal. Instead they say He was resurrected in the spirit. His body evaporated. If Jesus' resurrection wasn't literal and physical, why do they think theirs will be any different?

Encourage the Freedman

If God has used you to help rescue a slave of the Watchtower, you should help her replace the error with truth and to repair the reflexes that have been developed in her JW training. She will have a natural hunger for the Word of God, because now it makes more sense. She can read the Bible as she would any other book. Encourage her to go to church and get involved in a small-group Bible study. There brothers and sisters in Christ will take the place of JW friends who no longer speak to her.

Another help for the ex-JW is to meet with other ex-JW's in a local support group, which she can find in most large cities. The Internet is a good source of contact with fellow ex-JW's. (Some of those websites are listed in Additional Resources and Glossary of Terms.)

Loving the LORD More and More

Previously I heard people talk about loving the LORD. I didn't love Him. I was scared of Him. Then after I surrendered to Him, repented of my sins, and begged forgiveness, I felt reverence for Him. I felt gratitude that He had died to pay the penalty for my sins and had forgiven me. I had joy in my heart. I felt as if a great weight had been lifted from my fatigued back. I felt completed; I knew who I was and to where I was going. I was filled with gratitude to the LORD, but still I didn't love Him. I had no feelings of affection, no *philos* love, and certainly no *agapae* love, the most perfect, unselfish kind of love.

As I attended church and Bible study and learned more about the LORD, I grew closer to Him. Gratitude and reverence grew into affection. Now two generations later my heart is filled with love for the LORD when I think about what He has done for humanity and for me.

Before He made the world, He knew you and I someday would be born. The odds against us ever being born were billions to one. Think of all the billions of sperm cells our fathers produced and the hundreds of eggs our mothers produced and the odds of two of them getting together to make one unique human being. That was not a problem for God. He knew you and I would be born before He made the earth and separated the water from the land.[188]

He also knew we would use our free will and sin against Him. His permitting sin did not mean He caused it.[189] Before He made the world, He made provisions for our redemption from the penalty of sin.

God is holy and just. He cannot have sin in His presence. How could His justice be satisfied so He could forgive us, perfect us, and allow us to live with Him in heaven? The answer is *propitiation*—the atoning sacrifice. One person uniquely qualified would pay our penalty.[190] Jesus the Christ, the only One qualified, would satisfy the justice of God.

That was God's plan for our redemption. Throughout human history we can see events that lead up to it.

Many times the LORD Himself was sent to the earth in the form of an Angel of the LORD. Without personally visiting the earth He could know what was going on with the builders of the Tower of Babel, but still He visited earth and took a look.[191] "Who was running the universe while the LORD was checking out Babel?" the Watchtower might ask? The answer: He was. While He, God the Son, was checking out Babel, the Father was on the throne and the Holy Spirit was everywhere all at the same time.

Many times the LORD Himself visited the earth as the Angel of the LORD and talked to people such as Hagar, Abraham's slave who had run away with his young son, Ishmael.[192]

The LORD visited the Oaks of Mamre, sat down with Abraham, and ate some of Sarah's fresh-baked bread. He allowed Abraham to bargain with Him over the fate of Sodom. Then the LORD standing on the earth rained down fire from the LORD in heaven and destroyed Sodom and Gomorrah.[193]

As Melchizedek, the king of Salem (later named *Jerusalem*), the LORD visited the earth and ruled as King of Peace.[194] He visited earth and at the Brook Jabbok personally wrestled with Jacob.[195]

The LORD Himself visited Egypt to see how His people Israel were being mistreated.[196] Who was running the universe then? He was the one God manifest in three persons.

Finally the LORD was sent to earth and became flesh in the form of a little baby born to the virgin Mary. To do so He lay aside the free exercise of His power and limited Himself. He learned like other kids. He grew like other kids. But unlike the rest of us, He never sinned. He went about doing good. He performed miracles of healing and raising the dead to prove He was the Messiah, *Immanuel*, and *God with us*.[197]

He fulfilled the prophecies of the Old Testament. He, the *arm of the Lord*, was wounded for our transgressions.[198] He allowed Himself to be nailed to a cruel Roman cross and to die an agonizing death. This was the *propitiation* or the sacrificial offering to God to pay the penalty for our sins.

Yes, God Himself, in the form of His Son, died to satisfy the justice of God the Father. Jesus said, *I and my Father are one.*"[199]

To this day I am awestruck at what the LORD has done for humanity and for you and for me. He loved us with an *agapae* love—unselfish and unconditional. He loved us first, before we ever loved Him.[200]

When my mind goes back to the nothing that existed besides God, and then He spoke and the universe was created, I remember that even then, He had us in mind. My heart is filled with love for Him when I think of how patient He has been with humanity to allow the human race to continue to fumble around and make mistakes. Often someone has asked me, "Why does God allow evil to continue? Why doesn't He just pull the plug and stop it?"

My answer is, "grace". The grace of God allowed more people to be born who could be redeemed and have a home in heaven with him. Eventually time will stop, but neither you nor I nor any prophet, false or otherwise, knows when that will be.

Then I think of the assurance the LORD has given me of my relationship with Him. I know I have not always been faithful to Him, but He has to me. I'd like to think I never will sin again until I go to be with Him, but that isn't realistic. I can rely on His promise that *He is faithful and just to forgive our sins and cleanse us from all unrighteousness.*[201]

I grew to love the LORD; so can you. Make sure you belong to Him—that you trust in Jesus Christ the LORD. Pray without ceasing; talk to Him frequently. Read His Word. Attend worship services and Bible study. Share the good news with other people. Get involved in a small-group Bible study.

Rescuing Slaves of the Watchtower

My wife, Marona, and I are members of a large church.* Many of the members I don't know. But the 50 people in my Sunday-school class are as close as family. A group like that exists somewhere for you. As a reflection of God's love they will welcome you with open arms and love you unconditionally.

Slaves of the Watchtower can be rescued. The old stone prison is held together with crumbling mortar, institutionalized lying, more than a century of false prophecies, 180-degree turns in dogma, and dictatorial rule by the whims of a totalitarian hierarchy, toleration and shielding of sex abusers of children, and glaring contradictions of biblical truth. When the mortar crumbles and the stones collapse, we who know the real truth must not abandon the escapees but lead them out of the dust and debris and into the light of Christian liberty.

---

*Note: My first wife, Marilu, died in 2001. I married Marona in 2003.

Appendix A

Evangelism Approaches

You might want to start a telephone ministry to Jehovah's Witnesses. If so, please feel free to use the following 15 messages. They also can be used in letters to and conversations with family members *studying* with JW's.

Franz Admitted Christ Is Not Present on Earth
(2:39 Minutes)

Did Jesus Christ start making mistakes in 1914? Those familiar with Jehovah's Witnesses doctrines are aware that JW's claim that in 1914 Jesus Christ returned to earth invisibly and now rules and reigns through the Jehovah's Witnesses.

The Watchtower Bible and Tract Society, parent organization of the Jehovah's Witnesses, continually changes its mind about things. For example it said that Armageddon would occur in 1925. It said Abraham, Isaac, and Jacob would be resurrected in 1925. Just before Judge Joseph Rutherford died in 1945, he expressed his disappointment in not having seen them. Throughout World War II the Watchtower Society continued to say Armageddon could be only a few months away. Then later the Society claimed that Armageddon would occur in 1975.

When confronted with these false prophecies Jehovah's Witnesses say, "We all make mistakes." That's true—we all do make mistakes. But Jesus Christ does not make mistakes. Either He returned in 1914 or He didn't. Either He is ruling through the Jehovah's Witnesses or He is not.

Frederick Franz, the late president of the Watchtower Society, admitted that Jesus Christ is not present. In a 1975 discussion about the authority of the president of the Society, Frederick Franz said that Nathan Knorr, then president, was the chief executive of the Society and that he was the chief executive of the Lord's people here on earth.

He also said, "Jesus Christ is not down here on earth and so is using agents to carry out His will." We know Jesus Christ has not returned and is not present; Frederick Franz knew it too—and admitted it.

We know Jesus Christ is not directing the Watchtower Society. The whole idea of an invisible return is contrary to Scripture. Blaming on Christ the Watchtower's mistakes and false prophecies makes the Society's position more shaky.

The Watchtower Society is lying when it says Christ returned invisibly and now rules through the Society; Frederick Franz even admitted it.

If you trusted in the Watchtower Society as God's prophet on earth, please read your Bible. Believe what the Bible says, not what the Society says it says.

(The end of each three-minute recorded message gave the following invitation: "For further information please leave your name and address after the tone. And call again next week for a new message.")

Literal Resurrection of Believers (2:03 Minutes)

In 1 Corinthians 15:20 the apostle Paul said: *Now is Christ risen from the dead, and become the firstfruits of them that slept.* In other words Christ is the first of many who would be resurrected. Many times Jesus said believers in Him would be resurrected.

The Watchtower Society denies the literal and physical <u>resurrection</u> of Jesus and also denies the literal and physical <u>return</u> of Jesus. However, it claims that in 1941 He returned invisibly. The Society also does not deny the literal resurrection of faithful people. As a matter of fact the Society promises to diligently working, obedient, door-knocking Jehovah's Witnesses a physical resurrection and eternal life on earth. If you agree with the Watchtower's doctrine, let me ask you this: if Jesus was not literally resurrected, what makes you think you will be? If Jesus' resurrection was invisible and unseen, how do you know millions of others already haven't been resurrected invisibly and unseen? If Jesus' return only was spiritual and invisible, how do you know Armageddon won't be just spiritual, invisible, and unnoticed? Such ideas make no sense, because they are contradictory to reason and contradictory to Scripture. But so are the Watchtower doctrines.

Jesus literally and physically was resurrected from the grave. He was seen and touched by His disciples. He ate with them. The angels assured the apostles that Jesus would return as He left: visibly.

If you have been trying to earn your own salvation by obeying the Watchtower, listen to the apostle Paul's words in Romans 10:9: *. . . that if thou shalt confess with thy mouth the lord Jesus, and shalt believe in thine heart that God hath raised Him from the dead, thou shalt be saved.*

False Prophets
(2:00 Minutes)

If a person tells you one thing and the Bible tells you something else, whom do you believe? How about if the person or group of people claim to be a prophet of Jehovah God? Does that make a difference? Joseph Smith claimed to be a prophet of God.

Jim Jones claimed to be God Himself. David Koresh claimed he was the Lamb of God—Christ.

What's the difference between these so-called prophets? The Jehovah's Witnesses agree that Joseph Smith was a false prophet. They agree that Jim Jones was a fraud and that David Koresh was a false Christ. Millions of other people believe sincerely that Joseph Smith was a true prophet of God. Some are willing to stake their lives on it. People believed so strongly in Jim Jones and David Koresh that for these two men they laid down their lives and their children's lives. Many thousands devote full time and pay their own expenses to try to convince the world that Sun Myung Moon is preaching the truth.

All would agree that sincerity on the part of a cult's followers does not necessarily mean that the cult speaks the truth. Those who sincerely believe the Watchtower is God's prophet need to step back and look at their situation. This is the same as the followers of Joseph Smith, Jim Jones, Sun Myung Moon, and David Koresh need to do.

Jesus does not contradict Himself. But the Watchtower, which claims Jesus returned in 1914 and now rules through the Jehovah's Witnesses, does contradict itself. God cannot lie, but false prophets do lie. Ex-Jehovah's Witnesses who know the real truth want to help you.

Jesus Is the Truth
(2:26 Minutes)

I have been privileged to preach the gospel to groups of Jehovah's Witnesses outside many Watchtower assemblies. My message is simple: "Jesus Christ loves you. He died for you. He was resurrected from the dead. If you believe and trust in Him as the LORD, He will forgive your sins and give you eternal life."

The responses to this message were varied. One especially stands out in my mind. On hearing my message a gray-haired man I guessed to be in his 50s said:

"I've been in the truth too long to believe that stuff."

This response was unusual because the man said it out loud. I believe it reveals the belief of a great many Jehovah's Witnesses: regardless of the truth of a statement and regardless of how scriptural it might be, the Watchtower deems it false if it arises from any source outside the Watchtower.

What is truth? Please read John 8:32 through 36. Jesus explains it. *Ye shall know the truth, and the truth shall make you free.* The Jehovah's Witnesses have distorted the meaning of this verse. Read the Scripture in context; you will see that Jesus is talking about Himself. To know Him—the Truth—is to be set free from sin. He said, *If the son therefore shall make you free, ye shall be free indeed.* In John 14:6 He said, . . . *I am the way the truth and the life.*

Yes, Jesus is the Truth. If you know Him as your personal savior—if you accept Him as the LORD, as Romans 10:9 says, then He will give you the gift of eternal life. When I trusted Jesus as the LORD, I was set free—not only from sin but also from the confusion and contradictions of the Watchtower.

Jesus Is the *I AM*
(2:02 Minutes)

More than 2,000 years ago in Jerusalem, in the courtyard of the temple, in which Jesus Christ was teaching, the scribes and Pharisees, representing the religious establishment of the day, feared that Jesus was a threat to their organization. They wanted things left as they were. They did not want their positions of leadership disturbed. They went to great trouble to try to discredit Jesus. They even accused Him of being demon-possessed.

To those who would keep His Word Jesus promised eternal life. Not being able to differentiate between spiritual and physical death, the organization people asked:

"Art thou greater than our father Abraham, who is dead? And the prophets are dead: Whom makest thou thyself?"

Jesus first explained his state of humility: He was subject to the Father in heaven. Then He declared that before Abraham became existent, *I AM*. Yes, Jesus declared Himself to be the *I AM*

—the same LORD that spoke to Moses from the burning bush, the *I AM*—the One who always was and always will be.

The Jews understood clearly what Jesus said and what He meant. Their immediate reaction was to pick up stones to kill Him. Their actions were quite similar to that of the reactions of some organization people of today.

The Watchtower Society, just as the scribes and Pharisees did, goes to much trouble to try to discredit Jesus. It doesn't want to admit that Jesus Christ is the *I AM*—the second person of the name which is transliterated *Yahweh* or *Jehovah*.

Changing the Word of God
(2:33 Minutes)

In Alexandria, Egypt, some 250 years before the birth of Christ, a group of 70 Jewish scholars were commissioned to translate the Hebrew Scriptures into Greek, the language of the people.

During the New Testament days the language of the people of the entire Mediterranean area including Palestine was Greek. It was called *Koine Greek*, or common Greek—the language of the common people. The New Testament was written in Koine Greek.

In the New Testament we find many quotations and paraphrases of Old Testament Scriptures. These quotations for the most part are from the Septuagint Bible, that translation made by the 70 scholars in Alexandria, Egypt.

In John 8:58 Jesus proclaimed Himself to be the *I AM*. He said, *Before Abraham was, I AM*. He used the same words that are found in the third chapter of Exodus when God spoke from the burning bush. Moses had asked God who Moses could say sent him. The Lord said, *I AM hath sent thee*. He declared that *I AM* was his name. In the Greek Septuagint (Old Testament) the words were *ego aime*, literally translated, *I AM*.

In every honest Bible Jesus is quoted correctly as saying, before Abraham was, *ego aime*, also literally translated *I AM*.

However, one dishonest Bible has changed the translation to, *Before Abraham came into existence, I have been.* That dishonest Bible is published by the Watchtower Society. The reason the Watchtower Society has changed the clearly revealed word of God is because the Society denies the deity of Jesus Christ. It denies He is the *I AM*. Jesus' words are crystal-clear. He intended to say what he said. The Jews to whom He spoke understood immediately; they took up stones to kill Him. Now the modern Pharisees throw blasphemous insults.

Reading the Bible in Context (2:51 Minutes)

For many years Raymond Franz had been a missionary for the Watchtower Society. Then he was appointed to Bethel, the international headquarters in Brooklyn, NY. One of his tasks was to help write the book, *Aid to Bible Understanding*. During his research for the first time Raymond Franz learned to study the Bible in context. That was the beginning of his ability to see through the falsehood of some of the Watchtower doctrines. In his book *Crisis of Conscience*, published by Commentary Press, Atlanta in 1983, on page 23 Franz says:

"Now having both time and access to the extra Bible helps, the lexicons, commentaries, Hebrew and Greek concordances, and so forth, was an aid. But above all it was seeing the need always to let the context guide, always let the Scriptures themselves control, that made the major difference. There was no overnight change of viewpoint, but, over a period of years, a gradual deepening of appreciation of the crucial need to let God's word speak for itself to the fullest extent possible . . .."

The end result of Raymond Franz's reading the Bible in context was that he began to think for himself and to read the Bible in context. The end result was his being disfellowshiped by the Jehovah's Witnesses. The Watchtower Society doesn't want people to think for themselves. They teach people to say, "I think for myself." But if one actually begins to think for himself and to question any of the Watchtower's doctrines, he may, like Raymond Franz and many others, get kicked out.

The Almighty Creator God gave us the Bible to enlighten us and not to confuse us. We need no Watchtower literature to explain what the Word of God clearly reveals.

Many people have read the Bible alone without any aid or explanation from any person and have trusted in Jesus Christ as the Lord and committed their lives to Him. But none have become Jehovah's Witnesses by reading the Bible alone.

I urge you to read the Bible in context. Believe what the Bible says; don't believe what some group of people say it says.

Forbidding to Marry
(2:19 Minutes)

In his first letter to Timothy the apostle Paul warned that in the latter times some would depart from the faith and that some of the wrongs they would do included *speaking lies in hypocrisy* and *forbidding to marry*. (Read 1 Tim. 4:1-3.)

When we read this, we automatically think of the Roman Catholic Church, which forbids its priests and nuns to marry. For many years another religion discouraged marriage for all its young people. That organization is the Watchtower, the parent organization of Jehovah's Witnesscs.

An example of obedience to the Watchtower, which said in 1941 that Armageddon was just a matter of months away, can be seen in the life of Raymond Franz. Franz was 19-years old when he heard the president of the Watchtower Society urge young witnesses not to marry. As an obedient Jehovah's Witness he didn't marry until he was 36-years old.

Raymond Franz believed the false prophecies of the Watchtower Society. He believed Armageddon was just a matter of months away. Now in his later years of life he has missed some of the greatest blessings of this life—the blessings of children and grandchildren. The Bible says: *Now the Spirit speaketh expressly, that in the latter times some shall depart from the faith, giving heed to seducing spirits, and doctrines of devils; speaking lies in hypocrisy; having their conscience seared with a hot iron; forbidding to marry.*

Do you just believe everything the Watchtower Society says? Raymond Franz did. But he learned better. Perhaps you also can learn better. Raymond Franz learned the truth about the Watchtower Society; he saw it from the inside as a member of the Governing Body. He saw the lies, contradictions, and hypocrisy. He got out.

I personally read the Bible in context and saw from God's Word the contradictions and lies of the Watchtower Society. I got out.

Six-Thousand Years Prophecy (2:33 Minutes)

The Watchtower book entitled *Daily Heavenly Manna* said 6,000 years of human history ended in 1872.

The Watchtower book entitled *The Time Is at Hand* said 6,000 years of human history ended in 1873.

The Watchtower book entitled *The Truth Shall Make You Free* said 6,000 years of human history ended in 1972.

The *Awake* magazine of October 8, 1968, said 6,000 years of human history ended in 1975.

This same Watchtower Society claims that Jesus Christ returned invisibly and now rules and reigns through the Society; that same society keeps making these mistakes. Does Jesus Christ make mistakes? Does Jesus Christ keep telling the Watchtower Society wrong dates?

Somebody is making false prophecies—and it's not Jesus Christ. In Deuteronomy 18:21-22 Moses wrote, *And if thou say in thine heart, how shall we know the word which the LORD hath not spoken? When a prophet speaketh in the name of the LORD, if the thing follow not, nor come to pass, that is the thing which the LORD hath not spoken . . ..*

The Watchtower has said a lot of things that were wrong. The Watchtower Society claims to be God's prophet. According to the Word of the LORD it is a false prophet.

In Matthew 24:11 Jesus said, *And many false prophets shall rise and deceive many.*

In that same chapter, verse 23, Jesus also said, *Then if any man shall say unto you, lo, here is Christ, or there; believe it not.*

What if they say He is in Brooklyn and is ruling through the Watchtower Society? *Believe it not.* Want to know the truth? Read the Bible. It also tells us, *For as the lightning cometh out of the east, and shineth even unto the west; so shall also the coming of the Son of Man be.*

When Jesus returns, everyone will see, just like they see lightning. The Watchtower has been lying about this. But the Bible tells the truth.

Ex-JW's for Jesus
(2:14 Minutes)

The Watchtower book entitled *Millions Now Living Will Never Die* and the Watchtower book *Salvation* both said that in 1925 Abraham would arise from his grave. The Watchtower book entitled *Thy Kingdom Come* said the millennial kingdom of Christ began in 1873.

The Watchtower book entitled *The Finished Mystery* said the churches would be destroyed in 1918.

From its very beginning to the present time the Watchtower Society has made false prophecies. Yet it claims to speak by God, by angels, by God's Holy Spirit, by divinely provided light, and by the direction of Jesus Christ.

How many times does a friend of yours lie to you before you quit trusting her? Most Jehovah's Witnesses have been in the organization such a short time that they don't know about many of these false prophecies. But others have been involved for many years and close their eyes to reality.

How can adult, intelligent people continue to be hoodwinked by the Watchtower Society? The only answer is that they are so mentally disciplined that they will believe anything the Watchtower says, no matter how contradictory it may be.

Some brainwashed Jehovah's Witnesses, however, have shaken off the Watchtower's enslavement. With open minds hundreds of them have read their Bibles in and have begun to realize that the Watchtower could be wrong. Then continuing to read their Bibles they have realized that the Watchtower is a false prophet and that Jesus Christ is LORD indeed, not just another, lesser, angel god.

Ex-Jehovah's Witnesses for Jesus have shaken off the Watchtower control and trusted in Jesus Christ as Lord and Savior. They care about you.

Anti-Education
(2:19 Minutes)

Why has the Watchtower Society discouraged Jehovah's Witnesses from going to college? Why have some Jehovah's Witnesses encouraged their children to drop out of high school?

Why are Jehovah's Witnesses encouraged to do simple, menial work even though some of these individuals may be capable of doing much more interesting and more rewarding work?

By looking at the long-term results of these actions we can see the desired result. The result is that most Jehovah's Witnesses are not as educated as the rest of the population is.

College or seminary education is not an end in itself, but education teaches people to reason, to study, to analyze, and to think. Those are things the Watchtower Society does not want its people doing. The Society wants its people to obey. Usually when a Jehovah's Witness goes against the grain and gets a higher education, she stops being an active, door-knocking Jehovah's Witness. Why? Because she now more easily can see the contradictions in the Watchtower doctrines.

Lorri MacGregor was an 18-year-old college student. She became a Jehovah's Witness and was told to drop out of college, because Armageddon would occur before she could graduate. But many years later Lorri did learn to think for herself. She shook off the Watchtower's enslavememt and now is teaching the truth about Jesus Christ.

According to Raymond Franz, who was a member of the Witnesses' governing body, one of the questions studied by the governing body has been "whether one qualifies as an elder if he approves of his son or daughter taking higher education".

If you are a Jehovah's Witness—or are studying with the JW's—please think. Almighty God gave you a brain; use it. See that you are being used by a dangerous cult.

Playing God
(2:38 Minutes)

The Watchtower Society has tried to tell husbands and wives what to do in the privacy of their own bedrooms. Embarrassed wives have been called before elders and asked questions about the most intimate details of their lives.

The governing body of Jehovah's Witnesses said a married couple would be disfellowshiped because the Watchtower leadership did not approve of their sexual foreplay.

Raymond Franz, who was a member of the governing body, in his book, *Crisis of Conscience*, says:

"The governing body's decision in 1972 resulted in a sizable number of 'judicial hearings' as elders followed up on reports of confessions of the sexual practices involved. Women experienced painful embarrassment in such hearings as they responded to the elders' questions about the intimacies of their marital relations. Some marriages broke up with resulting divorce."

According to Franz, after five years the disfellowshiping policy was reversed. He said, ". . . the governing body in effect now withdrew itself from that intimate area of others' lives. Again the body assigned me to prepare material for publication—this time

Appendix A: Evangelism Tools

advising of the change. I found it personally satisfying to be able to acknowledge, even though rather obliquely, that the organization had been in error."

Here an organization played God. It claimed to be led by Jehovah God and intruded into the private lives of husbands and wives, caused marriages to break up, and then admitted it had made a mistake.

Almighty God does not make mistakes. This is additional proof that the Watchtower Society is not guided by God as it claims to be. Jesus Christ does not make mistakes. The Watchtower Society claims that Christ now is ruling and reigning through the Watchtower Society. That is a false claim by a false prophet.

If you are a Jehovah's Witness or are studying with the Witnesses, please look at the facts. Realize this is a false and dangerous cult.

Lord's Supper
(2:02 Minutes)

Jesus said, *Take eat: this is my body which is broken for you, this do in remembrance of me.* That is plain enough, isn't it? Jesus told his disciples to take and eat the bread of the Lord's Supper.

The Watchtower teaches Jehovah's Witnesses that they are not to take and eat. Each Passover in Kingdom Halls across the nation, Jehovah's Witnesses and people who are studying with them gather to observe what they call "the Lord's evening meal", but in most cases none will eat or drink. The Watchtower says only 144.000, most of whom now are dead and gone, are to take and eat. When they deny that ordinary Christians are to take and eat, are they also denying that His body was *broken for you*? No. As often happens, in mid-sentence the Watchtower switches doctrines.

Those who are disciples of Christ are to take and eat because Christ's body was broken for them. All of them! Christ didn't say there were certain classes of disciples—upper class who were to eat and lower class who were not to eat. He said, *Take eat* . . . . Later the apostle Paul said, *Let a man examine Himself, and so let him eat of that bread and drink of that cup.* This is just one more instance of the Watchtower changing God's Word to fit its own doctrines. Please read your Bible. Believe what the Bible says and not what the Watchtower says it says.

This message is brought to you by Ex-Jehovah's Witnesses for Jesus, people who once were brainwashed by the Watchtower Society but now are free in Christ.

Discerning the Lord's Body
(1:55 Minutes)

This is my body, Jesus said when He broke the bread and gave it to His disciples. What did He mean, *This is my body*?

For 76 years the Watchtower Society taught that Jesus was not speaking of His physical body but of the Christian congregation. Then in 1956 the Watchtower changed its doctrine and said the bread represents *Jesus' body of flesh.*

If the Watchtower changed its mind before, might it not change it again? Jesus said, *This is my body, which is broken for you.* How can the Watchtower, or anyone else for that matter, decide to change the Bible's meaning?

The Bible clearly states that those who eat and drink unworthily eat and drink damnation to themselves, not discerning the Lord's body.

One time or the other the Watchtower was not discerning the Lord's body. Why follow an organization that claims to speak for God but that can't make up its mind?

The Watchtower Society denies that this body of Christ, which was broken for us, ever was resurrected. The Bible teaches that believers in Christ will be resurrected as He was resurrected. The Watchtower denies the literal and physical resurrection of Christ but promises Jehovah's Witnesses a literal and physical resurrection.

Thousands have left the Watchtower because of the contradictions and changes in doctrines. Many of these people have decided to trust in Jesus Christ instead of trusting the Watchtower.

Literal Resurrection
(2:40 Minutes)

When faithful women brought spices to anoint the body of Jesus, an angel told them He had risen from the dead. The angel showed them the empty tomb. The angel told them to go tell the disciples to go into Galilee, where they would see Jesus. In 1 Corinthians 15:6 the apostle Paul says that Jesus was seen by 500 people at one time.

In Jerusalem after His resurrection Jesus appeared to the 11 apostles. They were frightened because they supposed they had seen a spirit. Jesus assured them that a spirit did not have flesh and bones as they saw Him have. He urged them to touch Him and to see that He was real. Then He ate with them as further proof of his literal and physical resurrection.

After Jesus returned from Galilee, He met with the disciples in Jerusalem. At this time He told them to wait for the Holy Spirit to be given. Then going on to the Mount of Olives Jesus talked with the apostles. While they were looking at Him, He ascended up into heaven. Two angels promised that this same Jesus would return in like manner.

After His resurrection Jesus was seen by His disciples. He was touched by his disciples. He ate with His disciples. The apostles saw Him ascend into heaven; they were promised that in the same way Jesus would return.

How, then, can some mere human being tell us that Jesus returned invisibly and that when He returned, no one saw Him?

The Watchtower Society once taught that in 1874 Jesus would return. Then later it began to teach that in 1914 Jesus returned. But the Bible says Jesus' disciples saw Him when He left and will see Him when He returns.

So whom do you believe—the Bible or the Watchtower Society, composed of people who claim to be modern-day prophets of Jehovah? Many people who once were Jehovah's Witnesses and were brainwashed by the Watchtower Society now are true believers in Jesus and want to help you.

Appendix B

Understanding the Trinity

Scripture does not explain or defend the doctrine of the trinity but assumes its existence as it does the existence of God. However, just as people throughout the ages have tried to prove the existence of God, we also find proving the truth of the trinity to be necessary. Both efforts often are futile, because they are casting seed on hard, dry ground. Individuals who have experienced a personal encounter with Jesus Christ need little explanation of the unity of God. When we realize that He is without limits, we don't need to be convinced.

God is everywhere present. He exists in everything. He is all-powerful. He is all-knowing. He can take the form of a person and eat Sarah's home-baked bread and talk to Abraham face to face while at the same time existing everywhere to the farthest galaxy and at the same instant sitting on heaven's throne as He prepares to rain fire down on Sodom and Gomorrah.

The Watchtower Society leaders try to reduce God to fit their own limited understanding. We struggle to understand the things God has designed and created. How much more difficulty we have understanding the LORD Himself. We can't any more understand Him than a new puppy can understand nuclear physics. The puppy trusts his master to deal with everything beyond his understanding. So must we.

The LORD, however, has left us with positive information about the trinity. (To avoid duplication, in this chapter I have made many statements without elaboration because the subjects have been dealt with in earlier chapters. I have, however, furnished references for each statement of fact.)

Trinity Part 1

Seeing God

The Bible must be interpreted by the Bible. Any verse that is not clear or seems to contradict other parts of the Bible should be interpreted in the light of that which is clearly revealed.

People in the Old Testament days believed that to see God meant they would die. Some believed they saw God and did not die.

Job believed he would see God, his redeemer.[202]

Jesus promised that Christians would see God. *Blessed are the pure in heart: for they shall see God.*[203]

John said we would see God *as he is.*[204]

John said evildoers have not seen God. *Beloved, follow not that which is evil, but that which is good. He that doeth good is of God: but he that doeth evil hath not seen God.*[205]

John said no man had seen God.[206]

Jesus said no one had seen the Father except, . . . *he which is of God,* or *the One Who is from God,* apparently referring to Himself. *Not that any man hath seen the Father, save he which is of God, he hath seen the Father.*[207]

After he wrestled with the Angel of the Lord, Jacob said . . .*I have seen God face to face, and my life is preserved.*[208]

Gideon also feared he would be killed because he had seen an angel of the Lord face to face. *And when Gideon perceived that he was an angel of the LORD, Gideon said, Alas, O Lord GOD! for because I have seen an angel of the LORD face to face. And the*

Appendix B: Understanding the Trinity

LORD said unto him, Peace be unto thee; fear not: thou shalt not die.[209] (Notice that the angel of the Lord speaks as the LORD in first person. The LORD has taken the form of an angel and is speaking for Himself. This only can be a preincarnate manifestation of Jesus Christ.)

The parents of Samson feared they would be killed because they had seen an Angel of the LORD face to face. *And Manoah said unto his wife, We shall surely die, because we have seen God. But his wife said unto him, If the LORD were pleased to kill us, he would not have received a burnt offering and a meat offering at our hands, neither would he have shewed us all these things, nor would as at this time have told us such things as these.*[210]

The writer of Hebrews implies that with holiness we shall see the Lord. *Follow peace with all men, and holiness, without which no man shall see the Lord.*[211]

Moses speaks of seeing the LORD face to face.[212]
God is spirit and cannot be seen by human eyes.[213]
(Christ) . . . *is the image of the invisible God . . . .*[214]
God is invisible.[215]

Jesus said people have not seen the Father. *And the Father Himself, which hath sent me, hath borne witness of me. Ye have neither heard his voice at any time, nor seen his shape.*[216]

The Hebrew words translated *see* or *seen* are equivalent to our English words, so we should have no problem understanding them. In Job 19:26, . . . *mine eyes shall see God*, the Hebrew word *chazah* is translated *see*. *Chazah* means to gaze at, perceive, behold, look. The Hebrew word *ra'ah* also is used and means to see or discern. In English both these words are equivalent to *see* or *seen*.

A Greek word translated *see* or *seen* is *hoptanomai*, the source of our words *ophthalmology* and *optical*. Another Greek word is *horao*, which means to stare at, see, or perceive. These words, too, can mean to see visually or perceptually, so they are equivalent to our English word *see*.

We *see* with our eyes and we see, perceive, or discern, with our minds. A blind man may say, "Yes, I see", which means he perceives or understands. This is proper usage in English, Greek, and Hebrew.

Therefore, the context must determine whether the meaning is to see visually, perceptually, or perhaps both.

If you read Job 19:25-27 in context we can have no doubt that Job speaks about seeing with his eyes, . . . *yet in my flesh shall I see God: Whom I shall see for myself, and mine eyes shall behold. . ..*

Who is Job's *redeemer*? Who would stand on the earth in the latter day? Christ Jesus is clearly the *redeemer*. Christ literally stood on the earth and died to redeem us from sin. Christ will return. Christ will resurrect Job. Job will see Christ. Then Job will see God. We cannot see a spirit. In that respect we cannot see God in His essence. But we can see a body. The Word, who always was in existence who became flesh (John 1:12, 14).

Matthew 5:8 could mean . . . *the pure in heart . . . shall see God* . . . either with their eyes, or perception. It could be either. To be pure in heart they already must have perceived something about God.

First John 3:12: . . . *when he shall appear*, refers back to God. God will appear; when he does, . . . *we shall be like him; for we shall see him as he is.* To the person who does not believe that Jesus Christ is God, this presents a problem. Will God the Father appear? Will we be like Him? Will we see Him as He is? Paul says, yes. If we believe Christ and the Father are one, we have no problem. In any case Paul has assured believers that God will appear and that we shall see Him.

So on His return we will see God.

Third John 11 says . . . *he that doeth evil hath not seen God,* and implies that the righteous have seen God. This has to mean perceptive seeing rather than visual seeing.

John 1:18 says *No man hath seen God . . ..* Does this mean that up until that moment no man had seen God? What about the Old Testament prophets that had already seen manifestations of God in the Angel of the Lord, in the Burning Bush, and in the Shekinah glory cloud? Is this a contradiction? Does it mean no man *would* ever see God? Or does it mean no man *could* ever see God?

Appendix B: Understanding the Trinity

Let's examine this difficult verse in other translations:

No one has ever seen God; the only Son, who is in the bosom of the Father, he has made him known. Revised Standard Version (RSV).

It is true that no one has ever seen God at any time. Yet the divine and only Son, who lives in the closest intimacy with the Father, has made him known. (PHILLIPS).

No one has ever seen God; but God's only Son, he who is nearest to the Father's heart, he has made him known (New English Bible—NEB).

No one has ever seen God, but God the only Son, who is at the Father's side, has made him known (New International Version—NIV).

No man has seen God at any time; the only Begotten God, who is in the bosom of the Father, he has explained him (New American Standard Version—NASV).

Dr. Randolph Yeager understood this verse to mean most intimate perceptive seeing and translates it:

Not one has ever understood God. God only begotten, the One Who is in the bosom of the Father he is the One Who reveals Him completely.

Yeager matches the sense of the two phrases, *No one has ever understood God*, with *he is the One Who reveals Him completely*.

Notice the common threads of meaning in all the modern translations. The *apodosis* is consistently *made him known* or *explained him*. Therefore, the context of *see* is perceive or have an intimate understanding.

Notice another common thread: affirming the deity of Jesus Christ. Rather than saying *only begotten Son*, as the King James Version does, the oldest and most reliable original Greek manuscripts say *monogenas theos*, which literally means *the only begotten God.*

In John 6:44-46 Jesus spoke of people being taught of God—hearing and learning of the Father. Jesus said a person who is *of God, he hath seen the Father.* This context suggests perception rather than visual sight.

Jacob, Gideon, and the parents of Samuel saw God face to face, but they did not see the essence of God, His spirit. They saw an *Angel of the Lord*, a manifestation of God who appeared as a man. These verses obviously were speaking of seeing with the eyes.[217]

In Hebrews 12:14, speaking of *holiness, without which no man shall see the Lord,* suggests that with holiness one could see the Lord. The context suggests perception rather than seeing with the eye.

In Numbers 14:13-14 Moses spoke of seeing the LORD *face to face.* Moses saw manifestations of God in the burning bush, in the cloud that went before Israel, and in the pillar of fire by night. Moses also saw *the back parts* of the LORD. The context of the following verses show that those *back parts* were more knowledge of God—His name, Yahweh, LORD, the I AM. Although Moses saw visual manifestations of God, the *back parts* allowed him to perceive more of the attributes of God, His sovereignty, His true justice, His true mercy, and His holiness.

Exodus 34:5-6 says, *And the LORD descended in the cloud, and stood with him there, and proclaimed the name of the LORD.* Apparently the LORD appeared in the form of an angel of the LORD who stood and talked with Moses. And the LORD passed by before him, and proclaimed, *The LORD, The LORD God, merciful and gracious, long-suffering and abundant in goodness and truth. . ..* The LORD proclaimed His name, office, authority, and attributes; these were so much more than just a set of letters forming a word for a name.

Appendix B: Understanding the Trinity

The Scripture does not err. If the Bible seems contradictory, we need to study it more. Then we find greater illumination.

No one can see God's true essence. He is spirit and invisible to us. If we visually could see Him, we would die.

Jesus Christ in the flesh is a manifestation of God. Christians can look forward to going to heaven and seeing God when we see Christ. At the resurrection we—as well as Job—will see Him with our physical eyes.

Trinity Part 2

Messiah Is God

The Bible presents Jesus Christ as a human being—the Son of Man, the Son of God, Messiah, the Lord, and God. As God, Jesus Christ is divine or He is deity. *Messiah* in the Hebrew and *Christ* in the Greek mean exactly the same thing, *The Anointed One*. In this study we will use *Messiah* and *Christ* interchangeably.

1. The deity of the Messiah is assumed in the Old Testament.

Job assumed that Messiah is God. Who was Job's *Redeemer*? Christ clearly is the *Redeemer* of whom Job speaks.

Isaiah said Messiah would be *Immanuel,*[218] *God with us.*

From Matthew 1:22-23 we understand that Jesus' birth was a fulfillment of Isaiah's prophecy. God the Son became begotten by God the Holy Spirit and became flesh through the virgin Mary.

Emmanuel sometimes is interpreted as meaning *God in the flesh*. This interpretation certainly fits the situation, because Messiah became flesh. He became *God with us.*

Rescuing Slaves of the Watchtower

The Watchtower Society claims that Jesus Christ was Michael the Archangel who became flesh. The organization stretches verses in Daniel to the breaking point and fills in generous amounts of imagination to *prove it*. Michael is called a *prince*.[219] That doesn't make him the Messiah. A time will occur when Michael will stand up for Israel.[220] That doesn't make him Messiah. If Michael had been the Messiah, Jude surely would have mentioned this fact when he wrote of Michael contending over Moses' body.[221]

A legend says that stone masons on the Isle of Lesbos used a pliable lead rule so if a stone wasn't the right length, they would form the ruler to make it correct. That exercise in using a pliable standard is called the *Lesbian Rule*. The Watchtower Society is the greatest practitioner of the *Lesbian Rule*.

Isaiah gave many Godlike titles to Messiah—a Child, a Son, a Governor, Wonderful, Counselor, The Mighty God, The Everlasting Father, The Prince of Peace, One Whose kingdom never would end.[222]

Isaiah clearly speaks about one person—the Messiah—who will rule forever *upon the throne of David*.

Messiah is called *the arm of the LORD*.[223] The LORD is spirit. He doesn't have a body as people do, so He is not divided into arms, legs, etc. These anthropomorphic expressions are used of the LORD as literary devices to help us understand more clearly. Messiah is not a severed arm of the LORD but is a manifestation of the LORD Himself as He would reach out with His arm. This same Messiah took the punishment for our sins upon Himself and paid our penalty— . . .*the LORD hath laid on him the iniquity of us all*.[224]

The *arm of the LORD* is He—a separate personality from the LORD, yet one with the LORD.

Appendix B: Understanding the Trinity

The prophet Micah said Messiah is eternal . . . *whose goings forth have been from of old, from everlasting.*[225]

Using this prophecy the elders of Judaism learned where Messiah would be born and told the wicked King Herod.

No one else but God can claim to be eternal.

In Psalm 110:1 David spoke of Messiah as his Lord.

The LORD hath sworn, and will not repent, Thou art a priest for ever after the order of Melchizedek.[226] The LORD still was talking to the Lord. This is fact is also referred to in Hebrews 5:5-6, *So also Christ glorified not Himself to be made an high priest; but he that said unto him, Thou art my Son, today have I begotten thee. As he saith also in another place, Thou art a priest for ever after the order of Melchizedek.*

The Bible describes Melchizedek as king of peace; he also is described as being without father, without mother, without descent, having neither beginning of days, nor end of life; but made like unto the Son of God; *abideth a priest continually.*[227]

Only the I AM had no beginning and will have no end. Therefore, Melchizedek was a pre-incarnate manifestation of the eternal Christ, Who had no beginning and will have no end.

In Zechariah 12:10 the LORD speaks of Himself as being pierced, . . . *and they shall look upon me whom they have pierced* . . .. Christ is the One Who was pierced when He was crucified. Clearly in Zechariah 12:1 the LORD is speaking. Verse 10 records the continuing words of the same LORD. When the Romans pierced Jesus' hands, they pierced the LORD.

We need not go beyond the Old Testament to see that Messiah is the LORD. If we believe Jesus, who was born of the virgin Mary in Bethlehem. is Messiah, the question is settled: Jesus is God in the flesh.

2. The deity of Christ is assumed in the New Testament.

The gospels declare Jesus, the virgin-born son of Mary, to be Christ. Anyone who claims Christianity as his faith claims Jesus Christ is the Messiah, so we will leave that as an established and accepted fact.

Christ had no beginning and will have no end.

Christ is the eternal Word.[228] (For a more detailed study of The Word, the *logos,* see Appendix D.)

The Greek word translated *Word* is *Logos.* The word was in common usage among the Greeks. *Logos* could mean a *word*, a *phrase*, a *speech, an accounting,* or *a body of doctrine.* Revelation 19:13 calls Christ *The Word of God.* In Greek religious thinking *logos* could mean a great hierarchy of gods of ascending rank from just above humanity all the way up to infinity. The Greeks didn't concern themselves much with the Creator God. But the *logos*, this plethora of gods, they believed was the link between humanity and the infinite first cause of all things.

In writing the Gospel of John the apostle used terms with which his readers were familiar. He served as pastor of a church mostly composed of Gentiles. He introduced Jesus as the *logos.*

(1) John proclaimed that the Word had no beginning.

> John declares the eternity of the Word and then emphasizes it. Just in case we didn't understand the first time, *The same was in the beginning with God.* Christ already was in existence in the beginning and He was with God, according to John's gospel.
>
> This Word, who had no beginning, made everything. This *Logos* not only is the link between God and humanity, but He is one with God. He became a person. *And the Word was made flesh . . ..*[229] He was the only begotten God and the only begotten of God.

(2) Christ proclaimed Himself to be the I AM.

Appendix B: Understanding the Trinity

Talking to the Samaritan woman at Jacob's Well, Jesus said he was the Messiah. He used the words *ego aime*.[230]

(3) Jesus is called the Alpha and Omega.

> *. . . I am Alpha and Omega, the first and the last.*[231]

Jesus clearly stated His eternity. He is the first and last. He is eternal. Only God can be eternal.

Not only is the voice clearly that of Jesus, but John describes him in Revelation 1:12-18.

> *And when I saw him, I fell at his feet as dead. And he laid his right hand upon me, saying unto me, Fear not; I am the first and the last.*

Again Jesus declared Himself to be eternal . . . *the first and the last.*

Later, in Revelation 21:6, God calls Himself the Alpha and Omega. *And he said unto me, It is done. I am Alpha and Omega, the beginning and the end . . . .*

Jesus is the *Alpha and Omega*. God is the *Alpha and Omega*. If you don't believe Jesus is God, you have a definite problem here.

Again in Revelation 22:13 clearly Jesus is speaking: *I am Alpha and Omega, the beginning and the end, the first and the last.*

(4) Jesus Christ is King of Kings and Lord of Lords.

Paul clearly was speaking of . . . *our Lord Jesus Christ*, when he said, *Who is the blessed and only Potentate, the King of kings and Lord of lords.*[232]

Again in Revelation 17:14 Jesus is called *Lord of lords and King of kings*. Revelation 19:16 says, *And he hath on his vesture and on his thigh a name written, KING OF KINGS, AND LORD OF LORDS.*

Does this mean that Jesus is Lord of the LORD God?
No. He IS the LORD God.
Jesus became a human being so He could be our Savior.
Jesus is the *Logos*, the link between God and humanity.
He is *the arm of the Lord*.
He is the LORD.
Realize how much He loved us—to span the great difference between God and humanity, to become one of us.

3. The Bible proclaims Jesus to be God in the Flesh.

Immanuel (or Emmanuel), mentioned previously, means *God with us*. Jesus was the fulfillment of Isaiah's prophecy that Messiah would be *God with us*.[233]

In Paul's first letter to Timothy the apostle said *the Mystery of Godliness . . . was manifest in the flesh . . .*[234] and *. . . received up into glory*. God became flesh in the person of Jesus. Jesus is the One Who was received up into glory. Obviously this *Mystery of Godliness* is Jesus.

The KJV translators, using the manuscripts they had at the time, have properly translated *God was manifest in the flesh*. However, long after the KJV was published in 1611, older manuscripts that say *He* instead of God were discovered. To be faithful to use the oldest and most reliable manuscripts, most modern translations use *He*. And here is testimony of the basic honesty of these scholars. If they had been willing to sacrifice scholarship for *an axe to grind* regarding the deity of Christ, they might have used the same manuscripts as the KJV to add strength to a theological position.

Personal pronouns are used, because a person was manifested in the flesh. Who was *manifest in the flesh*? *The mystery of godliness* was *manifest in the flesh*. Some translators say *The mystery of our religion*. But still this subject is a person. If the mystery of godliness is not God, who is He? Paul probably is quoting verses of a Christian song popular at the time:

> *He was manifested in the flesh,*
> *Vindicated by the Spirit,*
> *Seen by angels,*
> *Preached among the nations,*
> *Believed on in the world.*

A scriptural mystery is something that had to be revealed by God. We might call it a "mystery until God explained it", because it does not remain a mystery. The *Mystery of Godliness* is Christ revealed. He was manifest in the flesh. People saw Him in the flesh.[235]

The *Mystery of Godliness* is one and the same as the *arm of the Lord* and the *Logos*.

4. Jesus and the Father are one.

Jesus explained to Philip, *I am in the Father, and the Father is in me.*[236] Jesus told Philip, *. . . he that hath seen me hath seen the Father. . . .*[237]

Jesus also is in the bosom of the Father. To say God, a spirit, has a bosom is called an anthropomorphic expression—a literary device to convey divine attributes in human descriptions. Such an expression doesn't mean that God consists only of a body with arms and legs as human beings are.

When the infamous Texas outlaw John Wesley Hardin was apprehended by Texas Rangers on a train in Florida, he said "the long arm of the law" had gotten him. The *law* doesn't have a human body or an arm. Bible writers used the same kind of anthropomorphic expressions for God.

5. Jesus Christ is worshiped.

Only God is to be worshiped.[238]
The Angels worship Christ.[239]
Why does the writer of Hebrews say that Jesus was made *a little lower than angels*?[240]
To say the eternal Christ born of the virgin Mary was made *a little lower than the angels* is another way of saying He became a human being. He was made *a little lower than the angels* to suffer death for us. He did not take on Himself the nature of angels but took on Himself the nature of a human being as the physical descendant of Abraham. (If Christ were Michael the Archangel, as the Watchtower claims, this statement would make no sense, because He already would have been an angel.)
The Wise Men worshiped Jesus.[241]
Jesus permitted people to worship Him during His earthly ministry. If He had not been deity, He certainly would have forbidden them.
Jesus walked on the water during a storm on the Sea of Galilee. Matthew 14:33 says, *Then they that were in the ship came and worshipped him . . ..*
After Christ's resurrection He met His disciples. On seeing the risen Lord they worshiped Him. Rather than to rebuke them for worship Jesus told them to go and tell the brethren of His resurrection.[242]
Jesus healed a blind man at the Temple. The man's response was to worship Jesus.[243]
Should we worship Jesus? Yes. Should we worship God only? Yes. When we worship Jesus, we are worshiping God. Jesus is the Messiah, the Arm of the Lord, the Logos, the Word of God. Jesus is in the Father and the Father in Him. To redeem us from sin Christ became *a little lower than the angels* when He became a human being. But He never ceased to be deity.

6. Jesus Christ indwells Christians.

The Spirit of Christ and the Spirit of God indwell Christians. Romans 8:9-10: *But ye are not in the flesh, but in the Spirit, if so be that the Spirit of God dwell in you. Now if any man have not the Spirit of Christ, he is none of his. And if Christ be in you, the body is dead because of sin; but the Spirit is life because of righteousness.*

This speaks of the omnipresence of Christ. Being everywhere present is an attribute of God. Christ is bodily in heaven and sits at the right hand of the Father. His spirit also indwells millions of believers who are living on earth.

The Bible has more to say about the indwelling Holy Spirit.

Romans 8:11: *But if the Spirit of him that raised up Jesus from the dead dwell in you, he that raised up Christ from the dead shall also quicken your mortal bodies by his Spirit that dwelleth in you.*

Apparently both the Holy Spirit and the Spirit of Christ indwell Christians.

7. Who raised Jesus from the dead? The Holy Spirit raised up Jesus from the dead.[219]

Paul said God raised Jesus from the dead.

Romans 10:9: *That if thou shalt confess with thy mouth the Lord Jesus, and shalt believe in thine heart that God hath raised him from the dead, thou shalt be saved.*

According to Jesus' own words He was able to raise Himself from the dead.

John 10:17-18: *Therefore doth my Father love me, because I lay down my life, that I might take it again. No man taketh it from me, but I lay it down of myself. I have power to lay it down, and I have power to take it again. This commandment have I received of my Father.*

Therefore, if God raised Jesus from the dead, the Holy Spirit raised Jesus from the dead, and Jesus Himself had power to raise Himself from the dead, we have the three Persons of God Who were active in the resurrection.

If Jesus had the power to raise Himself from the dead, could he have done so if His total essence were dead? He gave up His spirit; His body died. In that condition He had the power to raise Himself from the dead.

8. Jesus is called *Lord*.

The Greek word *kurios* is equivalent to the English word *Lord*. It can mean a human lord or the Lord God Almighty. The Greek Septuagint Bible is a translation of the Hebrew Old Testament made in about 250 B.C. Because 70 scholars translated it, the Septuagint in theological literature often is abbreviated "LXX".

In the LXX, the Bible most used and most quoted during Jesus' earthly ministry, the Tetragrammaton is translated *kurios*. The New Testament was written in *koine* or "common" Greek, the language spoken in the marketplaces and among neighbors, and written in personal letters. In the Greek New Testament, God is called *kurios*. Human lords are also called *kurios*. Jesus and writers of the New Testament quoted from the LXX more than they did from the Hebrew Scriptures.

Therefore, in the Greek New Testament, just as in English, the context must determine whether we are talking about a human lord or the Lord God.

The salvation confession surely doesn't mean Jesus is just a human lord.

> *. . . confess with thy mouth the Lord Jesus, and shalt believe in thine heart that God hath raised him from the dead, thou shalt be saved.*[244]

This Scripture suggests that we must confess that Jesus is *the* Lord. Look at other translations:

> *That if you confess with your mouth Jesus as Lord, and believe in your heart that God raised Him from the dead, you shall be saved* (NASV, RSV).

Appendix B: Understanding the Trinity

> *If you openly admit by your own mouth that Jesus Christ is the Lord, and if you believe in your own heart that God raised him from the dead, you will be saved* (PHILLIPS).

> *If on your lips is the confession, "Jesus is Lord", and in your heart the faith that God raised him from the dead, then you will find salvation* (NEB).

To receive salvation a person must confess that Jesus Christ is Lord. What kind of lord? Certainly not just a human lord or angelic lord. Christ is the LORD.

9. The Sabbath is the LORD's. But Jesus is the Lord of the Sabbath.[246]

If Christ were not God, He would be usurping the authority of God by assuming lordship over the Sabbath.

In many places in the New Testament, Jesus is simply called *the Lord*.

Before Christ's triumphal entry into Jerusalem, which fulfilled an Old Testament prophecy concerning the LORD, He told His disciples to get a colt on which He was to ride because, He said, *The Lord hath need of them. . ..*[247] The prophecy was concerning the coming of the LORD, Jehovah. Jesus fulfilled that prophecy, and called Himself, the Lord (using the same Greek word used for both Lord and LORD).

Before He was born, Jesus was called *the Lord*.
Luke 2:11: *For unto you is born this day in the city of David a Saviour, which is Christ the Lord.*
Jesus is the same LORD Isaiah prophesied to appear. Isaiah 40:3: *The voice of him that crieth in the wilderness, Prepare ye the way of the LORD, make straight in the desert a highway for our God.*
John the Baptist clearly was the one Isaiah wrote about—the forerunner of Messiah. Zacharias, father of John the Baptist, rec-

ognized that his son would be the forerunner prophesied by Isaiah. *And thou, child, shalt be called the prophet of the Highest: for thou shalt go before the face of the Lord to prepare his ways;*[248] Matthew said John the Baptist was a fulfillment of Isaiah's prophecy, . . . *Prepare ye the way of the Lord, make his paths straight.*[249] The Gospel of Mark says the same. *The voice of one crying in the wilderness, Prepare ye the way of the Lord, make his paths straight.*[250] Luke did likewise. *As it is written in the book of the words of Esaias the prophet, saying, The voice of one crying in the wilderness, Prepare ye the way of the Lord, make his paths straight.*[251]

The LXX's Isaiah translates the Tetragrammaton *kurios* the same as in the New Testament. *Kurio* is Jesus Christ the Lord—the same LORD spoken of by Isaiah.

Jesus Christ is Lord. He always was Lord. He laid aside the free exercise of His power and was sent to earth—born a human baby in a barn. He lived a life of humility. Our human weaknesses were His. He was tempted in every way as we are, yet He did not sin. He demonstrated that He was the Messiah by doing miracles. He was resurrected from the dead, the final proof.

Seeing His humanity, the religious leaders choked on His deity. When Christ declared His deity, nonbelievers tried to stone Him.

"How could the Lord Jesus call the Father 'God', if Jesus Himself is God? How can God have a God?" Jesus called the Father *God* and *Lord*. The Father also called Jesus *God* and *Lord*.

The writer of the Book of Hebrews quotes God, Who is speaking of the Son, Christ.

Hebrews 1:9-10: *Thou hast loved righteousness, and hated iniquity; therefore God, even thy God, hath anointed thee with the oil of gladness above thy fellows. And, Thou, Lord, in the beginning hast laid the foundation of the earth; and the heavens are the works of thine hands.*

The writer of Hebrews quoted Psalm 45:6-7, *Thy throne, O God, is for ever and ever: the sceptre of thy kingdom is a right sceptre. Thou lovest righteousness, and hatest wickedness: there-*

fore God, thy God, hath anointed thee with the oil of gladness above thy fellows.

The LORD, *Yahweh*, Jehovah, calls Messiah the LORD (*Yahweh*, Jehovah).

The Prophet Jeremiah spoke of the coming Messiah and called Him *The LORD our Righteousness.*[252]

Like Thomas we can say to Jesus, *My Lord and my God.* We can understanding as Paul did that Christ was . . .*manifest in the flesh, justified in the Spirit, seen of angels, preached unto the Gentiles, believed on in the world, received up into glory.*[253]

Both the Old Testament and the New Testament assume the Messiah to be deity. Since Jehovah is the only God, Messiah must be God. Yet He prayed to the Father and was dependent on the Holy Spirit for power to do miracles during His humility. So Messiah was a personality distinct from the Father and the Holy Spirit. Yet God is one. The only solution to the seeming paradox is the Christian doctrine of the Trinity.

Trinity Part 3

The Holy Spirit is God.

In the Old Testament we see the Holy Spirit emanating from God as did the *arm of the Lord.* A man has a spirit and an arm, but neither of these has a separate personality. As previously demonstrated, Christ, also known as the *arm of the Lord*, the Logos, the Mystery of Godliness, the Messiah, has a separate personality from God the Father, yet is one with Him.

Likewise the Holy Spirit is one with God. We will see that the Spirit of the Lord, the Holy Spirit, also has personality. But first look at some of the Scriptures that indicate an emanating Spirit, much like the *arm of the Lord.*

The Holy Spirit was given to empower and bless people in the Old Testament. These verses indicate that the Holy Spirit is connected with God, and like the *arm of the Lord*, is God.

In Psalm 51:11 David said, . . . *take not thy holy spirit from me.*

Isaiah said . . . *where is He that put his holy Spirit within him?*[254]

Likewise in the New Testament, the Holy Spirit was given. Certainly this Spirit was of God, although as yet personality is not yet indicated.

Jesus said, *If ye then, being evil, know how to give good gifts unto your children: how much more shall your Heavenly Father give the Holy Spirit to them that ask him?*[255]

The apostle Paul said believers are . . . *sealed with that holy Spirit of promise.*[256]

The Holy Spirit has personality
Can a nonperson be vexed?
Isaiah 63:10: *But they rebelled, and vexed his holy Spirit . . . .* The word translated *vexed* means "provoked, grieved" or "moved emotionally". You can't vex an electrical current. Whatever is vexed must have personality, or it can't be vexed, provoked, grieved, or moved emotionally.

Can a nonperson lead?
And Jesus being full of the Holy Ghost returned from Jordan, and was led by the Spirit into the wilderness.[257]

The apostle Paul said, no *man speaking by the Spirit of God calleth Jesus accursed: and that no man can say that Jesus is the Lord, but by the Holy Ghost.*[258]

If a man leads a donkey with a rope, is the man or the rope leading the donkey? The rope may be the instrument, but the man leads. The Spirit was not an impersonal instrument such as a rope that led Jesus into the wilderness. The Word of God says the Spirit led Jesus. An impersonal object or force can't lead.

Appendix B: Understanding the Trinity

The Holy Spirit leads people to speak the truth that "Jesus is the Lord." This indicates personality rather than impersonal instrumentality.

Can a nonperson be grieved?

Paul said, *And grieve not the holy Spirit of God, whereby ye are sealed unto the day of redemption.*[259]

An impersonal influence, instrument, or electrical current cannot be grieved. Christians during bad behavior grieve the Holy Spirit. This more than indicates personality; it demands it. The Holy Spirit is a person. That doesn't mean He has a body like a man. It means He has a personality.

Can a nonperson be lied to?

Peter said Ananias had lied to the Holy Spirit.[260]

The Holy Spirit has a mind.

Romans 8:27: *And he that searcheth the hearts knoweth what is the mind of the Spirit, because he maketh intercession for the saints according to the will of God.*

Acts 15:28: *For it seemed good to the Holy Ghost, and to us, to lay upon you no greater burden than these necessary things.*

An influence or an energy field cannot have a mind. The Holy Spirit not only has a mind but a will and compassion to make intercession for the saints.

How could a mindless influence "seem" with the disciples and James to lay no legalistic burden on Gentile Christians?

The Holy Spirit gives spiritual gifts.

First Corinthians 12:8: *For to one is given by the Spirit the word of wisdom; to another the word of knowledge by the same Spirit.*

The Holy Spirit can be insulted.

Hebrews 10:29: *Of how much sorer punishment, suppose ye, shall he be thought worthy, who hath trodden under foot the Son of God, and hath counted the blood of the covenant, wherewith he was sanctified, an unholy thing, and hath done despite unto the Spirit of grace?*

The Holy Spirit can be blasphemed.

Matthew 12:31: *. . . All manner of sin and blasphemy shall be forgiven unto men: but the blasphemy against the Holy Ghost shall not be forgiven unto men.*

Jesus spoke of the Holy Spirit as a person.

John 14:26: *But the Comforter, which is the Holy Ghost, whom the Father will send in my name, he shall teach you all things, and bring all things to your remembrance, whatsoever I have said unto you.*

John 15:26: *But when the Comforter is come, whom I will send unto you from the Father, even the Spirit of truth, which proceedeth from the Father, he shall testify of me.*

John 16:7: *Nevertheless I tell you the truth; It is expedient for you that I go away: for if I go not away, the Comforter will not come unto you; but if I depart, I will send him unto you.*

John 16:13: *. . . when he, the Spirit of truth, is come, he will guide you into all truth . . ..*

In the Greek language words have gender—male or female—or are neuter. The Greek word for *spirit* is the same as the word for *breath* or *wind* and is neuter. Therefore, most of the time, to be grammatically correct, even the Holy Spirit is spoken of in the neuter gender. However, Jesus chose to use the masculine pronoun, *He,* anyway. This emphasizes the personality of the Holy Spirit.

Certainly Jesus thought of the Holy Spirit as a person. The Bible declares Him to be a person. The Holy Spirit took Jesus' place on earth and now dwells in the bodies of Christians.

The *Comforter* means "one who stands by your side" as a lawyer would. The Holy Spirit is our *Comforter.* In 1 John 2:1 this same word is used for Jesus: *My little children, these things write I unto you, that ye sin not. And if any man sin, we have an advocate with the Father, Jesus Christ the righteous.* This is as if Jesus were our lawyer, standing beside us and pleading our case. The same is true of the Holy Spirit. Lawyers have to be persons.

The Holy Spirit is God.

Peter, in his rebuke to Ananias, said, . . . *thou hast not lied unto men, but unto God.*

Trinity Part 4

Only One God Exists.

When people disagree, they often express their opponent's position in gross distortion. So if you want to find out what someone believes, ask the person and not his opponent. His opponent might set up a "straw man".

For example if you ask a Unitarian what Trinitarians believe, he might say, "They believe in three gods." If you ask a Jehovah's Witness what Christians believe, he might say, "They believe in a monstrous, three-headed god."

Both of these "straw men" are easily knocked down.

Rescuing Slaves of the Watchtower

For the first 200 years of the Christian church no difficulty with the doctrine of the trinity arose. Arius of Alexandria (A.D. 253-336) believed God the Father to be the only deity and that the Son and Holy Spirit were created beings. Arius believed Christ was called God because He is next in rank to God and was endowed with divine power to create. This caused a theological furor. Arius was condemned by a council in Nice in A.D. 325. Such condemnation never has yet stopped a doctrine, be it true or false. By A.D. 359 "Arianism", as the doctrine now was called, grew to be accepted in a great number of churches in the Roman Empire.[261] But Arianism died a natural death, as theologians and believers concluded that it contradicted Scripture.

Over a millennium later a man named Faustus Socinus (1539-1604) demoted Christ further than had Arius. Socinus taught that Christ was just a man. He also denied Christ's atonement for our sins. Socinus emphasized human reason and deemphasized the supernatural. This was the beginning of Unitarianism.[262]

Both the Arians and Socinians believed that Christ was to be worshiped.[263] However, Unitarianism evolved into denying worship to Christ and then to considering Him a mere man.

When I was in seminary, I thought learning about the many heresies that had developed in the past 2,000 years was a waste of time. *Why learn all that error? Why not just stick with the truth?* I later realized that we need to learn about past errors so as not to repeat them. Modern cultists Charles Taze Russell and Herbert W. Armstrong thought they had discovered something new and exciting. They did not realize the tired old heresy had been tried and found wanting. .

A scribe had heard Jesus talking to the Sadducees; He was explaining that God was the God of the living, not of the dead. The scribe, necessarily a man learned in the Scriptures, asked Jesus what was the greatest commandment. Many times scribes or lawyers asked Jesus questions as they tried to trap him. Al-

Appendix B: Understanding the Trinity

though this scribe apparently knew the answer, he was carrying on a serious conversation, as indicated by Jesus' response.

Matthew 22:37: *Jesus said unto him, Thou shalt love the Lord thy God with all thy heart, and with all thy soul, and with all thy mind.*

Part of that greatest commandment involved a right belief. We must believe in but one God—one LORD.

First Timothy 2:5: *For there is one God, and one mediator between God and men, the man Christ Jesus.* We have only one way of reaching that one God; that is through Jesus Christ.

John 14:6: *. . . no man cometh unto the Father, but by me.*

John 3:36: *He that believeth on the Son hath everlasting life: and he that believeth not the Son shall not see life; but the wrath of God abideth on him.*

Just believing in the existence of God is not enough. Believing in the existence of Christ is not enough. We must believe in Christ, which involves commitment to Him. Loving God as stated in the Greatest Commandment involves aligning with Him on His terms, which is through Jesus Christ. When we love God with all our heart, soul, mind, and strength, we love Christ. When we love Christ with all our heart, soul, mind, and strength, we love God.

The deity of Messiah in the Old Testament is obvious; it also is found in the New Testament. To reconcile this and still deny the trinity, Arius and some of his modern counterparts have suggested that Christ is some kind of a lesser God. This is in direct contradiction to Scripture.

Deuteronomy 4:35: *. . . the LORD He is God; there is none else beside him.*

First Kings 8:60: *. . . the LORD is God, and that there is none else.*

First Corinthians 8:6: *But to us there is but one God, the Father blotteth out thy transgressions for mine own sake, and will not remember thy sins.*

Without the doctrine of the trinity we would find a terrible contradiction with the New Testament.

Ephesians 4:32: *. . . even as God for Christ's sake hath forgiven you.*

The LORD forgives sin for His own sake. God forgives sins for Christ's sake. No contradiction is there, because the LORD God and Christ are one.

Without the doctrine of the trinity the Unitarians would be right in forbidding worship to Jesus, a mere human being. The Arians would have been wrong to worship a lesser God.

Exodus 34:14: *For thou shalt worship no other god: for the LORD, whose name is Jealous, is a jealous God.*

The scriptural evidence overwhelms claims against worshiping Christ and even requires it. Therefore, we worship one God. We worship the Father, the Son, and the Holy Spirit—three Persons but one essence.

Ephesians 4:4-5: *There is one body, and one Spirit, even as ye are called in one hope of your calling; One Lord, one faith, one baptism, 6 One God and Father of all, who is above all, and through all, and in you all.*

A person doesn't have to have a body to be a person.

Some people can't imagine a person apart from a human body. God is a person, but He is spirit.

The devil is a person, but he does not have a body like a human being.[264] In the Garden of Eden he manifested Himself as a serpent and in Babylon as a king.[265] The devil was personified as Judas and will be personified as Antichrist.[266]

The devil is not a human body, although he has taken those forms. Yet the devil is a person.

God is not a human body, although He has taken forms of an Angel of the Lord, and as Jesus Christ. Yet God the Father is a person, as is God the Holy Spirit.

God is spoken of as three persons. Second Corinthians 13:14: *The grace of the Lord Jesus Christ, and the love of God, and the communion of the Holy Ghost, be with you all. Amen.*

The Matthew 28:19 baptismal formula names all three: . . . *baptizing them in the name of the Father, and of the Son, and of the Holy Ghost.*

The Great Commission assumes the Trinity.[267] We are to baptize not in the *names* but in the *name* of the Father, Son, and Holy Spirit. We baptize in the authority, with the authorization of, the one God.

Understanding the Trinity

Conclusion

What constitutes our nation may help to illustrate the trinity. What is the United States of America?

Is it a population of more than 300 million people? Yes.

Is it land from shining sea to shining sea with islands beyond? Yes.

Is it a government? Yes.

How many U.S.'s are there? The population is one; the land is one; the government is one. Does that add up to three countries? No. Only one U.S. exists, but it exists in three distinct ways: people, land, and government.

The United States invaded Kuwait to wrest it from the Iraqi dictator Saddam Hussein.

Did the whole population go to Kuwait and then to Afghanistan and Iraq? No.

Did all the land of the 50 states go? No.

Did all the government go? No.

Only a small part of the population went, but that expeditionary force went with the full authority of the U.S.; it went in the name of the U.S. The U.S. was in Kuwait, Afghanistan, and Iraq.

Did the U.S. have to abandon its homeland to go to Kuwait, Afghanistan, and Iraq? No. The U.S. at the same time was in

Kuwait, Afghanistan, Iraq, Alaska, Hawaii, and the Continental 48, plus Western Europe, South Korea, and many other places.

Can the U.S. be in more than one place at one time? Yes.

Does the U.S. have more than one personality? Yes—more like 300 million personalities. We have three branches of the government: legislative, judicial, and executive. Each of the three carries the authority—the name of the U.S.

Congress speaks in the name of the U.S.

The U.S. Supreme Court speaks in the name of the U.S.

The President speaks in the name of the U.S.

How many U.S.'s are there? Congress is one; the Supreme Court is one; the executive administration is one. Does that mean three U.S.'s exist? No. The three distinct branches of the government, with different personalities and functions, make up one indivisible government and not three governments.

Just as the U.S. went on a mission to Kuwait, Afghanistan, and Iraq, God, in the Person of Jesus Christ, was sent to earth. God still was in heaven on the throne, just as the U.S. government still was in Washington, and just like all the U.S. land still was in its place.

When Jesus Christ was in humility on the earth and was doing the Father's will, God still was omnipresent on every planet, star, and asteroid in the universe. While the U.S. was in Kuwait, Afghanistan, and Iraq, Americans were in every other nation as well. They were there as tourists, business travelers, resident aliens, members of the U.S. armed forces, and diplomats representing our country.

Just as the U.S. military forces hit the Taliban and Saddam Hussein's armies with modern, sophisticated weapons and overwhelming air superiority, so the Holy Spirit empowered Jesus—hearing His prayers and enabling Him to do miracles. (Remember that Jesus laid aside His power in heaven to arrive on the earth in humility.)

The U.S. in Kuwait, Afghanistan, and Iraq was in constant communication with the U.S. homeland. Jesus, while on earth, prayed often to God in heaven.

Appendix B: Understanding the Trinity

The U.S. at home dearly loved the U.S. abroad; the U.S. there dearly loved the U.S. at home. They were one. Jesus loved the Father; the Father loved Him. They are one.

Appendix C

An Objective Look at Cults

Mormonism

Once a person has been rescued from the Watchtower, he can see the similarity between it and other cults.

Mormonism has a homemade Jesus who has little resemblance to the biblical Jesus. Mormons teach that Jesus was a spirit brother of Satan and that He lived on a remote planet with the Father, a God who once was a human being. The Father asked for a plan of redemption for people on the faraway planet Earth; both Jesus and Satan proposed one. The Father favored Jesus' plan over Satan's, so Satan got sore and rebelled.

To Mormons, Jesus is just one of many gods along with the Father, the Holy Spirit, and the Holy Ghost. They teach that "As man now is, God once was. As God now is, man may become." If you ask a Mormon, he will tell you that he believes in only one God, the Father. But ask how many gods exist. He will tell you millions. Each god the Father used to be a man and was so good he became a god—and his father was the same way, and so was his father, and his father, and on and on millions of times stretching back into infinity. Mormons don't believe in an infinite God; they believe in an infinite number of gods.

Joseph Smith, whom Mormons believe was a true prophet of God, made many false prophecies.

Like the Watchtower, Mormons get "new light" from heaven and change the rules. Polygamy was practiced by Mormons until they needed to achieve statehood for Utah. Polygamy didn't wash with the rest of the country, so the 12 Mormon Apostles got new light that polygamy no longer was allowed, so Utah could join the United States. Mormons once prohibited dark-skinned people from becoming Mormon bishops until social pressure became so great that in 1979 they got *new light* from heaven that blacks were OK to become bishops.

Mormons believe in three levels of heaven. The top heaven is for light-complexioned (which indicates they were valiant warriors in a previous life) Mormons who have been obedient to all the temple rituals. The middle heaven is for good Mormons. The bottom heaven is for other good people. Hell is reserved for Mormons who have left the faith; these they call *apostates*.

In the top Mormon heaven a man is eligible to earn his own planet and harem of wives to repopulate the planet so he can become a father god.

Mormonism has more in common with Greek paganism than it does with Christianity. The Mormons have dressed up their gods as though they were Christians and have given them biblical names, but that doesn't make them Christian.

Armstrongism

Herbert W. Armstrong's World Wide Church of God was greatly influenced by Jehovah's Witnesses and Seventh-Day Adventists.

After Armstrong's death his church split. The church's new president, Joseph W. Tkach, led the church out of its cultish doctrines and established it as a Christian church. Others, however, split off and continued Armstrong's cultish beliefs. These included such things as:

God is a family, not trinity—a false, pagan concept.

Appendix C: An Objective Look at Cults

The Holy Spirit is not considered a person but the power through which the Father and the Son work.

Jesus was not God in the beginning but became a son of God and part of the godhead when He was resurrected from the dead. Thus at the time of the resurrection, all members of humanity who believe in God instantly shall be changed and become part of the God family and thus God.

Armstrongites believe the blood of Christ saves people only from the death penalty of sin. To be saved one must be baptized and receive the Holy Spirit through the laying-on of hands. One is not truly born again until the resurrection, when that person attains immortality and becomes part of the God Family.

Armstrongites deny the existence of hell. When one dies, his mind, body, and soul also die. They believe adherents will be resurrected and will become part of the God Family.

Like Seventh-Day Adventists, Armstrongites meet on Saturday and observe dietary laws.

These cults may seem crazy. But they can be as crazy as they want, since they make up their own rules and change them in the middle of the game. In that respect the Watchtower is like the rest.

Rastafarians

Rastafarians, mentioned in chapter 4, *The Truth about the Watchtower's Custom-Made Bible,* don't claim to be Christians, but they use the Watchtower's NWT Bible and have adopted some of its language. When you see someone with long hair twisted into long strands that wildly protrude in every direction, it's either a *Rasta man* or a lookalike who probably doesn't know the significance of the *dreadlocks.*

Rastafarians, like other cultists, have redefined the Bible to suit themselves. For example they don't believe in "everlasting life", because they say "Everlasting life doesn't last." They believe in "ever-living life" that just keeps on going.

A real, committed Rastafarian smokes Ganja, "holy herb" (marijuana or hashish), and regularly praises Jah (one of the names of God in the Watchtower Bible) and Ras Tafari, the late Haile Selassie, former emperor of Ethiopia. The Rasta man believes Haile Selassie, the Christ, will be resurrected. And the Rasta man believes he never will die. When an elderly Rastafarian dies, the fellow believers are shocked to realize the deceased must have had some secret sin; otherwise he wouldn't have died.

Rastafarians keep promising each other they will live forever, but they keep on dying anyway. Their failed promises are much like those of the Cargo Cult and the Watchtower Society.

Moonies

When I was pastor in Richardson, a florist delivered to my office a beautiful bouquet of flowers. It contained an invitation to a meeting of pastors of different denominations. I learned that every pastor in the Dallas area had received flowers. The invitation was to a meeting conducted by Sun Myung Moon, head of the Unification Church.

Billionaire Sun Myung Moon spent a fortune trying to lead Christian churches into some kind of alliance with him. Few accepted the offer.

We don't hear as much about the followers of Sun Myung Moon as we did several years ago. This probably is because his Unification Church controls so much news media, including United Press International and *The Washington Times*.

Moon believes Christ failed in His earthly mission and that Moon himself is the Second Advent Christ who is destined to rule the world. He believes his family is the holy family and has qualities of deity. His second son, Heung-Jim Moon, died after an auto accident in 1984. Moon proclaimed his dead son to be king of the Spirits in heaven.

Typical of other cults, the Moonies believe they have exclusive truth, all the answers, and the only way to God. Something else Moon has in common with the Watchtower: he has loads of money but lots of people work for him for nothing.

Appendix D

The Word

John 1:1 from Greek New Testaments

Westcott and Hort, 1881

εν αρχη   ην   ο λογος και ο   λογος ην προς τον θεον
'In-beginning was the Word and the Word was with the God

και   θεος ην   ο λογος
and God was the Word'

Scriviner New Testament 1894

1εν αρχη   ην ο   λογος και ο λογος   ην προς τον θεον
'In-beginning was the Word and the Word was with the God

και θεος ην ο   λογος
and God was the Word'

Rescuing Slaves of the Watchtower

Stephanas New Testament, 1550

1εν αρχη ην ο λογος και ο λογος ην προς τον
'In beginning was the Word and the Word was with the

θεον και θεος ην ο λογος
God and God was the Word'

The various Greek New Testaments agree on John 1:1. The Watchtower uses the Westcott and Hort Greek New Testament for *The Kingdom Interlinear Translation of the Greek Scripture* (Watchtower Bible and Tract Society, New York 1969 by New World Bible Translation Committee).

The interlinear portion on the left column of the Interlinear is faithful to the original translation as that above. However, in the right-hand column the Watchtower translation is quite different:

In [the] beginning the Word was, and the Word was with God, and the Word was a god.

The Watchtower translators put in brackets added words, such as [the], above. However, the indefinite article *a* in . . . *the Word was a god* is treated as if it were in the original Greek.

Word order in Greek sentences often is different from word order in English. However, the Greeks had a means of emphasis that we don't use in English. To emphasize a phrase we might put it in boldface type or italic type or maybe underline the word or put it in all capital letters. The original Koine Greek New Testament had no such devices. Rather the text was written in all capital letters without punctuation and without space between words.

To emphasize a word or a phrase the Greeks put it last in the sentence. John's emphasis in the first chapter of his gospel is . . . *the Word was God*. We might have emphasized it thusly: . . . *the WORD WAS GOD*.

Appendix D: The Word

Inserting the rogue *a* obviously is a dishonest attempt to distort the clearly revealed Word of God. The NWT translation committee, uneducated in Greek, has chosen to overrule Greek scholars who have spent lifetimes studying the language.

Another attempt to demote Christ is seen in the Watchtower's departure from all the three Greek New Testaments quoted above by translating προς (*pros*) *toward* God instead of *with* God. That translation is not without basis. *Pros* could be translated *toward*. However, the best translation is *with*. A. T. Robertson's *Grammar of the Greek New Testament* (Broadman Press, Nashville 1934) on page 623 says:

"'Near' rather than 'towards' seems to explain the resultant meaning more satisfactorily. The idea seems to be 'facing'. . . In ο λογος ην προς τον θεον (John 1:1) the literal idea comes out well, 'face to face' with God.'"

This is but another example of the WT Society's attempt to muddy the water about the deity of Christ and to cover plagiarism by frequent use of synonyms.

Additional Resources

Hewitt, Joe, *I Was Raised A Jehovah's Witness*, Accent Book, Denver 1979 and Kregel Publishing, Grand Rapids 1997.

Magnani, Duane, *The Watchtower Files*, Bethany, Minneapolis 1983.

Martin, Walter R., *The Kingdom of the Cults*, Bethany, Minneapolis 1965.

Countess, Robert H., *The Jehovah's Witnesses' New Testament*, Presbyterian and Reformed, Phillipsburg, NJ 1982.

Franz, Raymond, Crisis of Conscience, Commentary Press, Atlanta 1983.

Gruss, Edmond C., *We Left Jehovah's Witnesses a Non-Prophet Organization*, Presbyterian and Reformed, Phillipsburg, NJ 1974.

Schnell, William J., *Thirty Years a Watchtower Slave*.

Trombley, Charles, *Kicked Out of the Kingdom*, Whitaker House, Monroeville, PA 1974.

Ortega, Helen and Joe, New Light Ministries, PO Box 670751 Marietta, AR 30066.

Ex-Jehovah's Witnesses for Jesus annual convention each October at New Ringgold, PA. Contact Joan Cetnar, RD 3 Weir Lake Road, Kunkletown, PA 18058.

Christian Apologetics Ministry, *www.carm.org*

Child Custody Consultation, JWCC, 800-762-9227. (This organization assists families in child custody fights against Jehovah's Witnesses.)

http://exjehovahswitnessforum.yuku.com

www.freeminds.org

Official Watchtower website, *www.watchtower.org*

Jansma, Nils and Sherry, *www.exJW's.net*

Macgregor, Keith and Lorri, MM Ministries, *http://mmoutreach-inc.com/mminfo@gmail.com* Magnani, Duane, *www.christian-witnesses.com*

Reed, David, Witness for Jesus, Inc., *http://4jehovah.org*

Watchman Fellowship, a national counter cult and apologetics ministry, *www.watchman.org*

Watters, Randy, *www.freeminds.org*

Witness Incorporated, *www.witnessinc.com*, *jwbooks@sbcglobal.net*

Glossary of Terms

Term	Watchtower's Definition
Antichrist	All Christian pastors
Apostate	A former JW
Babylon the Great	Any faith or religion apart from the Jehovah's Witnesses
Bethel	Watchtower Society Headquarters in Brooklyn
Bethelite	A non-salaried worker at Bethel
Circuit Overseer	Salaried supervisor over several Kingdom Hall congregations
Congregational Overseer	Equivalent of a pastor, although he is not paid
Disfellowshiped	Same as excommunicated; a JW who is shunned
District Overseer	Salaried supervisor of several circuits

Elders	Governors of the local Kingdom Hall, equivalent to elders in a church with Presbyterian form of church government
Goat	Anyone who rejects the Watchtower teachings
Governing Body	Group that is in charge of the Watchtower Society. Members: Carey W. Barber, John E. Barr, Samuel Herd, Theodore Jaracz, M. Stephen Lett, Garrit Loesch, Guy Pierce, Albert D. Schroeder, David Splane, Daniel Sydlik[268]
In a sense	This is the Jehovah's Witnesses' way of saying something means other than what it says
In The Truth	An active Jehovah's Witness in good standing
Jonadabs	Same as the other sheep; not eligible for heaven
Judicial Committee	Group of Elders who put JW's on trial
Kingdom Hall	The place in which a local congregation of JW's meets
Ministerial Servants	Equivalent of Deacons, each with specific responsibility
New Light	Doctrinal changes from heaven given through the Society
NWT	(New World Translation of the Holy Scriptures) The Watchtower Bible

Glossary of Terms

Other Sheep	JW's who can't go to heaven but hope to live eternally on earth
Pioneer	Full-time worker (not paid but allowed to make a small profit on literature sales)
Public Talk	What others would call a sermon
Publicly Reproved	A person who has been publicly disciplined by the elders
Publisher	An active, baptized JW who witnesses at least 10 hours a month
Reinstated	One who has been disfellowshiped and is received back
Required Weekly Meetings	*Book study* (Usually in the home of a prospect)
	Ministry School (Instruction and role play for door-to-door and speaking)
	Service Meetings (Instructions from Bethel, Watchtower Headquarters)
	Public lecture (Weekly sermon)
	Watchtower Study (Group study, article in the Watchtower magazine)
The Anointed	Members of the 144,000; JW's who go to heaven
The Little Flock	Same as The Anointed; the 144,000 who go to heaven
The Elect	Same as The Anointed and The Little Flock, the 144,000
The Society	The Watchtower Society headquartered in Brooklyn, NY

Theocratic School	Training program for door-to-door witnessing and public speaking
Theocratic	An adjective describing an enthusiastic and obedient JW
Unspiritual	A weak JW
Untheocratic	A weak JW
Watchtower Society	Mailing Address: Watchtower, 25 Columbia Heights, Brooklyn, NY 11201-2483
Watchtower Study	Weekly meeting during which the Watchtower magazine is studied
Worldly Person	Anyone who is not a Jehovah's Witness in good standing
Zone Overseer	Salaried supervisor of several Districts

References

[1] Canada Library of Parliament, Research Branch, report by Susan Alter, Law and Government Division
[2] Randall Watters, *My Story*, Part 1
[3] Love and Norris, Attorneys at Law, 314 Main Street, Suite 300, Fort Worth, TX 76102. *www.lovenorrisattorneys.com*
[4] Matthew 8:9-10
[5] Luke 3:14
[6] Acts 10:1-48
[7] Acts 26:14
[8] John 8:44
[9] Revelation 21:8
[10] David Reed's Website, Comments from the Friends, *http://www.cftf.com/online/main.html*
[11] Watch Tower Bible and Tract Society of Pennsylvania, 1969, 1971, *Aid to Bible Understanding*, page 1060
[12] Watchtower's official website: *www.Watchtower.org/e/jt/article_08.htm*
[13] Watchtower Official Website, *www.watchtower.org/e/jt/article_08.htm*
[14] According to the New York and Pennsylvania Secretary of State offices, these are the Watchtower corporations with dates of formation: Watchtower Bible and Tract Society of New York, Inc., a Domestic Not-For-Profit Corporation, formed March 4, 1909, in Putnam County, NY; Watchtower Associates, Ltd., a domestic

business corporation, formed July 22, 1966, in Nassau County, NY; Watchtower Enterprises, L.L.C., a Domestic Limited Liability Company, formed March 29, 2002, in Kings County, NY; Watchtower Foundation, Inc., a Domestic Limited Liability Company, formed April 12, 2002, in Kings County, NY; Watchtower Ventures, Inc., a Foreign Business Corporation, formed in Nassau County March 7, 2007, with jurisdiction in Nevada. Watchtower Bible and Tract Society of Florida, Inc., formed February 11, 2008, in Putnam County, NY. According to the Pennsylvania Department of State, the Watch Tower Bible and Tract Society of Pennsylvania, was incorporated as a non-profit, non-stock company, October 7, 1955, and is headquartered in Coraopolis, PA. The Watchtower Bible and Tract Society of New York was also incorporated in Pennsylvania as a non-profit, non-stock, foreign corporation on June 22, 2000, with addresses in Coraopolis, PA, and Brooklyn, NY. According to Wikipedia, the online encyclopedia, the following are also Watchtower corporations: Christian Congregation of Jehovah's Witnesses, incorporated in New York in 2000; Religious Order of Jehovah's Witnesses, incorporated in New York in 2000; and Kingdom Support Services, incorporated in New York in 2000

[15] Watchtower Official Website, *www.watchtower.org/e/jt/article_07.htm*

[16] *http://en.wikipedia.org/wiki/Governing_Body_of_Jehovah's_Witnesses*

[17] Wikipedia the Internet Encyclopedia, *http://en.wikipedia.org/wiki/Watchtower_Bible_and_Tract_Society_of_New_York#Revenue*

[18] DUMBO: A business and industrial area in Brooklyn, "Down Under Manhattan Bridge Overpass"

[19] Rich Calder in *The New York Post*, May 14, 2007, quoted in http://www.rickross.com/reference/jw/jw295.html

[20] *http://www.jehovahs-witness.net/jw/friends/53692/1/WTBS-Financial-Empire*

[21] Harold Farber in *The New York Times*, April 7, 1991, quoted in *http://www.rickross.com/reference/jw/jw76.html*

[22] *The Dallas Morning News*, August 15, 2009, page 1-A

[23] Matthew 19:29

[24] John 1:12-13

[25] Isaiah 7:14

[26] Isaiah 53:1-5

References

27. John 14:1-4
28. Jay Walker, *My Six-Year Journey out of the Watchtower,* Chapter 5, E-book at *www.xJW's.net/pioneers*
29. Personal interview with Dr. Julius Mantey, New Ringgold, PA, 1983
30. *http://www.carm.org/jw/false_prophecies.htm*
31. January 1886, *Watchtower,* page 817
32. *The Time Is at Hand,* page 101
33. Watchtower *Reprints*, VI, April 1, 1915, page 5659
34. *The Watchtower*, April 1, 1972, page 197
35. Deuteronomy 18:22
36. *Millions Now Living Will Never Die,* pages 97 and 105
37. *Life,* pages 170, 332
38. *Light,* II, page 327
39. Matthew 25:1-13
40. *Vindication, I,* page 147
41. Franz, Raymond, *Crisis of Conscience,* Commentary Press, Atlanta, 1983
42. *Salvation,* pages 310, 361
43. The Watchtower, September 1, 1940, 265
44. Matthew 7:15-16
45. Jeremiah 25:11
46. Isaiah 7:14
47. Judges 6:8
48. Matthew 7:21-23
49. Matthew 15:32
50. Matthew 25:34-46
51. James 1:27
52. Matthew 9:36
53. James. 5:14
54. John 20:27-29
55. Philippians 4:6
56. Luke 11:24-26
57. Acts 16:28-30
58. Acts 16:31
59. Romans 8:26, KJV
60. Mark 1:1
61. Luke 1:32
62. John 18:36
63. Matthew 5:5
64. Exodus 34:14; Nehemiah 9:6; Psalm 29:2
65. Psalm 5:7; 95:6
66. Matthew 2:2, 11
67. Matthew 8:2; 9:18; 14:33; 15:25; 20:20; 28:9, 17; Mark 5:6; Luke 24:52; John 9:38
68. Hebrews 1:6
69. 2 Chronicles 7:3; 29:28
70. Exodus 20:7
71. John 14:6
72. 1 John 2:18-19
73. 1 John 2:20-22
74. Exodus 29:29
75. Matthew 28:19
76. *The Watchtower, April 1 2006,* pages 21-25
77. *The Truth that Leads to Eternal Life,* page 79
78. Matthew 8:11
79. 1 Thessalonians 4:14-17
80. Exodus 34:26; Deuteronomy 14:21
81. Firsthand knowledge spoken of by Joan Cetnar based on personal experience
82. Acts 20:28
83. Ephesians 1:7
84. Hebrews 9:14
85. *www.ajwrb.org* (Associated Jehovah's Witnesses for Reform on Blood)

[86] *http://www.ajwrb.org/experiences/mary.shtml*
[87] Genesis 9:4
[88] Leviticus 11:4
[89] Leviticus 19:19
[90] Romans 8:4; 13:8; Galatians 5:14
[91] Acts 15:24, 28,29
[92] Romans 14:1-3, 14.
[93] Luke 8:12; Acts 16:31; Romans 10:9
[94] Acts 15:11
[95] Matthew 8:11
[96] Genesis 2:7
[97] Psalms 42:2
[98] Psalms 56:13
[99] Psalms 84:2
[100] Revelation 16:3
[101] Genesis 35:18
[102] Exodus 12:15
[103] Matthew 10:28
[104] Luke 16:22-31
[105] 2 Corinthians 5:8
[106] 1 Samuel 18:1
[107] 2 Samuel 5:8
[108] Job 14:22
[109] Mark 14:34
[110] Psalm 107:26
[111] Luke 2:35
[112] 1 Kings 17:21-22
[113] Matthew 10:28
[114] Revelation 19:20; 20:10, 15
[115] 1 Thessalonians 5:10
[116] 2 Corinthians 5:8
[117] Revelation 6:9-10
[118] 1 Corinthians 15:44
[119] I Thessalonians 5:23
[120] *The Truth That Leads to Eternal Life,* page 38
[121] Genesis 1:27
[122] John 4:24
[123] John 3:6-7
[124] Proverbs 20:27
[125] 1 Corinthians 2:11
[126] John 11:33
[127] *Aid to Bible Understanding,* Watchtower Society, page 1395 pgph 3
[128] *Aid to Bible Understanding,* Watchtower Society, page 1395 pgph 4
[129] *Aid to Bible Understanding,* Watchtower Society, page 1396 pgph 1
[130] 1 Corinthians 15:12-20
[131] Gerhard Kittel, *Theological Dictionary of the New Testament,* Wm B. Eerdmans, Grand Rapids
[132] Ant., 18:14; Bell., 2, 163
[133] Matthew 22:32
[134] 2 Corinthians 5:6
[135] Hebrews 9:27
[136] Revelation 22:12
[137] Psalm 45:17
[138] Matthew 5:22
[139] Matthew 5:29, 30; 18:9; Mark 9:43, 47; Luke 12:5
[140] 2 Peter 2:4
[141] Randolph Yeager, *The Renaissance New Testament,* Pelican Press, New Orleans, Vol. 17 page 235
[142] *Reasoning From the Scriptures, Watchtower Bible and Tract Society,* page 173
[143] Mark 9:46
[144] Mark 1:23; Luke 4:14
[145] *Op cit,* page 174
[146] Psalm 72:2
[147] Psalm 89:14
[148] Psalm 103:6

References

[149] Isaiah 5:16
[150] Luke 18:7
[151] 1 John 2:22
[152] John 4:26
[153] John 10:30
[154] *Then Is Finished the Mystery of God,* page 249
[155] Deuteronomy 6:4
[156] Deuteronomy 4:35; see also Deuteronomy 6:4; 32:39. 2 Samuel 7:22; 1 Chronicles 17:20; Psalm. 83:18; 86:10; Isaiah 43:10; 44:6; 45:18; Mark 12:29; 1 Corinthians 8:4; Ephesians 4:6; 1 Timothy 2:5; 1 John 5:7
[157] Micah 5:2
[158] Isaiah 43:11
[159] Luke 1:47
[160] John 4:42
[161] Psalm 106:21; Isa. 45:15, 21
[162] Isaiah 45:22-23
[163] Romans 14:10-11
[164] Philippians 2:9-12
[165] Isaiah 49:26; 60:16
[166] Job 19:25
[167] Luke 2:11
[168] Acts 5:31
[169] Philippians 3:20; 1 Timothy 1:1; 2:3; Titus 1:3-4; 2:10, 13, and 3:4, 6; 2 Pet. 1:1, 11; 2:20; 3:2, 18
[170] John 1:1-3
[171] Exodus 20:3
[172] Exodus 3:14
[173] John 8:58
[174] Luke 2:51-52
[175] 2 Peter 3:18
[176] 1 Timothy 6:13-16; Revelation 1:7
[177] *The Watchtower,* 15 Sept., 1910, 298
[178] *The Dallas Morning News* March 31, 2008, page 1B
[179] Galatians 4:7
[180] Romans 3:23, 10
[181] Romans 10:9
[182] Matthew 6:20
[183] Luke 10:20
[184] 2 Corinthians 5:1
[185] Revelation 21:2
[186] Hebrews 12:22
[187] Luke 20:35-36
[188] Matthew 25:34
[189] James 1:13
[190] 1 John 2:22; 4:10
[191] Genesis 11:15
[192] Genesis 16:7-11
[193] Genesis 19:24
[194] Genesis 14:18-20; Psalm 110:4; Hebrews 7:1-6
[195] Genesis 32:24-30
[196] Exodus 3:7-8
[197] Matthew 1:23
[198] Isaiah 53:1-7
[199] John 10:30
[200] 1 John 4:19
[201] 1 John 1:9
[202] Job 19:25-27
[203] Matthew 5:8
[204] 1 John 3:1, 2
[205] 2 John 1:11
[206] John 1:18
[207] John 6:46
[208] Genesis 32:30
[209] Judges 6:22-23
[210] Judges 13:20-23
[211] Hebrews 12:14
[212] Numbers 14:13-14
[213] John 4:24
[214] Colossians 1:15
[215] 1 Timothy 1:17

[216] John 5:37
[217] Genesis 32:30, Judges 6:22-23, and 13:20-22
[218] Isaiah 7:14
[219] Daniel 10:21
[220] Daniel 12:1
[221] Jude 1:9
[222] Isaiah 9:6-7
[223] Isaiah 53:1
[224] Isaiah 53:6
[225] Micah 5:2
[226] Psalm 110:4
[227] Hebrews 7:1-3
[228] John 1:1-3
[229] John 1:14
[230] John 4:26
[231] Revelation 1:11
[232] 1 Timothy 6:15
[233] Isaiah 7:14; Matthew 1:23
[234] 1 Timothy 3:16
[235] John 1:18
[236] John 14:6-11
[237] John 14:9
[238] Matthew 4:10
[239] Hebrews 1:5
[240] Hebrews 2:7, 9
[241] Matthew 2:2
[242] Matthew 28:9
[243] John 9:38
[244] Romans 8:11
[245] Romans 10:9
[246] Exodus 20:10; Matthew 12:8
[247] Matthew 21:3
[248] Luke 1:76
[249] Matthew 3:3
[250] Mark 1:3
[251] Luke 3:4
[252] Jeremiah 23:5
[253] John 20:28; 1 Timothy 3:16
[254] Isaiah 63:11
[255] Luke 11:13
[256] Ephesians 1:13
[257] Luke 4:1
[258] 1 Corinthians 12:3
[259] Ephesians 4:30
[260] Acts 5:3
[261] Job 19:25-27
[262] Funk & Wagnalls, 1983, Vol. 24 page 71
[263] *Systematic Theology*, A.H. Strong, Third Edition 1890, page 159
[264] John 8:44; 14:30; 1 John 3:8
[265] Genesis 3:1; Isaiah 14:4-22
[266] John 17:12; 2 Thessalonians 2:3
[267] Matthew 28:19-20
[268] *http://www.ajwrb.org/reform/database.shtml*

Index

144,000 16, 22, 36, 52, 117, 118, 119, 120, 141, 182, 183
1874 205
1876 176
1881 241
1886 83
1889 83
1894 83, 241
1904 83
1914 58, 76, 83, 142, 191, 192, 194, 205
1925 84, 200
1945 127, 129, 130
1975 60, 82, 83, 88, 192
1998 35, 55

A

Abraham 116, 120, 133, 134, 135, 145, 157, 159, 186, 191, 195, 196, 197, 200, 207, 220
Adam 133
Adams, Don Alden 51, 52
Adopt-a-child 95
Afghanistan 233, 234
Africa 95, 125
Aid to Bible Understanding 6, 35, 36, 139, 197
Alexandria 196, 230
America 2, 6, 20, 95, 153, 233
Ananias 227, 229
Angel of the LORD 155, 186, 208, 209, 210, 212, 232
Anointed 52, 115, 154, 213, 224, 225
anti-education 75, 77, 201
antichrist 114, 115, 116, 154, 232
apostate 22, 24, 47, 72, 107, 114, 174, 176
arbitrary 56, 57, 58
Arianism 230
arm of the Lord 67, 115, 161, 162, 187, 214, 218, 219, 220, 225
Armageddon 6, 10, 11, 19, 22, 34, 38, 39, 41, 42, 82, 83, 85, 86, 87, 88, 96, 104, 127, 154, 169, 170, 171, 176, 178, 180, 191, 193, 198, 202
Armstrong, Herbert W. 230, 238
Assembly 37, 49, 58, 170, 171, 172, 177
atheist 99
Athens 37
authority 5, 7, 10, 13, 19, 43, 52, 53, 54, 56, 57, 58, 59, 66, 68, 72, 109, 113, 115, 117, 137, 142, 144, 165, 192, 212, 223, 233, 234
Awake 15, 117, 126, 199

B

bad grammar 157
bait-and-switch 39
baptize 113, 116, 233
BBC 14
beard 11
beards 11, 164
Bethelite 22
birthday 164
Bithynia 161
Blizard, Paul 22, 23
blood 7, 18, 22, 23, 33, 35, 38, 39, 43, 45, 62, 73, 89, 98, 123, 124, 125, 126, 127, 128, 129, 130, 131, 169, 176, 228, 239
blood transfusion 7, 22, 23, 35, 38, 43, 73, 89, 123, 124, 125, 127, 128, 130, 169, 176
bondage 6, 7, 20, 89, 180
Bonham 52
Bowen, Bill 14
Brady, TX 22
branch 52
Butler, Kimberly 175

C

Campbell, Timothy 56, 57
Canada 55
Cargo Cult 87, 240
Catholic 16, 51, 53, 81, 100, 104, 105, 166, 198
Cetnar, Bill 25, 48, 81, 117, 126, 180
Cetnar, Joan 48
chess 30, 165
Christendom 41, 85, 96, 174
Christmas 43, 164, 165, 169
Circuit 52, 72, 159
clergy 51, 55
Coca-Cola™ 153, 154
Comments from the Friends 35
communism 35
compartmentalized thinking 67
Congress 2, 234
conscience 7, 23, 31, 48, 57, 58, 72, 85, 127, 182, 197, 199, 202
Constitution 170

255

construction 55, 97
contradictions 6, 17, 57, 67, 69, 140, 188, 195, 199, 202, 205
control 2, 5, 6, 9, 42, 43, 49, 51, 52, 53, 58, 59, 60, 63, 68, 95, 99, 119, 168, 169, 170, 171, 172, 197, 201
Convention 24, 25, 75, 79, 85, 172, 177, 179
Countess, Robert H. 81
Cousins, Alison 14
cross 50, 91, 102, 108, 153, 159, 164, 165, 168, 172, 173, 174, 175, 187
cruelty 25, 45, 71, 72, 73
cult 6, 31, 35, 41, 42, 43, 44, 45, 60, 81, 87, 99, 137, 194, 202, 203, 240

D

Daily Heavenly Manna 199
Dallas Morning News, The 177
Dallas Theological Seminary 166
David 35, 108, 127, 135, 155, 158, 194, 214, 215, 223, 226
deacon 11, 91
deceive 5, 6, 36, 200
deception 38, 39, 41
deity of Christ 216, 218, 243
DeMayo, Alex 24
demon 25, 65, 90, 99, 195
depression 10
Depression 68
devil 34, 94, 96, 232
disciples 9, 18, 19, 95, 97, 112, 116, 131, 143, 151, 160, 176, 193, 203, 204, 205, 206, 220, 223, 227
disfellowship 5, 12
disfellowshiped 11, 13, 19, 22, 24, 30, 38, 47, 56, 57, 71, 85, 92, 96, 113, 123, 127, 171, 181, 197, 202
disfellowshiping 35, 202
District 52, 75, 170
divorce 43, 56, 89, 202

E

Easter 164
Ecclesiastes 145, 146
Edmond C. Gruss 48, 180
Egypt 89, 186, 196
elders 5, 10, 11, 12, 13, 14, 16, 21, 22, 23, 24, 25, 33, 36, 37, 42, 43, 49, 52, 56, 57, 72, 73, 89, 90, 96, 114, 172, 181, 182, 202, 215
Elect 16, 21, 52, 183, 184
Emmanuel 156, 213, 218

emotional 6, 7, 10, 22, 42, 61, 73, 103, 138, 169
employees 34, 55
Europe 125, 234
evidence 29, 64, 81, 82, 138, 141, 232
Ex-JW's 17, 49, 73, 81, 114, 177, 178, 179, 180, 185, 200

F

failure 6, 10, 57, 120
false prophecies 34, 47, 49, 81, 88, 188, 192, 198, 199, 200, 201, 238
false prophets 88, 90, 193, 194, 200
family 9, 10, 12, 22, 24, 28, 30, 31, 34, 39, 44, 59, 60, 61, 62, 63, 68, 72, 82, 100, 125, 126, 169, 170, 172, 175, 176, 181, 188, 191, 238, 239, 240
father 5, 14, 15, 23, 34, 45, 59, 60, 61, 62, 63, 64, 68, 94, 108, 109, 111, 112, 113, 114, 115, 116, 134, 151, 154, 155, 157, 158, 160, 161, 162, 167, 170, 186, 187, 195, 208, 209, 210, 211, 212, 214, 215, 219, 220, 221, 223, 224, 225, 226, 228, 229, 230, 231, 232, 233, 234, 235, 237, 238, 239
fathers 59, 185
Finished Mystery, The 200
First Amendment 49
fishing 164
flag 17, 18, 20, 29, 169
forgiveness 6, 50, 93, 127, 129, 158, 185
Fort Worth, TX 4, 13
founder 9, 11, 83, 104
Frederick Franz 36, 38, 52, 192

G

Galilee 148, 205, 220
Gehenna 135, 136, 147, 148
Gethsemane 18, 135
Gideon 154, 208, 212
Gordon, Al 16
gospel 4, 6, 15, 20, 31, 37, 49, 50, 83, 86, 87, 93, 95, 107, 108, 109, 117, 120, 127, 140, 152, 153, 161, 178, 194, 216, 224, 242
gospel of the kingdom 86, 107, 108, 109
government 35, 38, 48, 53, 55, 56, 58, 95, 155, 170, 176, 233, 234
Greek 36, 37, 38, 48, 49, 79, 80, 81, 110, 139, 144, 154, 157, 159, 174, 196, 197, 209, 210, 212, 213, 216, 222, 223, 229, 238, 241, 242, 243
Greenville, TX 64

Groenveld, Jan 13

H

heaven 16, 20, 21, 22, 36, 50, 52, 62, 67, 90, 103, 108, 109, 118, 119, 120, 121, 136, 137, 139, 141, 142, 157, 158, 160, 168, 176, 180, 182, 183, 184, 186, 187, 195, 205, 207, 213, 221, 234, 238, 240
Hebrews 110, 112, 125, 161, 184, 209, 212, 215, 220, 224, 228
hell 30, 43, 66, 100, 101, 134, 136, 144, 146, 147, 148, 150, 176, 238, 239
Henderson, TX 172
hepatitis 23
Hewitt 2, 4, 103
hierarchy 6, 51, 53, 54, 55, 57, 59, 61, 72, 120, 188, 216
high school 22, 37, 104, 201
hippies 11
history 20, 51, 53, 83, 88, 110, 127, 129, 140, 186, 199
Hitler 45, 149, 150
holiness 209, 212
Holy Spirit 94, 103, 113, 116, 137, 139, 158, 160, 170, 186, 200, 205, 213, 221, 225, 226, 227, 228, 229, 230, 232, 233, 234, 237, 239
homeschooling 72
homicide 23
hunting 164
hypocrisy 6, 12, 17, 25, 29, 33, 34, 40, 57, 68, 85, 154, 198, 199

I

Immanuel 67, 89, 115, 154, 155, 187, 213, 218
immortality 140, 239
in a sense 30, 142
In The Truth 114, 169, 194
income 7, 52, 54, 63, 66
indictment 88, 90
indoctrinated 44, 104, 165, 166, 170
informers 23
intellectual 6, 7, 44, 80
Internet 13, 14, 185
interrogation 57
Iraq 233, 234
Israel 36, 89, 115, 118, 119, 120, 134, 151, 152, 155, 156, 158, 159, 186, 212, 214

J

Jacob 119, 120, 133, 145, 146, 186, 191, 208, 212, 217
jail 12, 93, 94, 102
Jews 18, 36, 84, 116, 118, 131, 138, 144, 147, 160, 196, 197
Job 34, 35, 39, 115, 117, 135, 157, 165, 208, 209, 210, 213
John 18, 19, 28, 30, 62, 75, 80, 115, 116, 127, 140, 143, 156, 158, 159, 160, 167, 184, 195, 196, 208, 210, 212, 216, 217, 219, 221, 223, 224, 228, 229, 231, 241, 242, 243
judge 15, 23, 53, 84, 85, 93, 149, 158, 176, 182, 191
judicial hearing 13, 23, 25, 73
justice 13, 149, 150, 186, 187, 212

K

Katrina 175
king 2, 18, 48, 52, 89, 94, 137, 161, 186, 212, 215, 217, 218, 232, 240
King James Version 2, 48, 212
kingdom 7, 10, 15, 16, 18, 20, 21, 23, 24, 28, 29, 31, 38, 40, 52, 55, 56, 57, 62, 68, 69, 73, 74, 76, 80, 82, 83, 86, 88, 90, 96, 100, 101, 104, 107, 108, 109, 114, 120, 169, 170, 171, 181, 200, 203, 214, 224, 242
kings 115, 137, 161, 217, 218, 231
Knorr, Nathan 52, 126, 192
Koine 37, 159, 196, 222, 242
Korea 234
Koresh 194
kurios 157, 222, 224
Kuwait 233, 234

L

lake of fire 34, 42, 136, 139, 183
land 118, 185, 233, 234
lawyers 52, 53, 229, 230
Lazarus 134, 135, 144, 145, 146
liar 30, 34, 37, 38, 115, 116, 154
lies 20, 25, 30, 33, 34, 36, 38, 45, 137, 198, 199
literature 7, 16, 18, 37, 38, 47, 49, 52, 53, 76, 81, 90, 96, 164, 167, 168, 169, 172, 173, 182, 198, 222
logos 216, 218, 219, 220, 225
Lopez, Rene 166
Lord's evening meal 21, 203
Lord's supper 127, 203
Love and Norris 13

lying 6, 31, 34, 35, 60, 61, 85, 188, 192, 200

M

Manson 59, 60
Miller, Mr. 39, 40, 41
missionaries 38, 126
missionary 22, 85, 93, 197
money 39, 41, 52, 54, 55, 58, 63, 92, 94, 154, 165, 240
mortar 5, 7, 33, 35, 37, 39, 41, 43, 45, 50, 60, 117, 152, 188
mother 5, 9, 17, 18, 20, 25, 34, 35, 36, 39, 40, 41, 59, 60, 61, 63, 64, 66, 67, 68, 69, 73, 74, 82, 84, 86, 104, 123, 125, 129, 141, 142, 161, 175, 176, 181, 215
mourning 164

N

Nazi 15, 45
New American Standard Version 24, 48, 211
new light 53, 84, 173, 176, 238
New Orleans 175
New World Translation 6, 21
New York Post 54
news media 35, 128, 240
NWT 21, 30, 38, 48, 49, 81, 117, 141, 155, 157, 159, 160, 239, 243

O

ordained 15
organization 4, 6, 7, 9, 10, 12, 13, 14, 17, 25, 27, 28, 35, 41, 47, 48, 54, 56, 57, 59, 61, 68, 71, 81, 82, 84, 85, 96, 97, 114, 116, 137, 151, 166, 169, 170, 172, 176, 180, 182, 191, 195, 196, 198, 200, 203, 204, 214
organized religion 48, 53, 176, 177
Ortega, Helen 20, 21, 22
Ortiz, Ray and Lisa 73
other sheep 142

P

Paradise 38, 39, 44, 65, 107, 108, 109, 120, 135, 168
Paradise earth 38, 39, 44, 65, 107, 108, 109, 168
paranoia 63, 103
parent 12, 13, 64, 128, 191, 198
parking lot 37, 49
parole 10, 60

pastor 52, 60, 65, 66, 73, 74, 81, 84, 91, 101, 102, 103, 114, 131, 153, 166, 176, 182, 183, 216, 240
perception 7, 107, 210, 212
personality 134, 135, 138, 139, 148, 159, 169, 214, 225, 226, 227, 229, 234
phonograph 15
physical return 193
ping pong 165
pioneered 181
plagiarism 80, 243
Pliny the Younger 140, 161
Pneuma 148
Pontus 161
Pope 53, 127
population 92, 93, 201, 233
prayer 21, 68, 92, 96, 97, 99, 103, 109, 111, 160, 168
press 13, 33, 197, 240, 243
priest 12, 81, 215
Prince of Peace 115, 155, 214
prison 9, 12, 19, 20, 29, 33, 60, 94, 98, 102, 117, 126, 179, 188
prisoners 4, 7, 49, 93, 94, 126, 127, 179
profits 54
publisher 11, 21, 52, 171

R

Rastafarians 137, 182, 239, 240
reinstated 57
religion 28, 35, 42, 48, 53, 58, 67, 94, 95, 99, 123, 155, 164, 176, 177, 198, 219
religious 5, 10, 12, 39, 42, 43, 51, 92, 100, 119, 124, 164, 170, 176, 177, 195, 216, 224
resurrection 41, 84, 97, 109, 116, 136, 139, 140, 141, 142, 143, 183, 184, 192, 193, 204, 205, 213, 220, 221, 239
Revelation 36, 61, 83, 118, 136, 157, 216, 217, 218
Roman Empire 20, 37, 230
Romans 157, 166, 173, 182, 193, 195, 215, 221, 227
Russell 9, 11, 52, 53, 83, 84, 86, 104, 142, 166, 167, 176, 230
Rutherford, Joseph 15

S

Sabbath 128, 131, 223
Samaritan 217
Samuel 212
Satan 16, 28, 30, 34, 69, 96, 97, 109, 111, 154, 168, 178, 237

Savior 25, 50, 103, 116, 132, 152, 154, 156, 158, 182, 195, 201, 218
Schnell, William J. 24
scholar 37, 38, 80
school activities 165
school dances 164
Scotland 14, 38
Scriviner 241
seeing God 208, 213
Septuagint 196, 222
servant 11, 15, 52, 72, 151, 152, 176
Seventh-Day Adventists 238, 239
sexual abuse 7, 13
smoking 11
snare and a racket 176, 177
soldiers 19, 20, 163, 165, 166, 173
soul 133, 134, 135, 136, 137, 138, 139, 141, 143, 144, 145, 147, 148, 149, 231, 239
sound bites 77, 177
South America 95
spirit 94, 103, 113, 116, 127, 133, 135, 136, 137, 138, 139, 140, 141, 143, 145, 146, 147, 148, 149, 158, 160, 170, 184, 186, 199, 200, 205, 209, 210, 212, 213, 214, 219, 221, 222, 225, 226, 227, 228, 229, 230, 232, 233, 234, 237, 239
Spirit of Christ 221
stauros 174
stone 7, 9, 11, 17, 33, 116, 160, 188, 214, 224
Strong's Concordance 174
studies 24, 48, 90, 123, 166, 167, 169, 171
study 10, 11, 21, 23, 25, 37, 47, 76, 80, 88, 112, 113, 165, 167, 168, 169, 171, 174, 183, 185, 187, 197, 201, 213, 216
studying 7, 21, 24, 66, 117, 166, 167, 191, 202, 203, 243
suicide 10, 43, 65
Sun Myung Moon 194, 240
Supreme Court 234

T

telephone ministry 177, 191
territory 15, 52
testimony card 15
Tetragrammaton 110, 222, 224
theocratic 10, 15, 21, 23, 36, 56, 65, 169
theologian 29, 166
Thirty Years a Watchtower Slave 24, 47
throwing rice 165

time is at hand 86, 199
torture stake 168, 174, 175
translator 80, 154
truth shall make you free 195, 199
two witnesses 12, 13, 14

U

U.S. 17, 51, 67, 71, 98, 233, 234, 235
University of Cincinnati 36, 38

V

vaccination 38, 126
Valentine's Day 164
verbal gymnastics 31, 42, 137
victims 12, 13, 128
vindicated 30, 219
virgin Mary 156, 186, 213, 215, 220
volunteer 7, 25, 55
vote 169

W

Walker, James 166
Watchtower magazine 15, 129, 171
Westcott and Hort 241, 242
Wichita 15, 40, 41, 73, 141
Wise Men 220
Word 7, 25, 27, 45, 50, 73, 80, 81, 88, 89, 103, 110, 111, 113, 115, 126, 134, 139, 144, 145, 147, 148, 154, 156, 157, 159, 167, 174, 178, 184, 187, 195, 196, 197, 198, 199, 200, 204, 209, 210, 212, 216, 220, 222, 223, 226, 228, 229, 241, 242, 243
work 7, 10, 12, 20, 22, 27, 29, 30, 34, 39, 40, 41, 48, 54, 57, 64, 66, 86, 89, 90, 96, 104, 165, 171, 172, 178, 181, 183, 201, 239, 240
worked 6, 29, 39, 40, 62, 68, 114, 117, 149, 180, 181
working 119, 165, 181, 193
works 54, 71, 90, 96, 127, 149, 173, 174, 180, 182, 183, 224
worldly 6, 11, 12, 35, 36, 52, 91, 99, 113, 164, 170, 171, 172
wounded 10, 162, 187

Y

Yeager, Randolph 80, 211
youth 12, 76, 164, 172

Z

Zechariah 215